DATE DUE

DEMCO 38-296

DENG'S GENERATION

Also by Ruth Cherrington

CHINA'S STUDENTS: The Struggle for Democracy

Deng's Generation

Young Intellectuals in 1980s China

Ruth Cherrington
Lecturer in British Cultural Studies
Veliko Turnovo University
Bulgaria

!1 6XS and London
the world

A catalogue record for this book is available from the British Library.

ISBN 0–333–67099–X

First published in the United States of America 1997 by
ST. MARTIN'S PRESS, INC.,
Scholarly and Reference Division,
175 Fifth Avenue, New York, N.Y. 10010

ISBN 0–312–17461–6

Library of Congress Cataloging-in-Publication Data
Cherrington, Ruth, 1955–
Deng's generation : young intellectuals in 1980s China / Ruth
Cherrington.
    p.   cm.
Includes bibliographical references and index.
ISBN 0–312–17461–6 (cloth)
1. Intellectuals—China.   2. China—Intellectual life.   3. China–
–Social conditions—1976–   I. Title.
HM213.C444 1997
305.5'52'0951—dc21   97–5331
                                                              CIP

This book is printed on paper suitable for recycling and made from fully managed and
sustained forest sources.

10   9   8   7   6   5   4   3   2   1
06   05   04   03   02   01   00   99   98   97

Printed and bound in Great Britain by
Antony Rowe Ltd, Chippenham, Wiltshire

Contents

Acknowledgements

This book probably would not have been envisaged let alone written without the advice and encouragement of Stephan Feuchtwang and Stuart Thompson, my Ph.D. examiners and I would like to express my sincere gratitude to them. Elisabeth Croll, my long-suffering supervisor, is also thanked for her help over many years. Colleagues in Britain, China and more recently Bulgaria, have all played their parts in terms of advice, ideas and support for this project and I am deeply indebted to all of them.

Many thanks to Brian Boulton, formerly of Harrow College of Higher Education, for finding time for me to conduct my research in the first place and Morry van Ments at Loughborough University for his practical advice and support.

Friends and family are never forgotten. This is for them and especially my parents, John and Freda Cherrington.

List of Abbreviations

BR	*Beijing Review*
CCP	Chinese Communist Party
CD	*China Daily*
CQ	*China Quarterly*
CR	*China Reconstructs*
CYL	Communist Youth League
ECMM	*Extracts from China Mainland Magazines*
FBIS CR	*Foreign Broadcast Information Service China Report*
FEER	*Far Eastern Economic Review*
GMD	Guomindang (KMT) Nationalist Party
GMRB	*Guangming Ribao (Bright Daily)*
NPC	National People's Congress
PRC	People's Republic of China
RMRB	*Renmin Ribao (People's Daily)*
SCMP	*Survey of China Mainland Press*
SEC	State Education Commission
SWB/FE	*Summary of World Broadcasts, Far East*
TOEFL	Test of English as a Foreign Language
ZGFN	*Zhongguo Funu (Women of China)*
ZGQN	*Zhongguo Qingnian (Chinese Youth Magazine)*

Introduction

This book is the outcome of several years of contact with young intellectuals in China and, it must be admitted, is only partly the result of conscious planning and preparation. Some of the following description and analysis is due to accidents of history that placed me in China in certain places at certain times and this can be seen as both a strength and a weakness of the project. Readers must decide for themselves the relative degree of each after considering the evidence.

I almost stumbled into the study of 'Deng's generation' in the first place after going to China out of curiosity in 1984 but a year of teaching in a small city on the Yangtse River only served to heighten that curiosity. My attention was drawn in particular to the students I came into contact with and the young teachers only a few years their senior who were all caught in the midst of the great changes sweeping the country at that time. China was in the early stages of opening up to the outside world and the reforms were just beginning to have an impact on the smaller towns and isolated regions considered as 'backward' (luohou) by more sophisticated urban Chinese. It was very noticeable that young people, especially those in higher education, were more in tune with the changes than their older counterparts and more likely to adapt to them. They could identify with the spirit of the new, post-Mao era as laid down within the official discourse and all the influences it brought, right down to the clothes they wore.

In this sense, even features such as fashions can be viewed as what I term 'generational accessories', as well as the key trends of thought and behaviour. Watching students tentatively discard Mao-style tunics in favour of tee shirts with misspelt English words printed on them strengthened my belief that a new generation was in the making. Their position was not, however, enviable as on the one hand they were encouraged by Communist Party leaders to embrace reforms yet simultaneously to adhere to the 'socialist road', and this was not an easy task. They were promised much from the reform programme yet in reality appeared to be struggling to find a suitable position for themselves in a changing society and remained bound by many traditions. Any advantages on offer appeared elusive.

1

In some ways, and at particular points in time, these young people were over zealous in embracing reforms and all things western and this caused clashes between them and the authorities. These clashes will be an important part of this work and can be placed into a generational perspective. Looking to the West was one key point stressed by the reform-minded leadership who wanted young people to learn from more technologically advanced societies in order to strengthen China. Wearing tee shirts may appear a superficial feature but there were other, more serious characteristics of this generation, such as their desires for political reforms to match those taking place within the economy. The official discourse and the extent to which it helped shape the generation will be considered. It may have set certain boundaries in terms of ideological development but young people could clearly go beyond these under certain circumstances.

As a result of this interest in their situation and the desire to see how it would all end I undertook research into this socio-demographic social group of 'educated youth' or *qingnian zhishi fenzi* and went back several times to China, notably to conduct ethnographic fieldwork in Beijing during 1988. I did not realise that this would turn out to be such a crucial year in contemporary Chinese history and it was fortuitous that I was there when so many things were happening around young intellectuals.

I left Beijing in early 1989 with an acute awareness of their deep frustrations, both intellectual and social, and believing that something could happen at any time. It soon did after the death of former Party Secretary, Hu Yaobang, in April and the resulting democracy movement made my research more immediate and pressing. It was difficult to be objective at that time given the nature of the unfolding events and my original aims were complicated by Tiananmen and its aftermath. A return trip and further investigations, as well as calmer, if not depressing, times enabled me eventually to complete the doctoral thesis which provides the basis of this book.

It has to be acknowledged that sympathetic involvement with some of the participants of this study and the witnessing of the latter stages of the 1989 student-led campaign affected the results of this project but it remains the result of sober post-Tiananmen reflection. Partiality is not in itself a bad thing as long as it is acknowledged (Pilkington, 1994) and some generalisations can be drawn from what is essentially a case study of this particular group. The originally envisaged account of 'contemporary' young intellectuals became, in effect, more of a historical record of the 1980s since the 1990s were already well under way by the time writing began. This book is, therefore, more about contemporary history than current social commentary but this is often the fate of such endeavours. It is still worth trying to understand a generation inextricably linked with those famous but tragic scenes on Tiananmen Square in 1989.

There is certainly more to their story, and this book sets out to recount in greater detail what the key characteristics of this generation were as well as how they were shaped by historical factors, constructed by official discourses and how they ultimately attempted to reconstruct themselves by creating space within the confines of what remained an authoritarian political system. The nature of this space will be explored as well as its boundaries.

What's in a Name? The Notion of Deng's Generation

It might be asked why this label was selected since this leader ultimately spurned his protégés and ordered the repression of young protesters. An alternative label of the 'reform generation' is feasible because they came to maturity during the period of *gaige kaifang* (reform and open door) policies. The rapid economic and social changes in China were, however, largely the work of the post-Mao regime led by Deng Xiaoping and those who passed into maturity as intellectuals during the years dominated by his leadership have been designated as his generation.

The term 'Thatcher's generation' was frequently used in the 1980s to describe British youth and this remains a valid description of young people who grew up during that period. Chinese youth during the 1960s and 1970s were often referred to as the 'Mao generation' (Siu and Stern, 1983; Chan, 1985) or more negatively as the 'lost generation'. The labelling of successive generations in this manner is not new but these easily recognisable terms taken from different social and political contexts stand for what are actually complex mixes of social and economic forces of specific historical periods which helped to shape distinctive generations. The labels 'Thatcher's' and 'Deng's' generation can be viewed, therefore, as summaries of much less simple processes and events which have to be unravelled in order to understand the generational characteristics and features. This book attempts to unravel the various strands which combined to produce a new generation of young intellectuals within the wider socio-demographic category of youth in China.

Deng's generation is a distinctive group of young people who I studied intermittently for over a decade. I have many memories of them as well as notes and observations which will all be drawn upon in this work. I can recall, for example, a party I gave near the end of my first stay in China when the students behaved in a far more relaxed manner than during previous gatherings. Their obvious desire and enthusiasm for dancing, singing pop songs and even commiting minor 'sins' such as kissing in public, showed some extent of the changes that had occurred within the short space of less than one year.

These personal recollections are indicative of more serious and widespread changes that occurred throughout the 1980s which greatly affected young people, particularly the rising generation of intellectuals. I shall endeavour to bring this group to life in order to enable the reader to envisage their characteristics, imagine their responses in certain situations and understand why they thought and behaved as they did, even why some of them stubbornly took on the government in 1989 with all the resulting tragic consequences. There will be an attempt to write the generational biography with all-round descriptions, from what films they liked, their career aspirations, their disappointments, to their experiences of political activism. In doing so, this book should fill some gaps and will make important links between the spheres of culture, society and history that produced this generation.

Much has already been written about Deng Xiaoping and the impact of reform policies upon Chinese society. This work frequently includes significant attention to the position of intellectuals in China, especially after the suppression of the 1989 pro-democracy movement. Indeed, the continued repression of voices oppositional to the regime which has implemented radical economic policies but largely denied political change, remains the focus of interest for many concerned scholars. This interest is regularly renewed, such as with the rearrest of one of China's best known dissidents, Wei Jingsheng in 1994 and his controversial 14-year prison sentence in late 1995.

Students, as young members of the Chinese intelligentsia have figured predominantly in some of these works which have certainly assisted in raising our awareness of their social position and spheres of influence. (Goldman *et al.* 1986; Ownby, 1986). It can be argued that there has not been so much attention paid to the precise defining features of young intellectuals in 1980s China. Whilst the main contributory factors to their social position have been described and analysed, especially in explanations of the 1989 protests, there has been an insufficient account of the generational nature of their thinking and behaviour. Those researchers who have attempted to analyse this generation have not usually implemented a generational perspective although it has been present in varying degrees of explicitness (Luo Xu, 1995; Kwong, 1994; Rosen, 1993; Hooper 1991).

It was noticeable during my visits to China that a clear generational consciousness and identity were emerging, expressed not only in predominant trends of thought but also in terms of behaviour and 'crazes'.[1] Their similar circumstances were translated into common traits and this is particularly true for students who lived closely together in cramped conditions with an official as well as unofficial emphasis on the peer group, as will be shown. There was a break between them and the previous generation and this was encouraged by the authorities who wanted to mould what can be described as 'modernisation successors' to replace the 'revolutionary successors' who had become, in fact, the 'lost generation' of the Cultural Revolution.[2] The new generation would ideally match the official discourse and assist the Party in implementing its policies but in actuality this was not always the case. Deng's generation had to find a way between the heavy baggage of cultural tradition and more recently arrived modernity, and this included managing official messages on both of these.

The 1980s saw regular demands for more human rights and personal freedoms and it will argued that there was a self-consciousness amongst Deng's generation as being 'braver' than their predecessors. Such a sentiment was expressed by one of the 1989 leaders, Li Lu, who sensed 'a central characteristic of my generation: the concept of the individual standing up against an autocratic system that sought to eliminate individuality. Many did not know how to develop as individuals but had a strong desire to rebel against convention and society: they did not want to be slaves like their fathers.' (Li, 1990:98). It will be shown that other young intellectuals shared this view, seeing themselves as a thoughtful and independent-minded generation who were ready and able to be agents of social change.

Plan of the Book

Chapter 1 will describe the application of the generational perspective to the Chinese context, beginning with an outline of the key concepts and a description of how, as well as why, these have been used. It is intended that this exercise will not only enrich the understanding of a specific section of Chinese youth and add to the expanding field of Chinese Studies but also make links with mainstream sociology. By employing a sociological concept usually applied in the western context, it will be seen that Chinese youth share similarities with their European and American counterparts which can be explained by the familiar, if perhaps underdeveloped, generational perspective (Mannheim, 1952; Remmling, 1975; Pilcher 1994).

The deconstruction of the category of '*qingnian zhishi fenzi*' follows in Chapter 2 with the consideration of the differences between young intellectuals and their contemporaries. This will draw upon the sociology of youth where relevant. Whilst similarities will be found in terms of generational links, the relative elite status of those young people with academic credentials set them apart from the others. Deng's generation will be described as a group of similarly placed social actors sharing a number of common characteristics. As an elite section of youth they can be seen to be both applying and subject to processes of 'social closure' (Parkin, 1979) which add to the specificity of the generation and its various units. The relevance of generations in the Chinese context will also be considered with an outline of intellectual generations of the communist era.

The attention of subsequent chapters will focus on description and analysis of the characteristic features of the generation. Chapter 3 considers the educational crazes and crises of the decade. The initial rush into higher education, for example, will be shown as an important generational marker, but later on enthusiasm was dampened by doubts and frustrations. Going abroad will be discussed within this context as one possible strategy for remedying this unsatisfactory position. The cultural achievements of Deng's reform generation and its identity as a self-conscious elite with a particular historical role and duties to perform will be considered in terms of technical skills and qualifications and, once again, perceived political duties.

Chapter 4 discusses predominant 'fads' and feeling of the decade such as the 'business craze' (*jingshang re*) amongst students in the late 1980s, which is understandable if they are viewed as 'the newborn children of the economic age' (*jingji shidai de chan er*) (Zhang and Cheng, 1988:34). Their preferred tastes in leisure pursuits and cultural activities will also be analysed in terms of generational characteristics and generational accessories. Important links will be shown between these activities and aspects of ideological explorations which eventually went so far as to question the essence of the Chinese identity in a rapidly changing context (Tu, 1993; 1994). Young intellectuals were particularly caught up in the mid-decade 'cultural re-examination fever' (*wenhua fansi re*) (Kelly, 1990) and the 'roots seeking craze' (*xungen wenzu*) (Wang, 1991). The controversy caused by the television series critical of traditional Chinese culture, *He Shang* (River Elegy), is included here. The ongoing ideological crisis was usually accompanied by economic, educational and political ones as the breakdown of Marxism led to a search for a suitable alternative.

Political activism will be shown in Chapter 5 as one outcome of the frustration felt by Deng's generation about the relative lack of liberalisation in political and personal spheres. Having been led to believe that they would benefit more than they actually did from economic reforms, the protests of young intellectuals will be shown not only as politically inspired but also as part of the overall concern about their social and economic position. The main strands of the 1989 pro-democracy movement were similar to previous protests and, in a sense, these disturbances were rehearsals for the larger scale and nationwide demonstrations. By this time the main features of the generation were observable and the predominant thoughts and actions were all present by Spring 1989. After this point they became a 'scarred' (Siu and Stern, 1983) generation just like their predecessors and this can be viewed as a watershed event. Deng's generation itself had to be superseded by another and the emergence of the 'post-reform' generation of the 1990s will be considered in the Conclusion.

The analysis of the generation will not assume that it was an homogeneous entity, acting the same throughout the 1980s. There were shifts and changes because they had to be adaptable to the multifaceted transformations of the decade as well as a number of policy shifts. The differences and divergences will be integrated themes throughout the work but it will be argued that a particular identity emerged from the interplay between the official discourse and young intellectuals' own attempts to define themselves. The nature of this identity increased the probability of an inter-generational clash with Deng's generation suggesting different solutions to China's problems and the consideration of generational features throws light on the events of 1989.

Their treatment by the authorities also varied with periods of '*fang*' and '*shou*', that is, relaxation and repression, according to which faction within the CCP leadership had the upper hand. The existence of such factions is usually denied but it is clear that behind the closed doors of Chinese government, power struggles occurred regularly throughout the 1980s and these affected their various supporters outside the gates of *Zhongnanhai*. Young intellectuals were watching and listening keenly to the outcomes because any policy shifts were bound to have repercussions in all areas of their future lives.

There were distinctive periods such as the early part of the decade with the efforts to leave behind the Cultural Revolution in both ideological and practical terms. This incorporated the apportioning of blame for the excesses of the period onto the 'Gang of Four'. Tentative criticism of Mao later became more direct with official questioning of the type of Marxism he chose for China. This included the much publicised 'seeking truth from facts' as well as the deconstruction and reconstruction of Chinese socialism, away from Maoism to Dengism with the official acceptance of a form of capitalist economics.

At several points the deconstruction of Marxism was halted and these periods were usually described as 'anti-bourgeois liberalism' campaigns, notably in 1983 and 1987. Deng's generation attempted to be flexible and willing to adapt to altered circumstances emanating from changes in official policies and capable of taking calculated risks based upon their readings and perceptions of what the CCP were doing. They did not always read the situation correctly and their risks did not always pay off, as was the case in 1989. It is important to note that we are considering predispositions and tendencies rather than fixed features as well as different preferences at various points in time.

One theoretical tool for understanding these predispositions is that of 'strategies of action', and the related notion of 'habitus' (Bourdieu, 1976; 1992) which will be described in Chapter 1 to further the analysis. Strategies can be seen as types of behaviour geared towards the attainment of certain goals and/or to overcome the impediments which may stand in the way of these goals. They may also involved 'adaptive behaviour' (Shirk, 1982:5) with the adjustment of original plans and changing of behaviour to fit the altered circumstances in order to maximise benefits. A diverse range of social behaviour can be described in this way, as discussed by a number of commentators.

Crow's (1989) characterisation of strategic action as involving choice which is conscious, rational, coherent and long term is not acceptable to everyone. Pickvance and Pickvance (1994) do not consider the distinction between conscious and unconscious as equivalent to that between strategic and non-strategic. They resolve this definition problem by claiming that there are two sub-categories of strategies, that is, conscious and unconscious, with the latter likely to be culturally transmitted rather than deliberately worked out by individuals. The reference to cultural aspects of strategies bears some similarity to Bourdieu's work which will be employed in this text.

It will be shown that some of the strategies of the generation led to different outcomes than those expected with their altered situation necessitating new courses of action. Unofficial political activism, for example, could lead to punishment rather than reward and in extreme cases, exile. Becoming involved in business and entrepreneurial pursuits also offered different possibilities and consequences which created further changes, generating additional strategy selection and behaviour in a continual feedback process. There were acts of resistance to official pressures in a society which, even in the relatively open 1980s, persisted with surveillance and control of the population. Young intellectuals will be shown as making efforts to lessen external controls and create their own personal, professional and social space which was distinctive and reflected their generational identity.

There were also notable contradictions. Whilst they frequently expressed confidence about their abilities, they were not immune from self-doubt and the more general anxieties affecting the Chinese intelligentsia, especially as the early promises of reform failed to materialise and social changes brought into question fundamental values. The contradictions and ambiguities of their status and role, some of which have historical roots, will be shown to have persisted until now, necessitating the development of strategies for coping with the problems caused by the changing parameters of intellectuals during this time. The shifting nature of the generation will be developed along with the fluidity of the concept as well as the disparities between the official discourse of young intellectuals and the actual realities in the reform era.

1 The Value of the Generational Perspective

It is generally recognised that in China, 'considerable attention (is) given to generational issues' (Yahuda, 1979:794), and this makes a generational perspective all the more relevant. Kwong (1994:249) referred to key social and political factors in recent Chinese history and how they may have affected groups of young people but did not 'elaborate' on 'how these factors shape youth attitudes'. She invoked a generational approach by stressing the importance of the 'common history' of Chinese youth who 'lived through the same major political and social events which shaped their views.' (*op. cit*:248). She then concentrated, as in this study, on Deng's generation who 'all experienced the more open political and economic climate of the 1980s'. For her purposes, however, a generational perspective was more implicit than explicit but this study was facilitated by drawing directly on Mannheim's work on generations.

It is accepted that Mannheim's 'seminal theoretical treatment of generations' (Pilcher, 1994:481) remains an underrated sociological legacy yet researchers who have applied it to empirical studies of contemporary social movements reached pertinent conclusions as a result. A number of American sociologists, for example, took up this concept in the early 1970s. Their interest was partly an academic reaction to the perceived radicalism of the youth movement and 'counter culture' which was often portrayed in the US media as an oppositional force threatening the stability of society.

There were also world-wide 'youth movements' in the 1960s, such as the anti-Vietnam war campaign and these were reflected in popular culture as well as in political protests. Some pop songs of the 1960s, for example, made by young people for their audiences of peers included references to revolutions and radical lifestyles as well as generational solidarity. Whilst such generational accessories arguably represented a revolt only at the level of style (Hebdige, 1979) it did appear that the younger generation were trying to bring about social and political change. There were, for example, specific single-issue protests such as the US

civil rights movement. In China, young people were, not always
by choice, preoccupied with 'class struggle' and their activities
gave them a specific generational identity.

The western youth movement phenomenon renewed interest in
generational analysis which, as Bengtson *et al.* (1974) remind us,
has been around since 'the beginning of recorded history' because older social members are usually concerned about the
behaviour of youth and how societies achieve both continuity and
change. The work of this period contributed greatly to the revival
of Mannheim's writings on generations which was largely neglected until this upsurge of interest. One reason given by Laufer
and Bengtson for the 'continuous anonymity' (1974:182) of the
generation theme was a perceived (rather than actual) lack of
discontinuity among age groups in US society up until the 1960s.
The society was reckoned to be fairly stable and social change
was slow and evolutionary rather than revolutionary. The protests of the 1960s showed this to be misguided with possible
threatening divergences emerging; hence the resulting academic
interest.

These attempts to analyse what is often described as the
'generation gap' tended, however, to conclude that it would not
bring about radical social change. Generational differences were
discovered but not ones so great as to wreck the existing status
quo. Kasschau *et al.* for example, found no evidence of a
'relentlessly mounting and uniform generational movement based
on conflict.' (1974: 91). The researchers set out to operationalize
the concept of 'generational unit' (Mannheim, 1952) and apply it
to the emergence of the 1960s youth movement as it manifested
itself in identification, ideology and behaviour of young people.
Whilst three quarters of all segments of their sample perceived
the young generation to be different and unique from others, this
was not always carried over in terms of identification and
ideology. Some were more likely to identify with social class
background rather than with other young people. Differences
between the sexes were also noted as well as between married
and unmarried members of the sample.

These results from studies of more than two decades ago are
relevant to the investigation of young intellectuals in 1980s China
where similar consistencies and divergences could be expected,
even though cultural variations mediate these to some extent.
The Chinese counterparts of the 1960s 'peace and love' gener-

ation (Starr, 1974) in the USA were also concerned with social and cultural issues but in different ways, usually through participation in the political campaigns of the Cultural Revolution.

Mannheim's work was also resurrected in Britain where it was incorporated into some of the Birmingham School's attempts to understand youth cultural developments (Murdock and McCron, 1976). It is reasonable to agree with Pilcher, however, that the use of this perspective remains, on the whole, underdeveloped with continued reliance on the explanatory powers of social class theory, and more recently, gender and ethnicity. The application of a generational perspective can, however, greatly assist the investigation of particular social groups and actually supplement these more frequently used ones. Whether generational identification and issues override other social features such as class and gender can be explored. In this sense, examining a social group in generational terms can further our knowledge about other forms of social differentiation, thus adding to these more common entry points rather than merely offering an alternative form of investigation.

Using generation as a discursive social category involves the identification of the shared features of the designated social group which, to some extent, unite them. We have to ask questions about what a generation actually is and how one can be distinguished from another before applying the perspective to the case study of 1980s young intellectuals in China.

Identifying Generations

The term 'generation' has common, everyday usage such as within the context of kinship groups where it can denote divisions within the family with senior, middle aged and younger members identifiable. Family generations are usually measured in terms of biological or genealogical cycles of birth, ageing and death. At the societal level, generations can be viewed as successive ages throughout history up to the present time and again may include biological or genealogical references. Bengtson *et al.* (1974) note that this usage was common before the nineteenth century but was one which Mannheim, in his own central thesis, rejected. It was unacceptable for him to take the 'Positivist' view that the succession of generations at regular intervals is 'the framework of human destiny in comprehensible, even measurable form' (*op.*

cit:276). The certainty of life cycles is not contested but the implication that these natural cycles can fully account for the totality of generational activity and change is debated. Age and ageing alone do not offer explanations for what groups of people do during their lifetimes.

It is also difficult to ascertain the beginning of one generation and ending of another because people are constantly being born and dying. They do not conveniently arrive in batches or cohorts which could be categorised as a generation in measured periods of years. Full intervals, as Mannheim noted, exist only in the individual family as people mature, marry and have children who then become the next generation. Pilcher suggests drawing a distinction between a social generation and a kinship generation, (1994:483). The former will obviously involve greater numbers of people from all social backgrounds and although it may be viewed simply as an aggregate of similarly aged people, Mannheim argued for the inclusion of significant social and historical events which play a role in the creation of generations. His shift away from the positivist ideal was probably shared by nineteenth century social philosophers who developed models of generations 'that were social and historical in nature, rather than biological or genealogical' (Bengtson *et al.*, 1974:3).

Some researchers prefer to use terminology similar to Mannheim's but retain the genealogical definition, such as in Gold's study of post 1949 Chinese youth (1991). He refers to generations as 'genealogical categories such as parents and children' (*op. cit*:594) but it is arguable that his preferred approach is actually more like Mannheim's. Gold suggests that the three birth cohorts which have passed through the youth stage since the founding of the PRC have had 'radically different relations with the Party-state' and can be best understood by the 'life course approach.' For him this offers 'a coherent way to link the progression of individuals and cohorts through the biological life span, with the socio-cultural context and historical events through which the progression occurs. It delineates the social construction of transition between stages in a life course and the definitions of the activities characteristic of each stage' (*op. cit*:594).

The similarity continues with his observations that 'Most scholars employing this approach trace cohorts over their entire life course or through particular stages and/or use major historical events such as the Depression, Holocaust or Vietnam War as a way to show how cohorts adapt and societies reconstitute themselves after such disruptions.' (*op. cit*:594). This use of the term 'cohort' is similar to that of generation employed in this study with Gold defining it as 'persons born in a given period who age together and have roughly similar experiences.' (*op. cit*:594). The exact definitions of terminology may differ but the approaches are comparable. The use of generational analysis in this study is similar to Gold's 'life course approach'.

Mannheim's perspective permits emphasis on contemporaneity but this is only sociologically significant 'when it also involves participation in the same historical and social circumstances' (1952:298). Age group identity cannot fully account for the specific self-consciousness of a particular generation which in turn may give rise to joint actions and experiences, whether it is the Red Guard (*weihong bing*) activities of the 1960s or the protests and pop songs of their western peers. Simple generational markers of age and life cycles are convenient measures but a proper generational analysis is more complex or, as Mannheim writes, 'The *sociological* [*sic*] problem of generations . . . begins at that point where the sociological relevance of these biological factors is discovered' (*op. cit*.291).

Whilst periods of ten to 15 years are usually viewed as suitable periods, this has to be reconsidered in the light of key events and historical forces shaping the different generations. The time period may be shorter or longer depending upon what is happening and how related events affect social members, as previously suggested. Starr writes that Mannheim considered generations to be 'age cohorts who occupy a common location in the sociohistorical process' but 'Mere contemporaneity does not, in itself, produce a common generation location' (1974:77). Age cohorts are not distinct generations unless there are social events which make them as such. Distinctive features may emanate from 'social and historical contexts' (Jones, 1988:708), with different experiences and the reactions to them, according to Yahuda (1979) being more significant than biological considerations of age.

The shift from one generation to another may be gradual with potential members having differential exposure to the key historical and social contexts, or it may be quick with a watershed event acting as a generational marker. Sudden, outstanding events such as revolutions may bring about an abrupt shift from one generation to another and demarcation is less problematic. Starr cites

Ryder who also distinguishes between 'traumatic' and 'evolutionary' social changes which 'have the effect of differentiating age cohorts,' (*op. cit*:79). Generational location is not always self-evident and blurred generational boundaries or '*dai ji*,' to use the Chinese term, have to be considered when operationalising the concept. This might at first seem one of the main problems with adopting the generational perspective but, in fact, it helps to identify points of reference between different parts of the generation.

In this book, Deng's or the reform generation will be linked to the reform era[1] and it is coincidental that this can be fitted into approximately ten years. The line of differentiation is drawn there because of the events of the period and how they affected young intellectuals. There are ambiguities on the peripheries of the generation and the point where Deng's generation begins and ends will be delineated as clearly as possible. It is recognisable both by the context within which it passed through the transition into maturity and in terms of its own resulting outlook or 'generational consciousness' (Clarke *et al.*, 1976:51) This has its origins in 'their shared social situation', and 'in the attitudes and responses developed by particular close-knit "concrete groups" in the course of responding to their shared "generation units" of similarly located contemporaries'. There is 'an identity of responses, a certain affinity in the way in which all move with and are formed by their common experiences' (Murdock and McCron, 1976:98) which can be summarised as a shared consciousness.

The policies of the British government in the 1980s set the context for 'Thatcher's generation' just as those of the post-Mao leadership in China were the context for Deng's generation. They helped to create such shared social situations, although other factors have to be taken into account because neither Thatcherism nor Dengism operated within a social vacuum without prior legacies and histories. What helps to set the scene for a generation is both the immediate as well as the not so immediate past but the former is very important in creating new generations and making them distinctive from their predecessors.

In the process, there develops amongst contemporaries a stock of responses related to their own generational identity but these may be stronger at certain points, especially in times of rapid social change. Without clearly recognisable events, there will be potentially blurred boundaries, as noted above. Each generation's characteristics are partly defined by those of others and reference to contemporary social and political change then becomes inevitable. In this study, it will shown that the key social and historical events are related to the reformist policies of the post-Mao leadership and the subsequent impact of these upon the group under scrutiny. Other generations within the Chinese context can be seen as similarly shaped by social and political events and movements.

The timing of generation-shaping events and sources of identity also has to be seen in terms of the human life-cycle to define more precisely at what point people fall into a generational category. We tend to belong to only one generation in our life time and cannot easily shift to another, even if we consciously try to adopt newer influences and trends. Older people may try to give the appearance of belonging to a younger generation, for example, but it is not only their biological age which may hinder this identification and acceptance by members of the desired generation. It may be easier to change our social class than generation and certainly 'generational mobility' is not a commonly used term, whereas social mobility is an accepted and well-researched phenomenon. We carry with us our own generational outlook and accessories which may be hard to lose, disguise or alter.

Even the language we use is associated with our generation and will give us away. According to Mannheim, when someone is placed in a new environment, they may consciously alter certain aspects of their thought and behaviour but they never fully acclimatise themselves in so 'radical and thoroughgoing a fashion' (1952:300). He includes language and dialect which persist from an earlier life stage and many sociolinguists concur that a person's linguistic identity is formed before adulthood. Certain words, phrases and slang, for example, come into use and then die out except perhaps amongst those who initiated or popularised their usage and it is difficult for people to change their early linguistic behaviour (Wells, 1988). Generational mobility, then, is a problematic, if not impossible, process.

There is some agreement that generational formation and subsequent identification often coincides with the formative years of life either childhood or youth but the focus tends to be on the latter. Up to a certain point of one's life, things are generally accepted, then a period of questioning ensues which evolves into a set of attitudes and responses. Mannheim links this to adolescence and to the notion of 'stratification of experience' (1952:297) within the generational equation. This takes us into the field of social psychology to some extent because he refers to consciousness and how events and data 'impinge' upon this with ideas of ' . . . "first impression", "childhood experiences" – and which follow to form the second, third, and other "strata"' (*op. cit*:298). Subsequent experiences may be superimposed upon earlier ones rather than having a direct impact. There may even be a form of filtering going on in the light of formative experiences which affect views, outlooks and ways of receiving new information and events.

As a result, there is a focus on the activities of young people, which is another reason why the generational perspective is relevant to this study. We really start to feel membership of a generation in our younger years as we move into adulthood and the youth peer group is 'one of the real and continuing bases for collective identities organised around the focus of "generation"' (Clarke *et al.*, 1976:51). Starr (1974) cites studies which support Mannheim's view that political identification specifically occurs during late adolescence and early adulthood so what is happening at this point in a person's life will probably form part of their generational consciousness.

To illustrate this point, for many 1960s Chinese youth, the years spent 'cleaning privies and feeding hogs coincided with childhood, adolescence, and young adulthood . . . For them, the Cultural Revolution was not a temporary setback to be endured, but the formative period of their lives' (Ownby, 1986:213). Raddock makes the point that young people were the group at the centre of this political movement which 'caught the young individual at a stage in his life when he [*sic*] was seeking to relate his childhood experience to an adult identity' (1977:1). Also noted by Laufer and Bengtson was the tendency for a concentration of interest upon student movements, with young intellectuals viewed as a particularly important part of a generation. Whilst this study does not break with this trend, it is recognised that generational analysis can be applied to all age cohorts and in all areas of societies.

This leads us into the consideration of heterogeneity. No generation experiences the key social and historical forces in exactly the same manner and Mannheim considered possible forms of differentiation. One division is between 'generations as mere collective facts on the one hand, and *concrete social groups* [*sic*] on the other' (1952:288). Not everybody within one generation will be part of a concrete social group, it would appear, because they have different locations within society as well as differential exposure to the key events of their generation. This involves another important distinction between generation as 'location' and as 'actuality' (*op. cit*: 288). Every generation contains a number of sub-units which may be more like concrete social groups depending upon their awareness of each other and sense of common identity or destiny. The latter implies some sort of mutual identification and common bond rather than mere placement.

Objectively speaking, all age cohort members exposed to generation-creating events may be counted as members but with acceptance of the differences between them. Some may feel the identification more strongly than others and this will certainly be explored with the specific case of 1980s young intellectuals. Mannheim stressed the need to 'clarify the specific inter-relations of the individuals comprising a single generation-unit'. This will be attempted since, as Starr points out, 'Any given actualized generation may contain several different generation units within it' (1974:77). The concept of a 'generation-unit' is important because any one generation consists of these sub-groups and there is the possibility of antagonism between them. In Mannheim's much quoted but extremely pertinent point,

> Youth experiencing the same concrete historical problems may be said to be part of the same actual generation; while those groups within the same actual generation which work up the material of their common experiences in different specific ways, constitute separate generation units. (1952:304)

The relevance of this extends to several main points. Firstly, it is correct to say that young intellectuals can be viewed as a 'generation unit' because of the different ways they experienced the reform decade compared to their less educated peers. They were part of the larger social group of 'youth', to be discussed in the following chapter, but had their own location. As Starr reminds us 'Any given actualized generation may contain several different generation units within it' (*op. cit*:77). Even within the category of *qingnian zhishi fenzi* it is arguably the case that other sub-generation units exist and this possibility will also be discussed with specific reference to the case study. Another point is that young intellectuals 'worked up' the material of their 'common experiences'. Consideration of the reform context will illustrate exactly what the material and common experiences could be and how the 'working up' led to certain trends of thought and behaviour.

Thirdly, there are factors of 'location' which affect the experiences of generation units and result in forms of differentiation. Without definable social structure, historical factors and social interaction, 'there would merely be birth ageing, and death' (Mannheim, 1952:291). In reality, this is not the case. Social class may be cited as one important locational factor and this creates, in his view, a 'tendency' towards certain experiences and reaction to them. Any particular tendency can be determined by consideration of the location which would point towards 'certain definite modes of behaviour, feeling, and thought' (*op. cit*:291). Certain locations give rise to variations within a particular generation but the use of the term 'tendency' avoids an over-deterministic model of behaviour and is similar in many respects to Bourdieu's notion of habitus.

This can be described as the 'organising framework of cultural dispositions' (Jenkins, 1992:39) within which individuals and groups operate or, in Bourdieu's own words, 'the strategy-generation principle enabling agents to cope with unforeseen and ever-changing situations . . . a system of lasting, transposable dispositions' (Garnham and Williams, 1986:120). He also described it as 'an objective relationship between two objectivities' (Bourdieu, 1992:101). Social actors can draw upon their resources of predispositions, cultural traits, perceptions and so on, in order to act in what they consider to be appropriate ways. Social class is an important source of habitus because it may lead to 'the set of agents who are placed in homogeneous conditions of existence imposing homogeneous conditionings and producing homogeneous systems of dispositions capable of generating similar practices' (*op. cit*:101). Like Mannheim's concept of location, it leads to certain tendencies in cognitive and behavioural terms. The habitus includes social practices and behaviour, even ways of talking and moving, and its theoretical ground is somewhere between the structuralism Bourdieu rejected and the opposite one of viewing society as the sum of different individuals' behaviours.

The habitus, as part of the social and cultural environment into which people are born and grow up, is transmitted through socialisation processes which are clearly mediated by factors of class, family background, racial identity and so on. Particular groups and collectivities have their own habitus which provides them with a source of 'objective practices' and also a set of 'subjective generative principles' (Jenkins, 1992:82). This is relevant for this case study with young intellectuals shown to be an elite group in Chinese society with a particular habitus leading them to certain predispositions or 'tendencies'.

Social class, as a common 'location', will affect generation-identity and consciousness. Upper class youth, for example, experience generational shaping events differently to their working class counterparts. The class dimension was shown to be important in a study by Kasschau *et al.* who sought to explore the various 'manifestations of generational consciousness or youth movement solidarity among various classes of youth', (1974:70), and found that class sometimes overrode generational solidarity. Adopting the generational perspective does not reduce other forms of differentiation to insignificance, the point being that young people may be exposed to similar historical events and become an 'actual' generation but different location leads to generation units.

As well as class, there are gender and ethnicity dimensions and in China the urban/rural divide is also important. These have to be considered to determine to what extent they affect the experiences of those within an actual generation and how they then 'work up' their generational material. It will be useful to consider what Starr (*op. cit.*) describes as the 'formative tendencies', 'fundamental integrative attitudes', and 'set of collective strivings' shared by members of the generation unit.

When treating the intelligentsia as a separate social category, with its own particular history and socio-economic, as well as political constituents, the younger members can be seen as a generation in themselves. Intellectual youth will, in this work, be treated both as a generation unit and a generation, necessitating consideration of dual location in terms of their non-intellectual peers and likewise for their more senior counterparts. They share certain generational characteristics of other youth with common elements and points of similarity but their elite position is a source of differentiation. Education is recognised here as a major generational issue because of the significance given to it at the outset of the reform decade, as will be shown in Chapter 3.

To determine the nature of generational heterogeneity, the key historical factors have to be delineated and related to people of similar ages in order to assess any differential exposure and experience. These events may not touch all those of the same age group or, if they do, not in quite the same manner due to factors of location and stratification of experience. The events and impact of the reform decade did not happen everywhere at the same time, for example. Rural youth were not initially exposed to all of the changes and had more secondary experience or contact with them, for example through watching television. This process of distinguishing the key events was carried out in this study first of all to determine how Deng's generation were distinctive from their predecessors and, secondly, how young intellectuals formed part of this generation. Thirdly, the analysis included identification of its own internal units and these distinctions subsequently helped to locate the respondents in this small scale case study.

This discussion of Mannheim's generational work raises the question of its precise importance or relevance for this study. Whilst it is useful to view a contemporary social group as a generation and then go on to explain its 'tendencies' in terms of thought and behaviour, this might be insufficient justification for adopting such a theoretical framework. So far this relevance has not been spelt out but, once again, it can be found within Mannheim's central text and was considered to be worth discussing separately here. This relevance relates to the relationship between generations and social change.

Delineating different generation units, for example, facilitates the identification of groups involved in attempts to bring about social change in China during the 1980s. Having discussed in some detail the component parts of the generational perspective, along with giving some indications of how they would be applied in this particular study, it will be useful to consider now this additional reason for developing some of Mannheim's key ideas. His own interest as well as that of the other researchers who have been cited in this area was partly led by the desire to better understand the process of social change. Some theoretical leanings can be examined before moving on to identify generations of Chinese intellectuals.

Generational Analysis and Social Change

Societies change over time, sometimes slowly and sometimes more suddenly and this is often, but not always, related to the activities of younger generations. Laufer and Bengtson describe how 'The concept of generations has served since antiquity to explain the process of social change' (1974:182). Why change occurs, or, on the other hand, why some things stay the same across historical periods in spite of successive biological generations being born, ageing and dying, is a key question at the base of much of this work. Mannheim was not the first to be curious about these factors and to seek answers in terms of social generations. He cites Hume who linked the biological continuity of the generations with political continuity whilst Comte 'toyed with' the idea of what would happen if the human life span were longer or shorter (Mannheim, 1952:277). The tempo of social change would alter accordingly in a stable society without sudden, revolutionary activity. It has also been the concern for social order and stability which has prompted much generational analysis, such as in the USA in the 1960s. This is why 'The problem of generations is important enough to merit serious consideration. It is one of the indispensable guides to an understanding of the structure of social and intellectual movements' (*op. cit*:286).

Examining generational issues can certainly assist the understanding of social change because young people engage with the legacies of their elders and they may accept, reject or change the cultural contents and social arrangements presented to them in the transferral process. This can happen consciously or unconsciously and to a greater or lesser extent. In modern societies, social change takes place at an accelerated pace and more extreme shifts may occur between generations thus making the younger generation of particular interest to 'social theorists and reformers interested in change' (Mann, 1983:45). Similarly, 'The more rapid the change, the greater the gap between generational sets of consciousness' (Brake, 1985:25). The youth of any society can be viewed potentially as a 'regenerative force' (Murdock and McCron, 1976:195) with the possibility of them creating sudden or revolutionary change. Starr cites Ryder who claimed that they are the age group 'containing the greatest potential for change' (Starr, 1972:78), being old enough to participate in social and political movements but not so commited in terms of work, family and so on. They have the time, energy and enthusiasm for consciously instigating social change. It is argued here that these considerations apply to young intellectuals even more so than their less educated peers who may marry earlier, for example.

In China, it is perhaps no coincidence that, as elsewhere, 'the renewed power from the enthusiasm for reconstruction which followed the armistice of 1918' (Murdock and McCron:196) was reflected in the actions of Chinese students. Ideas of transforming traditional Chinese institutional and cultural practices and modernising the language were very strong amongst the young intellectuals who participated in the 'May Fourth Movement'[2] (Chow, 1967) which remained an important cultural and political reference point in the 1980s. Ortega went so far as saying that it would be generational succession rather than class struggle which would act as the principal engine of change although there were few details of exactly how this process would evolve.

The crucial link between generational consciousness and social change affects the membership of generational units. Braungart notes how isolated youth, such as those in rural areas, 'have the potential for experiencing generational solidarity, but rarely become involved in generational movements. Membership implies participation in the social and intellectual currents of the day – which typically occur in urban centers experiencing rapid change' (1974:43). This predominance of intellectuals and particularly young intellectuals in any process of social change would seem to be supported in this study. Rural youth, it will be shown, have been 'activists' but in different ways to their urban peers. Without being swept up into 'dynamic destabilization' generational membership is questionable. This is why it is considered feasible to view young intellectuals as Deng's generation and because they were more involved especially as activists and instigators of change.

The US studies of 1960s protest movements, to draw a comparison, discovered that many activists had middle and upper middle class backgrounds. This not unexpected finding reinforces the link between change and certain key generational groups. The key group in the China is considered to be the young intellectuals especially when examining protest movements such as in 1989, which culminated in a violent clash between different generations. Whilst the generational perspective was valued from the outset of the study, it received more attention after this time as a way of understanding the differences between younger and more senior Chinese intellectuals. It is not proposed that this clash was purely a generational issue since there were clearly other factors involved but understanding the generations, especially Deng's, will provide further insights into the events of Spring 1989.

From the outset of the reform period, the likelihood of inter-generational conflict was quite high and may be considered as a characteristic feature. As Deng's generation was created at a time of systematic policy 'reversals', a wider generation gap could be expected than is normal when society is fairly stable. Hooper describes them as 'living through the period of greatest change in their lives – adolescence, finishing their education, competing in the job market, forming personal relationships – at a time of rapid economic and social change' (1991:264). They were characterised by these changes, striving to fashion themselves ultimately as suitable heirs to earlier generations whilst simulta-neously trying to achieve adulthood and find a suitable place for themselves in a rapidly modernising society. Any clashes between older and younger generations can be seen not only as the result of different ages but of different formative experiences and generational references.

Findings from this study have implications for research into generations in other social contexts since the application of Mannheim's 'seminal' concepts to actual examples can assist the analysis of social change and be useful in the search for the key groups involved in bringing this about. This application is not unproblematic, however, because of the difficulties involved in the empirical investigation of social generations (Pilcher, 1994:494). These problems will be discussed together with the impact of generational division on social processes in China. This raises important questions about the factors that single them out as a separate generation and how they carried the marks of their particular historical moment.

Additionally, it can be asked how these key factors help explain not only their political but also social and economic behaviour. In order to answer these questions adequately, we need to be clear about how the generational characteristics were shaped throughout the late 1970s and early 1980s. As a new generation, they tried to distinguish themselves from their predecessors and the relationship between them will be discussed with the key points and contact and divergence outlined. No generation, however, stands in isolation from others and there are clear links between the past and present. This will involve a summary of recent history and how the communist regime created concrete generational characteristics through its economic and other policy reforms. The relative lack of political reform was also influential in shaping generational features with many expecations left unfulfilled and adding to the frustrations which became transformed into various strategies of action including forms of political activism.

DRAWING GENERATIONAL BOUNDARIES OR WHO ARE DENG'S GENERATION?

As already noted, generations of youth have been shaped every decade or so since the communists took power and each of these 'has had its own defining characteristics, from 1950s idealism to 1980s disaffection' (Hooper, 1991:264). Gold prefers to talk in terms of 'cohorts', from the 1950s to the 1970s 'reform cohort, which was 'at the extreme of alienation' (1991:607). This last cohort is his equivalent of Deng's generation. Between 1949 and 1989, the four main generations all exhibited both continuities and differences related to their formative milieu.[3]

Zhang and Cheng (1988) include the communist founders of New China described as the'heroic generation' (*yi dai yinghao*). Also known as the 'Long March' generation, or the 'Old Guard' (Rice, 1992:125), those still alive in the 1980s remained politically influential, Deng Xiaoping being a prime example. Their successors, the 'pessimistic' generation, were disappointed by the initial results of communism and the regime's treatment of intellectuals but had mostly accepted the demands of the Party. They were succeeded by a 'political' generation in the 1960s which included young Red Guards spurred on by Mao Zedong to root out those intent on subverting socialism. Also known as the 'lost generation', their activism resulted in political disillusionment, even despair. The urban educated youth who were sent to the countryside are closely associated with the Cultural Revolution as are as those who were politically active Red Guards.

Gold identifies two 'cohorts' from the Cultural Revolution period. One consists of those in their youth during the 1950s and those in their childhood during the 1960s. The second group were affected more indirectly than the first since they were either too young to be sent to the countryside or went only for short periods. These differences affected their life chances and attitudes but both cohorts experienced problems as well as causing problems for the authorities. The younger ones had their education interrupted and could be unruly, even out of control because of losing early years of schooling and the associated discipline. They were able to resume their education, however, unlike many of the previous cohort.

The reform or the 'fourth generation' (*di si dai ren*) in Zhang and Cheng's reckoning, were called 'people on the edge' (Luo, 1995:558) because of the changes. The major forces shaping them arose from the different circumstances after the end of the Cultural Revolution with the deaths of Mao and Zhou Enlai in 1976 contributing to an end of an era feeling, as did the subsequent arrest of the 'Gang of Four' who had tried to usurp power.

The reinstatement of the college entrance examinations,[4] discussed more in Chapter 3, is viewed here as a generational marker or watershed event which in part distinguishes the former 'political' generation from the emerging 'economic' (*di jingji shidai*) one (Zhang and Cheng, 1988:4) and sent positive signals to the relatively 'unscarred' young intellectuals. Expectations of higher education as a route to improved life chances and social mobility can be seen as a generational characteristic. If these expectations were unmet, generational conflict could result leading to some form of social instability and political reaction, as will be shown. The reforms provided the socio-economic as well as the political background for heightened expectations amongst young intellectuals, who viewed higher education as a way of obtaining secure employment, high social position, status and a degree of influence in Chinese society.

This context can help determine the generational boundaries or *daiji* as well as taking into account those observations of Luo, Gold and Zhang and Cheng. Those born in the 1960s and early 1970s could be included as they would have experienced educational disruption during the Cultural Revolution but were probably not part of the wholesale transfer of urban youth to rural regions (*xiaxiang*), as previously noted (Bernstein, 1975; 1977). It is not possible to set an age or time limit, as already argued, because exposure to and experience of the Cultural Revolution varied from place to place to some extent. Those relatively free from the influences of the 'chaos', it can be argued, would be more exposed to and influenced by the succeeding reform years.

By adopting this approach, it can be seen that a number of sub-groups within Deng's generation are recognisable at the beginning of the reform period with some members exhibiting several characteristics of the previous 'lost' generation. There is some blurring of boundaries and it is arguable that some older youth belong more to the earlier rather than to Deng's generation. Luo also raises the problem of placing all young people of the 1980s together because this 'mixes up two distinctive age cohorts, or, as more commonly described in China, two "generations" that grew up in different social backgrounds and had different life experiences' (1995:559). The entrance examinations, however, brought some older and younger youth into the same generation. This can be described as an 'enlargement of contemporary Chinese youth' to include senior youth in their thirties who in some senses were already 'middle aged' (*Wei Ding Gao*, 1988, 14:3).

There were older youth who had completed middle school but had not attended university because of the Cultural Revolution; teenagers attending middle school; children at the upper levels of the primary sector; and, older youth who had completed higher education during the 1960s and early 1970s. There could be as much as 20 years difference in age if all of these were included in Deng's generation but age was previously rejected as the major generational indicator. Instead, the educational reforms from the mid-1970s onward play a crucial role in deciding generational placement. The inclusion of older youth is accepted as contentious because of their different life experiences, but within any generation there will be such sub-sections and the one being examined here is no exception. Not all older youth 'on the edge' could be included because of their identification with the past generation rather than the future one. Members of the reform generation, it is argued, were more forward-looking in terms of their own careers and development as well as that of their nation.

The first and final sub-groups outlined above, both at the top of the age range, had directly experienced the Cultural Revolution. The examinations offered those without tertiary education new opportunities. Those who had already completed their studies at this level were more likely to be viewed as belonging to the previous 'third' or 'political' generation. If some had succeeded in retaining the status of young intellectuals, even though they had not completed the entrance exams, and were actively involved in the changes taking place in Chinese society, they could be considered as belonging to the 1980s generation. Participation in further study could place them within this generation because of the importance of education for this social category and a prospective outlook, that is looking ahead, rather than a retrospective one could also identify older youth as members of the new generation.

At the other end are those who were at primary school when the reform decade began. They appear to have little in common with their seniors but there are reasons for placing them initially within the same generation, namely the educational and occupational aspirations they held after the key policy shift. Similar expectations of what might follow for them as an educated elite fostered a generational consciousness, it is argued, across a wider age span than might normally be expected. Variations in outlook arising from experiences and location *vis-à-vis* the Cultural Revolution and the reform programme have to be considered as possible 'fault lines' within the emerging generation. Older educated youth who had not progressed to university by the time the college exams were restored can be placed at the upper periphery of the reform generation if they fostered the ambition of pursuing higher education.

Those at the junior end represent the other periphery of this generation and, according to an article in *Zhongguo Qingnian*, experienced the 'least painful maturity' (1988, 10:14). '*Tongku de Chengshu*' considered a survey of 92 students enrolled in a university politics department between 1977 and 1978 and three levels of students were recognised altogether, similar to the four intra-generational units described above. Apart from the fortunate youngest group who were spared rural relocation, there was a level consisting of senior high school graduates from the 1960s whose progression into higher education had been interrupted. The other level was of junior and senior high school graduates from that period who were in the middle and suffered variable disruptions. The youngest were seen graduating from middle school during 1977 but were competing with their older counterparts during the first round of the examinations with their transition into adulthood likely to be through higher education rather than political campaigns.

The scene at examination centres was a literal and symbolic mixing of the generations. There were 'naive middle school students who had just graduated', and 'fathers and mothers in their thirties, with their own experience of suffering' (ZGQN, *op. cit*:3) Although years apart, they were all competing for the same places, all trying to gain the opportunity not only to study but to enter the social elite of young intellectuals being recreated by the reformist policies. They were 'the same generation with different age groups who would start from the same running track' (ZGQN, *op. cit*:3). All levels of youth were represented in the initial rush to take the examinations and numbers were very high with a considerable backlog of educated youth to be processed as well as the growing ranks of graduating middle school students.

The mixing of generations had disappeared by the 1980s with enrolment of students directly from senior middle school the official policy. Undergraduates at the end of the reform decade were peers and there was normally very little variation in age within each grade. It becomes easier after this time to place generational divides according to age rather than exposure to social and political developments. Although the young intellectuals interviewed in this study were a convenient sample, the participants could be viewed as fairly representative in this sense, with those still at university, as will be shown, all of the same ages because the entry of older applicants into higher education had been restricted. Once the backlog of rusticated youth who qualified for the examinations had taken them, members of this group were increasingly excluded from higher education and from Deng's generation itself.

At the time of conducting fieldwork, there were already indications that younger students were developing attitudes and behavioural trends different from their elders and perhaps, therefore, a different generational consciousness. The 'post-reform' generation to succeed Deng's was in the making by the late 1980s and a watershed event was probably necessary to clearly delineate it. 'Cultural re-examination' or 'cultural fever' had already taken off in 1985 according to Kelly (1990:30) against the background of this generational shift. It is arguably the case that the 1989 student movement with its serious repercussions provided such an historic, albeit tragic, watershed. Although it did not mark the end of China's economic reform programme, there was a temporary suspension of it and the government indicated little intention of making political reforms to match those in the economic sector.

The heterogeneity of a generation also includes social features which cross-cut each other, as previously suggested. Zhang and Cheng drew distinctions between university students, city youth (*chengshi qingnian*) and rural youth (*nongcun qingnian*). The rural/urban divide remains significant in China and it is rare for young intellectuals to have rural backgrounds, being more of an urban-based elite. Gender differentiation is another form of heterogeneity. Although they may share the specific generational milieu with male counterparts, women experience it differently because of social and cultural conventions. Traditional practices and beliefs persisted into the contemporary period although they were transformed in some ways. A similar argument can be adopted in terms of ethnic divisions within the generation with the majority Han Chinese having advantages, especially in education, over their minority counterparts. Bearing these sources of heterogeneity in mind, this is an appropriate point to describe those young intellectuals who contributed information to this study and also, more generally, data collection techniques.

COLLECTING DATA ABOUT DENG'S GENERATION

The study can be described as ethnographic in nature with much of the data obtained, as already stated, simply (or not so simply as the case may be) by being in China during the 1980s. Some of it is based on informal, unstructured observations and wanderings throughout the country and getting to know members of Deng's as well as some from the previous 'lost generation'. During 1988, however, more structured fieldwork was conducted which included interviews with a sample of 22 respondents supplemented by a number of semi-structured group interviews. There were also many opportunities to observe and join the reform generation at study, work and play for almost a year.

Numerous visits, such as to the nearby English Corner,[5] outings, parties, discos and so on all provided occasions to collect information even when the researcher was trying to get some 'R and R'. Some of the problems of conducting such fieldwork are described in the Appendix and will not be dwelt on here. Suffice it to say that by living amongst the group, a lot was learnt by listening and watching closely as well as asking pertinent questions.

Other data came from newspapers and magazines as well as the other media and common trends were noted. A high level of interconnectedness was apparent between what interviewees were saying, what students wanted to discuss in the classroom and what emerged during many private discussions. An unofficial social survey, referred to here as the 'Roots' survey,[6] was also useful. It was conducted amongst Beijing University (*Beida*) students during May and June 1988 with three questionnaires being administered before, during and after the June poster campaign or *xuechao*. The researchers undertook the study on their own initiative but under the auspices of one of the university's departments.

Their main objective was to investigate the attitudes and opinions of young intellectuals related to the issues previously identified as 'hot topics', such as the social position of intellectuals and the reform programme. As members of this social group, they shared many of the characteristics of their respondents. I was alerted to this research through informal channels and in many respects their concerns reflected my own with the questions they raised being similar to the ones I was preparing to ask. These key issues had emerged during a number of discussions with young intellectuals as well as from surveying the media and observing events at the time. The degree of overlap indicated the current major issues, and the questionnaires themselves, as well as the data provided by them, are relevant and informative.

The researchers quickly altered their schedules to include the June *xuechao* and its aftermath. They did not know when they initially administered the first questionnaire that the killing of a fellow postgraduate would soon spark localised student protest. Their presence on the scene of the *xuechao* was advantageous in one sense but it placed them in a potentially difficult position with the university authorities because they were investigating sensitive areas. At one point in early June they were told to end their research but the data collection continued and they were able to publish the results later in the year (*Zhongguo Fazhan yu Gaige*, 1988:10.). I was fortunate to be have a glimpse of the draft results from the questionnaires thanks to one of the researchers before they were analysed and written up as a published report.

Both the questions and the data informed the drafting of the interview schedule which was underway at that time. The survey also provided additional background material as well as quantitative data which supplemented my own basically qualitative data collected from the interviews. Personal observations of the conditions and main trends of thought among young intellectuals in general and more specifically the development of the June *xuechao* were confirmed to some extent by the 'Roots' survey.

It was useful in another way, acting as a link between the part of the research concerned with setting the context of Deng's generation where mostly secondary data was involved and the primary data from the interviews. Results from the three questionnaires can be considered as good indicators of attitudes and opinions but, as with other attitudinal research, there is some unreliability due to respondents not expressing their opinions frankly. This point is relevant for primary research conducted in China especially when views about political issues are sought. Concern about answering controversial questions caused genuine fear which should be borne in mind when analysing responses. I had to be sympathetic to the feelings of the researchers as well as my own respondents in order to protect them. The answers might not fully reflect their genuine views but the researchers were aware of possible limitations caused by the social and political situation because they were also young intellectuals and shared many experiences with their respondents. Putting aside these recognised problems, the 'Roots' survey offers a glimpse into the attitudes of Deng's generation. It is them speaking for themselves to some extent rather than through the official Party bodies.

Given such reservations, data from my own sample which was of a convenience or snowball type was considered carefully in terms of how representative it was. It is arguable that making generalisations based upon such a limited number of interviewees is problematic because they may not be representative of all young intellectuals. This issue has been raised by others who have relied on interviews for data collection, such as with Chinese émigrés in Hong Kong (Raddock 1977; Shirk 1982; Chan, 1985).

Interview volunteers may be different from those who either did not have the chance to talk or were unwilling to do so. It is often accepted, however, that interviewees may articulate views of their unheard counterparts. Leaving aside idiosynsracies, some trends of thought and behaviour are presented which can be compared, as they were in this study, with more general social trends and opinions.

My sample was obtained in a similar way to Raddock's sample, that is through social networks or *guanxi wang*[7] although his was Hong Kong rather than mainland based. He writes of being 'fortunate to gain introduction to two particular youths . . . and to win their confidence and friendship. These people then introduced me to several of their friends, who in turn introduced me to their friends. Thus, a snowballing technique, less oriented in reality to social science approaches than to the nature of interpersonal relationships in Chinese society, developed as a primary means of recruiting respondents.' (Raddock, 1977:12). Similarly, Unger's respondents, also émigrés in Hong Kong, were normally friends or the friends of friends (Unger, 1982).

The sample size was not decided in advance but grew according to people being introduced to me or by asking possible candidates. Occasionally, interviewees brought along their friends. 'It is common, in this style of research, to continue sampling by including additional interviewees until the researcher decides that the sample is of adequate size' (Rose, 1982:9). I heard similar themes being raised and certain patterns in the responses emerged. I felt that few, if any, further insights would be forthcoming by interviewing more than those 22 people, although some supplementary, informal group interviews were later arranged. There was constant observation of events in China as they unfolded throughout the year with particular reference to young intellectuals and these were useful guides to the more specific information provided by respondents. The generalisations made were considered carefully and set within the broader context of the reform period.

The opportunity to view at first hand the two poster campaigns, for example, assisted in this comparison, as did the collection of media items. Just as Raddock felt his snowball sample was adequate and fairly representative, this was my conclusion about my own sample. Overall, the 22 interviewees can be viewed as largely illustrative rather than representative of

Deng's generation because of the convenience nature of the sample. They were all studying in Beijing and included undergraduates as well as graduates from some years before. A number of them were known to me personally, others were introduced by colleagues who were interested in my research.

An important role was played by a key informant, 22-year old Chu[8] who not only supplied some of the interviewees but also much current information about the universities and related issues. He did this because of his own interest in Deng's generation, of which he was a part. This way of operating is not uncommon in China and in a sense I was gaining some positive advantages of the *guanxi wang* phenomenon. There were several other informants who were or became close friends and their ideas and reflections played an important role in terms of data collection and analysis. They shared some of the common traits of young intellectuals, such as the trend of going abroad to study, but sample members expressed their own personalities and views as well.

Members of three of the four sub-groups described above were present in the sample of interviewees but there were no older youth on the periphery, that is university graduates of the Cultural Revolution era. There were young students who were attending primary school when the reform decade began, middle school pupils who progressed straight to university and 'older' youth who seized the opportunity of higher education after the return of the entrance examinations.

The oldest sample members, Qiu, aged 31, and Gao and Zhou both aged 28, fitted into this last category. They had completed middle school in the mid-1970s but were not able to go to university at that time, having to wait until 1977. They all participated in the first sitting of the entrance examinations, along with hundreds of thousands of other 'rusticated' youth. Kelly also mentioned those who made it 'by the skin of their teeth back into the universities' (1990:42). These are the type of young intellectuals who arguably belong more to the previous generation but, as discussed before, their enthusiasm for and participation in higher education immediately after the reinstatement of the examinations gives them some characteristics of Deng's generation. They saw, however, the differences between themselves and their younger counterparts just out of school.

The largest generational unit consisted of 11 people in their mid-twenties in 1988 who were attending middle school at the start of the reform period. Wang, aged 23, was in his final year of study and about to graduate but the others in this sub-group had already graduated. They were: Xiu, Guo and Hua, aged 24; Zhang, Sun, Zhen and Yang aged 25; Lu, Jiang and Yu aged 26. They were spared from rural relocation and went straight into higher education. The *xia xiang* movement was probably, however, part of their consciousness with older siblings of the 'third generation' having been sent to the countryside throughout the 1970s. They were aware that without the reforms, they would have shared the same fate.

The youngest generational unit consisted of eight people who were at the higher levels of primary school when the reforms began. Li, Chen, Liu, Gu, Wen, Lili, all aged 20, and Deng and Zhao, aged 19, could take more for granted in educational terms than their senior generational members because they had experienced no discontinuities. The examinations were restored at the beginning of their educational careers and the significance of the reforms in terms of educational and occupational mobility may have been more indirect for them and conveyed through their parents and teachers.

This is in contrast to the oldest generational unit who grasped any opportunities that came their way because they were experienced enough to realise the importance of the policy shifts. Living through the Cultural Revolution distinguished them from these younger people but the shared 'dream' of higher education at this point offers a tenuous generational link. Potential educated youth still in primary school would not be reading the official messages but their parents and teachers would have been. This can be contrasted to the oldest intra-generational unit who were reading the messages and taking whatever opportunities they could.

The oldest interviewees were already in employment and two were married. One of them, Gao, identified himself as a 'young father'. More than ten years separate the eldest from the youngest members of the sample but they are juxtaposed here as intra-generational units within the same generation because of the reform context. The sample members had an important sense of proximity to what was happening at the political centre and also on the capital's major campuses by being based in Beijing during 1988. Being near Beijing University at that time was significant given this campus's reputation as a 'thermometer' of young intellectuals' thoughts and actions with a number of poster campaigns occuring there during the fieldwork period.

The range of higher education institutions attended by the sample varied from arguably the highest status ones in the country to a less prestigious teacher training college. Sun had studied languages and was teaching English, as was Zhen. The respondents ranged from first year undergraduates to the mature students who were taking special training courses, mostly to improve their English in preparation for going abroad. In terms of undergraduate subjects, there was some emphasis on science and technology in the sample and this was not restricted to the males. Two young women were studying chemistry, Li and Chen, and another one, Liu, studied computer science. One of the graduates, Lu, had taken a medical course and Zhen had an engineering qualification. The males Qiu, Jiang, Lu, Guo and Zhang had scientific, technological and medical studies background. Other subjects included philosophy, political science and science subjects.

Six respondents had either studied English during their first degree or were participants of an English language training course. This reflects to some extent the way in which the sample was gathered. With the researcher teaching English to both graduates and undergraduates, it was relatively easier to find people with some experience of formally taught English who were willing to be interviewed. This facilitated interaction during interviews and also, with several respondents known to the researcher, participation in extra-curricular social activities.

The social origins of the interviewees were largely those of middle class or 'bourgeois' backgrounds with teachers and government officials being the most common categories of parental occupations. Four described both parents as teachers whilst four had fathers who were government officials or cadres. There was only a minority of mothers or fathers from 'worker' and 'peasant' backgrounds with three in each category. This is significant because 'family and social class background play an important role' (Kwong, 1994:254). It was not clear how many respondents were offspring of earlier generations of rusticated youth whose parents lived in different regions from their original hometowns, examples being Inner Mongolia and Tibet. Although resettled in border regions, they may have maintained urban residence in small towns and non-manual ocupations. There was also an urban bias with most respondents from large or medium sized cities. Again, this may have been due to the nature of the sample but it tends to fall in line with other research findings. The historical and long-standing rural/urban divide was sharpened by the post-1976 policies and the traditional link between the educated elite and urban residence renewed.

There were no respondents from minority backgrounds. Although this could be due to the restricted nature of the sample it may also be indicative of the relatively fewer minority students in the capital. There were no formal contacts made with the institutions specialising in ethnic issues where most of the minority students can be found. There were some informal contacts, however, which provided additional information about certain minorities. Those interviewees who came from the less developed regions were Han Chinese whose families had been relocated. In this sense, Deng's generation is largely made up of young intellectuals of Han origin and this is reflected in the nature of the interview sample. It is accepted that it had limitations because of being drawn from educated youth studying in the capital and thus certain biases have to be borne in mind.

The research took the form of a case study with participant observation as well as interviews, both formal and informal, and is similar to other work within the field of education, such as Willis (1977). Whilst he also had a relatively small interview sample, the results were relevant when set within the context of working class underachievement. The results from this study can be justified as valuable because they are also set within a particular context, that is the economic and educational crises of late 1980s China. The fieldwork research for this study was completed at the end of 1989, just before the Spring student movement which displayed many of the key characteristics of earlier protests whilst having its own generational features. I was able to return to China before the end of the student demonstrations and conducted informal interviews with participants before the troops moved into Tiananmen Square. Further informal primary data was collected between February 1990 and August 1991 with some previous contacts reestablished inspite of increased vigilance by the authorities.

The 1989 movement can be accepted as the ultimate outcome of the disparities or 'aspirations gap' (Hooper, 1991:264) to be detailed in this work. These disparities were exacerbated in the late 1980s by the rapid economic and social changes of the reform period which led to many frustrations. Young intellectuals' own sense of group cohesion and the belief that they had a historic duty to fulfil also played their part in helping to shape the generation. It can, additionally, be viewed as symptomatic of the generation gap (*daigou*) with potential sources of conflict arising out of inter-generational differences which may have predisposed young intellectuals towards certain actions. Their attitudes and behaviour were at times considered problematic by those in positions of power, some of whom were once young intellectuals themselves. This was illustrated by the *yi dai yinghao* generation members still in power and making decisions affecting Deng's generation some six decades their junior.

In conclusion to her work on young intellectuals of the Cultural Revolution, Chan writes that it is 'the tale of only a single generation, unlike those that come before or after . . . the children of Deng are not the children of Mao' (1985:224). This will be illustrated throughout this book but the fact that there were similarities arising from their shared status as young intellectuals will be considered next.

2 Generations of Young Chinese Intellectuals

The term 'educated youth', an alternative to young intellectuals, was frequently used by the communist authorities until recently. It is a discursive category consisting of two major parts that need to be unravelled. The concept of youth in the Chinese context will be dealt with first, then the intellectual status. What we are considering here is not just a matter of definitions, although these are important especially when operationalising the concept of *qingnian zhishi fenzi* for research purposes. There are social, cultural, historical and political factors involved in the creation and shaping of this social group with an emphasis in the communist period on the official discourse as well as the treatment of the group.

THE 'YOUTHFULNESS' OF YOUNG INTELLECTUALS

As well as being a biological period of development occurring between childhood and adulthood, youth is also recognisable as a social and cultural phenomenon influenced by historical features. Transition is usually involved in varying ways, and the time involved is not universally fixed. Gold writes how the 'life course' is socially constructed and 'the actual content of socialization, education, citizenship and so on varies widely across and within countries', (1991:595). Definitions of youth differ both across time periods and at any given point and this observation holds true for China where the terms 'youth' and 'young people' are used just as loosely as in other societies, (Hooper, 1985a). The inconsistencies and ambiguities evident in the consideration of western youth are also found in the Chinese context.

The biological, physical and psychological developments that occur during puberty are seen here as only partial explanations of the features that constitute youth. Emphasising these developments is questioned as is the insufficient recognition of the cultural variations that give rise to different forms of youthful experiences. It is accepted that 'Although the basic biological processes are probably more or less similar in all human societies, their cultural definition varies – in detail at least – from society to society,' (Eisenstadt, 1956:19). The diversity of cultural, social and interactional features runs counter to the view of youth as a stage in the lifecycle beginning with the onset of puberty and ending once this is over. The limitations of bio-psychological explanations of youth and the subordination of cultural contexts lend support for viewing adolescence as 'a social rather than psychological phenomenon' (Jones, 1988:708).

Age limits also have their problems. Whilst the youth period can be delineated by age with both legal and official limits, the ascription of the youth label is subject to change with numerical age providing convenient measurable boundaries only. In China, Communist Youth League (CYL) membership, for example, extends from 14 to 28. In another official age definition, all those between 14 and 25 fit into the youth category and total approximately 300 million people, or over one quarter of the Chinese population, (Hooper, 1991:264). Age is a simple means of ruling people in or out of the youth group but does not explain the social and cultural features attached to the resulting category nor the problems that might arise from such placement in terms of social status and the accomplishment of adulthood. CYL members, for example, do not suddenly become adults upon expiry of their membership at the age of 28; they may already be considered and treated as adults. Age is more of an indicative rather than substantive definition of youth, as was suggested in the discussion of generational demarcations. Features of non-adult groups and their treatment by adults differ according to the specific social contexts within which they occur.

This is illustrated by the various social norms and values influencing the ways in which the behaviour of young people is assessed. Liu suggested that the violence of the Red Guard generation could only be partially explained in terms of the universal, adolescent tendencies such as 'youthful high spirits'. He writes that 'The actions of students and youths on mainland China between 1966–68 were largely determined by its political and social institutions . . . ' (1976:113). Wilson and Wilson, also analysing the Red Guards, suggested the adoption of 'broader studies of youth and the attitudes of young people in general' (1970:95). In the contemporary Chinese context, the societal factors will be shown to be related not only to the reform policies

but also to certain 'legacies' (Hooper, 1985a) which form part of
the habitus predisposing young people towards certain behaviour.
Cultural aspects can be seen exerting major influences and were
periodically called into question.

The key social institutions that played a role in shaping youth
are identified here as the family, work and politics. Their roles
can be considered both in terms of tradition and change with
'tradition' defined as 'those institutional patterns which for the
most part trace their pedigree with remarkably slight change well
back into Chinese history' (Levy, 1968:41). Social institutions also
act as filters through which wider social norms and cultural
legacies are disseminated through the socialisation process with
variations emanating from the nature of the prevailing social
stratification system. Young people in well-off families in urban
areas experience youth differently from poor young peasants, for
example, and such differences remain.

From Family to Work: Changing Transitions

The Chinese family can be viewed as central to the creation of
youth (Lethbridge, 1965). Current usage of the term '*qing nian*'
(youth) resembles the '*ch'ing-nien*' of the 'traditional' period. (Levy,
op. cit.). This was closely related to family position and relationships, social gradation and customary notions of authority. The
family 'was not only the basic production, consumption and
socialization unit, it was also invested with quasi-religious significance through the practice of ancestor worship' (Gold,
1991:597). It was stressed for centuries as 'the basic social unit
from which a sound society is constructed' (Lethbridge, 1965:38).
Individuals were frequently defined in relation to the kinship
group with youth and adulthood contingent upon family relationships. Junior members were ascribed subordinate positions not
only with regard to adults but also to older siblings. It was the
case that 'You define yourself within your own generation by
seniority and are taught from a very early age to be aware of the
subtle gradations of seniority and closeness of kinship within the
patrilineal descent line' (Jenner, 1992:107). Attaining a particular
age in itself was not the only determinant of position and status
within the family.

This seniority system (*lunzi peibei*) gave youth a role of dependency, assigning them to subordinate positions, and it could also

be seen in other social institutions. It was part of the 'Chinese tradition' (Kirby, 1965:v) with its emphasis on respect for authority, paternalism and fixed social gradations, and can be viewed as a form of social closure based upon seniority, with younger people excluded from the attainment of full material and social benefits as well as being assigned to less powerful positions. It has played an important role in the definition of youth, and aspects of this 'tyranny of history' (Jenner, *op. cit.*) or cultural 'baggage' continue to exert an oppressive influence on youth even though the role of the family has been reinterpreted and transformed. These factors were viewed in the 1980s as impediments to the successful attainment of certain goals but young people were attempting to confront this tradition and work out strategies for dealing with their exclusion, as will be shown.

The constricting nature of family relationships was also not always accepted in the past although individual nonconformity was difficult with youthful rebels having 'no place to go outside the family'. (Wilson and Wilson, 1970:97) The easiest strategy was probably to simply wait for one's turn in the status hierarchy, knowing that respect and authority would be the rewards for patience. This would tend to maximise conformist behaviour with a high level of social stability and a low degree of social change as appeared to be the case in traditional China. Those who were disadvantaged by the system early in life but saw gains awaiting them later on had a vested interest in retaining the status quo. Yet although there were many sources of convergence in the upbringing of young scholars at the turn of the century, they tended to exhibit 'deviant' rather than conformist behaviour by rebelling against the symbols of authority, such as during the 'May Fourth' movement (Rozman, 1981). Rapid social and economic changes caused disparities between the expectations of this social elite and actual experiences with traditional patterns of behaviour appearing as unreasonable both at the national as well as personal level.

A concerted onslaught on the Confucian tradition by youth took place in the early stages of 'May Fourth' with verbal attacks on the 'hopelessly encrusted . . . worn-out ways of thought' (Israel, 1966:4). Bringing about a 'family revolution' was one of the movement's aims, particularly in regard to youth and women. This latter group were continually ascribed low position and status with little to look forward to later in life. Wilson and

Wilson noted how during China's transitional period 'there had been widespread revolt against parental authority, particularly among the gentry' (*op. cit*:97).

Education and employment also played their part in the differentiation between youth and adulthood as they continue to do. The growing importance of the school and college peer group was an additional factor in this rebellion and within education there was a 'fundamental contradiction' (Hayhoe, 1992:15) as it straddled the old and new societes, creating a sense of ambiguity for its youthful participants. These factors contributed to 'May Fourth' which subsequently became incorporated into notions of youth, particularly the discourse of educated youth. Those involved in study are less likely to be considered as mature adults even if they are in their late twenties. This is because many aspects of dependency may remain in their lives and they are still completing their training for adult roles. Being involved in work may be more likely to lead to the adult status, although within work units (*danwei*) the seniority system will be in operation with gradations of status according to age and experience.

Modernisation processes affected youth even though traditional aspects of dependency and social subordination persisted and remained part of the habitus of young people in the reform period. China was a relative 'latecomer' to modernisation but by the end of the nineteenth century the institution of the family certainly experienced something of a 'revolution' (Levy, *op. cit.*). By finding their own way in life, young people could break away from the family and there appeared to be an inverse relationship between family control and independent incomes in the developed urban areas. As the latter increased, the former diminished but it was never completely negated. Family authority was transformed rather than eliminated by modernisation. With less reliance upon the family, young people could make more decisions for themselves, spend time with their peers and even behave in nonconformist ways. Both the concept and experience of youth changed as China moved from tradition to modernity.

Modernisation and industrial development were followed by political change. The domain of the family was deliberately encroached upon by the communists who sought to prioritise their own agenda and bring Chinese society in line with it. Social and political conformity were enforced wherever possible through political and social institutions and coercion remained a weapon just as it did in the traditional family. Youth became defined, then, not just by family position but by the developing official discourse. According to Gold 'The Party-state thus imposed its image of Chinese society as well as its definitions of reality, truth and the meaning of life on the nation's young people' (1991:600). This was carried out by mobilising not only the family but also other institutions and organisations such as the CYL, and the heavy involvement of the mass media.

After 1949, dependency shifted towards the state with a reduction of the family's functions and its influence over the transition into adulthood or, in Gold's terms, the 'life course'. The family was viewed suspiciously as 'the stronghold of values now destined for elimination' (Townsend, 1967:12). Dependency remained but was redefined in the altered political environment. As before, marriage was a major route out of youth, being in many ways the ultimate ritual marking the entry into adulthood. Jaschok (1986) writes that no matter how advanced in age is an unmarried youth, he or she cannot be considered as adult but lacking in maturity until marriage. These practices relate to the self-perception of the young. Being viewed by society as dependent and immature, they may view themselves as such. 'A young man of 29 may see himself as "childish" and act childishly until marriage transforms him miraculously into a person of weight and authority. This change is rapid, ritualised and inextricably linked with matrimony . . . ' (Jaschok:41).

Marriage may remain partly a family decision but the state and its various organs, such as the work unit, had a greater influence over the timing and incidence of marriage after 1949. The setting of legal ages for marriage at 20 for women, 22 for men (Croll, 1983:76) was part of the attempt to impose an official definition of youth and to control the entry into adulthood. The lower age limit for females reflects the sexual inequality already cited as a cultural norm. It is possible that this is part of the Confucian tradition and not necessarily an acknowledgement that women may mature earlier than men. Females in the contemporary period may be allowed to marry earlier because of lower educational participation and fewer opportunities to enter higher education than male counterparts. Social conventions continue to be influenced by traditional values such as the male preference for younger wives. There are also contemporary considerations of population control which may further restrict independent choice.

A good deal of propaganda was targeted at young people, particularly those in education, in an effort to dissuade them from what was described as 'early marriage'. Justifications for delaying marriage included allowing for full intellectual growth, political and ideological progress, making contributions to the 'motherland' and encouraging proper physical health and growth (ZGQN, June 1962). All of these were seen as threatened by early marriage which was officially viewed as detrimental to the individual and also to the nation as it concentrated peoples' efforts on their personal lives and away from more important concern with the 'masses' or collectivities. It was condemned as unpatriotic behaviour and not in line with the ideals of socialist morality. 'Youth is the golden age for study. It will be a very great loss to the country and to oneself if this study phase is not put to good use as fully as possible and if a portion of it is expended in falling in love' (SCMP, 2966, 1963:12).

This article queried the use of age markers between youth and non-youth. 'If a man gets married at the age of 27–28 and a woman at 25–26, they are married in their youth and within the age group of young people' (SCMP, *op. cit*:13). Youth was extended by the communists, especially for those in education whose priorities were deemed to lie outside the personal sphere. The passage into adulthood was no longer solely dependent upon family position but was linked to wider social and political objectives. Students 'talking love' (*tanlian ai*) were officially criticised and those who embarked upon sexual liaisons, if discovered, risked punishment. Even in the 1980s, students could not marry without official permission (Tournebise and Macdonald, 1987:50).

These practical aspects were not the only reasons for discouraging marriage. They form part of the normative evaluation of youth as a dependent group unable to make major decisions for themselves. The situation changed in more recent times, with official pronouncements in the reform decade that 'The subject of love has at last broken free from the shackles of Lin Biao and the Gang of Four.' (CR 28, no.1, 1979:10). Young people's personal relationships became 'more like those of youth elsewhere in the world. Gone is the public facade of pure comradeship and sacrifice of the personal life for the communal good...' (Hooper, 1991:267). Elements of the past, however, persist. It was still the case in the late 1980s that only the more senior sections of youth, that is those already in work, were likely to be married. Employment is important because a job provides some financial autonomy but most Chinese youth have until recently had little access to independent incomes and that may partly explain why marriage was not the norm amongst this group. Students tended to rely on their parents since scholarships or grants were limited but it will be shown to be a key characteristic that they did not always passively accept this dependency and sought ways out of it.

There was, however, often no avoiding the jobs assigned to them by the state which was the practice after 1949 with enforced dependency upon the state and the resulting *danwei*. When considered together with the increasing influence over education and family life, this shift towards state-controlled employment policies, both at local and national levels, was part of the official treatment of youth, with meanings and behavioural norms being laid down by the CCP. It could be argued that the nationwide system of job assignments, especially for graduates (*gaodeng fenpei*), has links with the pre-communist era.

The Imperial examination system determined not only who entered the ruling elite but usually where the successful candidates would be placed. Communist policies similarly offered few employment options with choice restricted further by a low level of economic development. The roots of the *fenpei* system can be seen as lying in the past with the traditional view of youth having to be placed into adulthood rather than attaining it themselves. This was integrated into more recent thinking and it is suggested here that without the antecedents of China's former expansive state bureaucracy and autocratic regimes, the nationwide system of job assignments would have been more difficult to implement.

Fenpei also acted as a control over young people whose destinies are affected by the nature of the work they do, at what level and in which part of the country. Rebellious youth were threatened with undesirable jobs and regions. Hooper noted that even a 'mundane job in a major city is considered preferable to the dreaded "remote province" assignment in Xinjiang or Tibet' (1991:266). This parallels earlier eras when careers could be helped or hindered by official bodies and those falling foul of the authorities were exiled to the outlying areas, considered to be uncivilised by Chinese standards. Internal exile to such places remains as a possible punishment for criminals and noncon-formists.

The mass reallocation of Chinese youth to rural areas throughout the 1950s and 1960s is a case in point. It was not the first time urban youth had been sent to the countryside[1] but was the most extensive with millions involved in '*xia xiang*' movements, perhaps with as many as ten per cent being sent to the countryside during the Cultural Revolution, (Bernstein, 1977:2). 'Going down to the villages and up to the mountains' encapsulated not only official definitions of youth and educated youth in particular but emphasised their dependency upon the state. 1.2 million were 'sent down' between 1956 and 1966, with the movement intensifying during the Cultural Revolution when as many as 12 million were transferred (Bernstein, 1975:xii). Whyte estimates that around 17 million urban youth were involved between 1968 and 1978 (1981:315) whilst Shirk claims that 'well over one million' were sent between 1962 and 1966 alone (1982:29).

These young people could not easily avoid this relocation with all the consequences that it entailed and were allotted their identity as *xia xiang* youth by the state. This generational label remained with them throughout their lives and 'rusticated youth' from the sixties are often viewed as having many problems as a result of their experiences during their formative years. The label itself becomes an easily recognisable explanation of a certain set of related attitudes, norms and behavioural trends.

The *xia xiang* policy further encroached upon the family as an agency of socialisation. Sending young people to the countryside overrode individual families reluctant to see their children leave home. Publicity emphasised the national imperatives of the campaign and families thus gaining 'revolutionary' credentials. 'The glorious duty of revolutionary parents is . . . to let the Party decide our children's future. You must never allow your own wishes to get in the way . . . ' (Chinese Sociology and Anthropology 11, 1978/79:69). Dependency shifted from the family to the communist authorities with clear links to the political arrangements of 'New China.' Political dependency, however, is also something of a tradition in China, as will be considered below.

Political Aspects

Post 1949 generations of youth were to inherit the mantle of their 'May Fourth' predecessors but under the strict guidance of the CCP with conformity promoted within a context of revolutionary rhetoric drawing upon the traditional role of China's young intellectuals. The idea of 'revolutionary successors' (*geming chen gongzhe*) was popularised in the 1950s and 1960s (Montaperto, 1972) but the model of 'revolutionary youth' propagated in, for example, the CYL's publication, *Zhongguo Qingnian* (ZGQN), was passive rather than active, appearing as a sanitised version of earlier youthful rebellion. There were descriptions of the League as a 'heroic shockforce . . . the new Long March' (FBIS CR 71, 1984:24). The dependency aspect of this was evident in the messages claiming young communists were to be 'trained and steeled. They do not grow up automatically.' (SCMP 3462 1965:9). The basic task of the CYL was to school youth in patriotism, 'fostering communist ideals of morality' (FBIS CR 71 *op. cit.*).

Political activism can be viewed as participation in campaigns and protest movements whether it is localised and targeted towards a specific policy or more widespread and generalised. Not all political activism is revolutionary, that is seeking to bring about a complete change in the government and political system but some is conformist in nature, organised by the existing regime to help foster support and enthusiasm for its own projects. The communists tried to incorporate the traditions of youthful protest into their organisations in order to produce an official version of educated youth. The conformity/rebellion dilemma predates 1919 and can be seen in the historical position and role of China's intellectuals who have carrried with them 'survivals of the past' (Goldman *et al.*, 1987:2) in their roles as servants of the state and moral critics of the ruler. The position of educated youth has tended to shift depending upon which side of the equation is emphasised at any one point in time. This has frequently created an ambiguous and unstable relationship between them and the communist authorities.

As most educated people in traditional China became bureaucrats and members of the ruling elite, they gave up intellectual autonomy to some extent and outspokenness, even if patriotically inspired, entailed risks. The role of 'remonstrance', clearly detailed by Nathan (1985) is an important part of the habitus of Chinese intellectuals, considered as their duty to the state and the people which predisposes them towards certain actions, including activism. Speaking out against injustices could lead to a 'righting of the wrongs' but intellectuals who did so took risks. Goldman *et al.* state that the intelligentsia were an elite conscious of themselves as autonomous critics of political authority if the need arose. This role was more developed than the professional one with the 'literati' seeing themselves 'in a special position to judge morality' (1987:6).

The 'May Fourth' participants saw themselves as censoring the Republican rulers of the day who had accepted the unfair terms of the Treaty of Versailles. The events of May 1919 showed the patriotic characteristics of the political component of the movement with students and other young intellectuals becoming 'the most articulate performers' in expressing personal dissatisfactions and political frustrations' (Levy, 1968:346). They were also at the forefront of a movement which extended beyond politics, into literature and other areas of social and cultural life.

These public airings of frustrations may have set a politically radical model but it was based upon a traditional role. Frustrations with their own social position and lack of opportunities also played a part but protests were couched in patriotic terminology. They were attempting to persuade the government to change their policies for the sake of the nation and this subsequently left a legacy for future generations who could adopt the strategy of political protest and activism. 'May Fourth' became part of the habitus of modern educated youth as well as being linked to the social and political identity passed down into the contemporary era. It reemerged to some extent during the 1989 movement with students attempting to set the agenda but this was seen as illegitmate by the authorities and too much like 'bourgeois liberalism'.

Since the 1950s, notions of fostering (*lingyang*), training and moulding (*peiyang*) were clearly related to the social and political objectives of the communist regime. As it could not be taken for granted that succeeding generations would support the socialist 'dream', their political socialisation had to include the correct values and behaviour. CYL members were expected to conform to its rules and codes with the propaganda warning of the 'temptations of bourgeois liberalism' which in CCP rhetoric was the opposite of true socialism. Youth were viewed as fickle, wanting an 'easy life' and 'won over to the bourgeoisie unwittingly' (SCMP 3410, 1965:2). The CYL offered not only protection from the temptations but also friendship and assisted in the cultivation of 'a new generation of revolutionaries' . . . (SCMP 3462,

1965:8). Young people were invited to look upon the League as 'their own good Friend' (*People's China* 14, 1955: 20) rather than just a Party mouthpiece.

The CYL, then, reflected rather than challenged the dominant cultural norms as did the manner in which it operated. With young people seen as politically immature, the League was to play a key role in their transition into maturity. Described as the CCP's 'junior assistant' it was conventional in its manner of steering young people into accepted adult roles. It permitted little participation in policy making nor did it lend itself to 'confrontational action strategies' (Rai, 1991:167). Dependency and lack of youthful autonomy were features of Chinese society criticised during 'May Fourth' but ironically they became part of CYL organisational arrangements. It did not really belong to its youthful members but to the CCP authorities. The *lunzi peibei* system discussed earlier is in operation with CYL officials (cadres) often older than the members. The paternalistic relationship between them and the members is evident in its propaganda but the persistence of this type of political dependency became increasingly unpalatable over the decades. There was a widespread sense of alienation by the time we reach Deng's generation, as will be documented in succeeding chapters.

The official discourse of youth, therefore, can be seen as retaining parts of a historical legacy in terms of definition and treatment of youth with political as well as cultural and social elements involved. By the 1980s, this discourse was being increasingly questioned, along with many other features of both Chinese cultural and communist practices. Young intellectuals were a group undertaking some of this questioning but the intellectual part of their title needs to be considered in order to complete the analysis of this social group. Before doing so, it will be useful to briefly examine the notion of youth culture in the Chinese context and how this adds further light on the increasingly problematic nature of the official discourse of *qingnian zhishi fenzi*.

The Nature of Youth Culture in China

Creating a youth culture can be viewed as a potentially less radical strategy for dealing with the ambiguities and problems of the youth status although it can offer resistance and rebellion, as will be shown. It is not the purpose here to outline the development of this concept and like Pilkington (1994) in her ethnographic work on Russian youth cultures, I will select the key points which were viewed as applicable in this study.

Youth culture as a relatively recent phenomenon is clearly linked to the lengthening transition from youth to adult status. Non-adults, being in a relatively weak social position, are 'marginalised' and this can cause conflicts between younger and older members of society. Having created adolescents, 'industrialised urban society provided no place for them' (Jones,1988:708), with a greater disparity between youth and adult roles in highly technological societies with few remaining traditional practices. Modernisation and educational expansion enabled young people to explore the cultural values presented to them by their elders as they spent increasing amounts of time with their own peer groups. In the Chinese context there may have been more freedom from the overbearing family and the possibility of alternative sources of identity centred around the youth group.

The practice of separating young people into age grades also encouraged peer group formation and identity with non-adults increasingly set apart from adults and adult responsibilities. The postponement of social maturity caused by extended periods in education may lead to 'pressure for youth groups to form' (Wilson and Wilson, 1970:96). There may have been negative results of the transfer of increasing numbers of young people into education for longer periods of time, with young people increasingly placed in a position of 'diminished rather than enhanced social status' (Musgrove, 1968:2), and experiencing status ambiguities.

The results of a social survey of 300 undergraduates in Shanghai in 1985 illustrate this sort of ambivalence. Most of the respondents claimed to be 'troubled' by the mixed feelings of being tied to their parents yet 'tasting the independent life' whilst at college (BR Vol. 28:27). Campus life gave them a degree of freedom but transition into adulthood life was suspended for the duration of their education because of their dependency. Students are less likely to enter adulthood by the marriage route with youth, in some ways, synonymous with participation in formal education because of the associated implications of immaturity. Education also formalises the transition from childhood into adulthood and can be viewed as an extended 'rite of passage' with associated dependency on adults, peer group affiliations and the formalisation of the socialisation process by secondary agencies. This frustration is a contributory factor in the formation of youth groups which attempt to gain a greater degree of independence for their members and enhance their social status.

Youth culture, then, can be viewed as a mechanism or strategy, depending upon whether a structuralist (Parsons, 1962) or social action perspective is employed, for overcoming problems caused by these discontinuities and marginalised status. In structural–functionalist terms, youth culture develops as a 'safety valve' helping to defuse some of the problems created by youth's ambivalent status on the verge of adulthood. As noted by Pilkington, Parsons stressed the role of youth culture as 'a mechanism of *maintaining social stability* [sic] rather than bringing about social change' (Pilkington, 1994:16). Young people can get together, share their experiences and be separate from the adult society which does not allow them entry, but overall their actions are not threatening. Delinquent youth cultures are more of a nuisance than a threat to social stability in this view. Youth culture also provides opportunities for leisure activities and has frequently been used in reference to teenage behaviour of western societies, especially the USA, but it is applicable in the Chinese context.

We can reject the idea of a homogeneous youth culture linked to the dominant culture of a given society. This is not to deny that youth from all sections of society do not have anything in common; they all have exposure and access to the dominant culture but it is worth noting the limitations of broad generalisations. The coexistence of several subcultures is probably closer to social reality (Brake, 1985; Frith, 1984; Hall and Jefferson, 1976). O'Donnell writes that 'almost no sociologist now believes that a general youth culture exists' (1985:26). Race and social class certainly cut across youth and this helps to produce a variety of youth subcultures which address specific problems of youth located in different social positions and milieux. Jones (1988) reminds us of the importance of gender differentiation because until recently girls were often either ignored or marginalised (MacRobbie, 1991).

When considering the historical development of Chinese youth culture, there was a growing sense of identification amongst young people in the late nineteenth century and recognition of their shared problems which assisted the development of a 'nascent youth culture' (Levy, *op. cit*). This would have been facilitated by the income-earning capacities of urban youth who found work in the new industries and occupied a similar social location, often away from their families. Even some young women found a degree of freedom and independence through work and could join in youth cultural activities. Simultaneously, changes in education and increasing numbers of institutions in the cities meant that student peer groups could also form collective identities. The subcultural idea allows for the heterogeneity of different youth groups developing their own specific solutions in terms of shared behaviour, language style, leisure pursuits and so on, with similarly placed peers.

Whilst these two sections of youth, that is students and workers, could be expected to share some similarities in terms of being in a period of transition and occupying a marginal status, their positional differences in terms of the stratification system and future roles would lead to any resulting youth identity and cultural features being different in nature. Yeh notes how even amongst young scholars and students, there were diversities and divisions, writing that 'one can hardly speak of a "national student culture", let alone refer to a generalized profile of Chinese students during the Republican period as a single social type' (Yeh, 1990:xii).

When rapid social change occurs, such as during the reform decade, 'it is youth that must chiefly cope with the strains . . . ' (Keniston in Wilson and Wilson, 1970:96). More specifically, it is often 'elite youth' such as student populations, according to Keniston, who feel these strains the most and may be inclined to act upon them in terms of subcultural developments. Not all youth were or are equally affected. The rural/urban divide is important as well as the differentiation between students and their less educated urban counterparts. Any youth culture developing in Chinese cities, for example, would be unavailable as a solution to the problems of rural youth trapped in more traditional circumstances and still closely tied to the family. Hooper (1985a) notes how this remains the case today with 'peasant' youth experiencing their transitional period into maturity differently from their urban counterparts.

It can be said that elements of youth subcultures developed in transitional China with 'May Fourth' being a possible outcome, in line with Keniston's observation. Participants attempted to resolve some of their own problems by adopting the patterns of behaviour, attitudes, speech and even dress codes of their peers. These were often nonconforming to the traditional modes. At the political level, they suggested solutions to the problems facing China. After the early decades of this century, however, social strife, civil war and the anti-Japanese campaigns diverted many youth into other areas and increasingly their autonomous youth cultural activities were dominated either by the Nationalist Party (*Guomindang*) or CCP. The communists, as with their GMD predecessors, attempted to impose an 'official ideology' (Kwong 1994) upon all youth groups with the aim of producing an 'official youth culture' which was, by its nature, conformist rather than rebellious. This has also been termed the 'service oriented' youth subculture in contrast to a more 'fun oriented' one seen in many American high schools in the 1960s (Hickrod and Hickrod, 1965:176).

The communist regime intended to prevent the rise of unofficial subcultures running counter to their own preferred conformist youth style. It was recognised that distinctive youth cultures may be read as oppositional or rebellious to the parent culture (contra-culture) and any such potential ones may have been 'nipped in the bud' (Hickrod and Hickrod:179). The extent to which they continued to be successful in the 1980s and whether they suppressed the 'fun' subculture is considered later. By encroaching upon the functions of the family and other social agencies, such as employment units, this aim was facilitated at least in the early stages of the communist regime. 'During the youth stage, Party-led organizations in schools, worksites, recreational associations and neighbourhoods were charged with inculcating the official values in youths and closely monitoring their behaviour and thoughts, testing their suitability as revolutionary successors' (Gold, 1991:599). There was little room for autonomous subcultural solutions to the problems of the youth status although some deviations were possible.

Even in a tightly controlled state like China, individuals attempt to create personal space and methods of avoiding surveillance. It has to be said, however, that youth culture was mostly of the official variety across the different sections of youth. Its ideal or 'advertised' form (Kwong, 1994:250) has been propagated in the media and through other channels such as schools, work units, local League branches and so on. It can seen as forming an important part of the social context within which educated youth operate.

The official ideal in recent times has been described as 'modernisation successors', that is scientifically advanced but politically acquiescent young intellectuals who will further Chinese socialism through their expertise. Dependency certainly remained a feature with the paternalistic Party organisations viewing young people as in need of close guidance in order for them to be responsible enough to take over the socialist project. This in itself gave Chinese youth new problems to overcome and subsequently presented the authorities with difficulties.

This outline of the discourse of Chinese youth has highlighted the fact that cultural legacies from the past still play a part in the definition and treatment of youth but that the communists set their own agenda and through exisiting social institutions tried to shape and mould youth in socialist terms. This tended to perpetuate the dependency and social subordination of young people. Not all sections of youth were dealt with in the same manner, however, and aspects of heterogeneity have already been alluded to. It is possible now to consider the elite status of young intellectuals, the second part of the discourse of educated youth, and describe not only who enters this group but what it means in the Chinese context. An elite is considered here as a relatively small group who have preferable life chances in terms of economic rewards, social status and political power. These three factors are key indicators of social position (*shehui diwei*) (White, 1981).

THE 'KNOWLEDGEABLE ELEMENTS' IN CHINESE SOCIETY

Young intellectuals are viewed here as both an intra-generational unit within the 1980s generation and as a generation in themselves in terms of their intellectual status and identity. They are a relatively small section of youth who reach the tertiary sector of the educational system and although exact definitions of 'knowledgeable elements' (*zhishi fenzi*) vary, the term is usually applied to young people qualified up to or beyond senior middle school. Chan writes of 'a great deal of unresolved controversy as to who exactly in China constitute intellectuals' and if nonmanual occupations are included, then the term 'applies to a larger group of people in China than is usually the case in western countries' (1992:91).

Similarly, Thogersen noted that 'intellectual' might refer to 'anybody with at least a senior secondary education, but is now used more narrowly to refer to people with a college or specialized middle school diploma, and to people who do not have such an educational background but who perform "mental" jobs' (1990:44). As in O'Boyle's definition of 'learned men' (1970), those with advanced school education are included as well as graduates and members of all the 'learned professions', whether or not they went to university. Kelly is not alone in contrasting the western meaning of 'intellectual' with the more general one used by the Chinese. 'We think of an egghead, a writer of books and learned papers, and exclude, rightly or wrongly most school teachers, engineers and medical practitioners. All of these people are considered intellectuals in China' (1990:25).

In Rai's view, it could be the case that 'all those who have secondary or higher education are called *zhishi fenzi*' (1991:129). Singer (1971) defined the group as middle school and college students and recent graduates, whilst the Chinese authorities have tended to apply the term to young people qualified up to or beyond senior middle school. White (1981) suggests that senior high school students, as well as those at college and university, can also be viewed as young intellectuals. In the contemporary period, this is more likely to imply 'key point' (*zhongdian*) secondary schooling, viewed as an elite education because of its links with university entrance, (Gasper, 1989). 'It is thus taken for granted that the key middle school students of today will be the university students of tomorrow' (Thogersen, 1990:79). The crucial indicator would now seem to be higher education, particularly at an established university or college where a full-time course of study is followed.

This book takes into consideration these comments about the official discourse of *qing nian zhishi fenzi* and will use the term to refer to college and university students and recent graduates. Those with a complete middle school education will be viewed as potential members of the group if attempting to enter higher education. Successful candidates are destined for a wide range of occupations from lower grade teachers to influential research scientists. All are classified as mental labourers even though there are clear gradations within their ranks.

Education is the main form of closure separating such people from manual workers (*gongren*) and peasants (*nongmin*) and more recently, *getihu*.[2] The 'gold' route, with 'the gold symbolizing the successful businessperson' (Hooper, 1991:265) contrasts with the 'black' of higher education. The growth of the private sector added another possible area of employment for the millions of young people graduating from middle schools each year of the 1980s and was encouraged by the reformist CCP leadership (CR 28 Nov. 1979:21). The *'qingnian qiye jia'* (young private business people) became a new social group. Feuchtwang and Hussain write that the 'proliferation of collective and private enterprises would help to "mop up"' urban labour exceeding the requirements of the State sector and this was encouraged by the government as the 'sole solution for what is in fact a massive problem of unemployment' (1983:36). As with the *zhishi fenzi* group, there were different types of entrepreneurs, ranging from the small street marketeer to large-scale businesses, *siying qiye*, legalised in 1988 (Young, 1992:64).

Those not within the *qingnian zhishi fenzi* category can be viewed as an alternative version of Deng's generation. Those failing to find any employment often fell into the *dai ye* (waiting for work) youth category. A Party report in 1982 put the figure at 14 million (Hooper, 1985a:84). *Dai ye* youth were often viewed as particularly prone to criminal tendencies, not only in China but elsewhere. 'Reports of illegal, anti-social youth activities appear frequently in Western and Hong Kong journals, and to some extent even in the Chinese press' (Ownby, 1986:214). This may be an unfair assumption but the Chinese authorities during the 1980s were concerned with the link between unemployment and youth crime.

Without the prospect of satisfactory work, the temptation to obtain money through crime might have been strong among the urban unemployed who possibly had too much time on their hands and lacked 'ideological' guidance even more so than students. There may have been some blurring of the boundaries between different youth groups due to the social and economic changes of the reform period but persistent differences and a special sense of identity distinguished educated youth from young workers or their rural counterparts.

China is not alone in restricting access to higher education although it is theoretically available for all. As in former times, it is often dependent upon factors of wealth, social status, power and proximity to schools and colleges. Higher education places increased after 1949 but competition was tight, however, given a doubling of the population over this time. In the 1950s and 1960s 'The lack of material abundance ... meant that only a small proportion of the population could be diverted from production to study' (Taylor, 1981:176). This remained the case in the 1980s with, according to one study, the proportion of 'intellectual workers' reaching only 8.8 per cent in 1990 with the goal set for the year 2000 being 10–12 per cent. This compares unfavourably to more developed countries where the proportion may have already reached 50 per cent (Zhu, 1993:43).

Although more young people progress beyond basic education levels, the proportion of highly educated persons in the population remains relatively small thus maintaining the exclusivity of the *zhishi fenzi* category. Key point students may have a sense of being special because of attending such schools and are placed in an advantageous position in terms of university entrance. In Beijing and other large cities 'the key schools have transition rates very close to 100 per cent and the large majority of their students are recruited by key universities' (Thogersen, 1990:81). While less than five per cent of senior high school graduates can enter higher education, key schools may have success rates of between 70–80 per cent (Hooper, 1985a:42). The concept of anticipatory socialisation is also relevant here as they are prepared and prepare themselves for higher education. Participating in the exams can be part of the process, giving the candidates a glimmer of high status having been selected from millions of other young people. They have to be reasonably successful even to take part.

Those who are not considered as higher education material, even if key point school students, could be treated as failures. It is as if two tiers of secondary education exist, one for those who are exam potential and the other for those who are not. The latter group need to consider finding another route through life. The negative repercussions include feelings of low self-esteem for those who cannot enter the higher education race and those who fail may find themselves in a social position different to the one they had anticipated and experience problems in adjusting to their changed status.

Yet even a junior middle school education remains a considerable achievement in China where high rates of illiteracy are still observable. Amongst 25 year olds, only around one per cent are

university graduates compared with 44.5 per cent illiterates
(Zhuang, 1988:47). Du (1992) also noted that less than five per
cent of the 6 to 7 million youth who leave senior middle school
annually could enter higher education in the 1980s. There is a
little less than one institute of higher education to each million
people in China and university places are 'extremely dear'. Other
figures show that only three per cent of the 19–24 year old age
group can acquire a university place (Tournebise and Macdonald, 1987:47). When referring to the youth group, the proportion of those who reach higher education appears to be even
lower with 'only 1.2 per cent' being enrolled (Hooper, 1985a:42).
The post 1949 educational expansion is undeniable but so is the
existence of a wide gap between those who complete education
and those with only a few years of schooling.

The social context of urban children of intellectuals is more
conducive to educational achievement and facilitates 'cultural
reproduction' (Bourdieu, 1973). On the other hand 'The habitus
of the subordinated class(es) will, in generating an acceptance of
the systems legitimacy, reinforce their disadvantage by inhibiting
their demands for access to the higher reaches of education by
defining it as "not for the likes of us."' (Jenkins, 1992:112). Urban
youth could be expected to be more ambitious in terms of
educational success than their rural counterparts because of their
social background and this will be supported when considering
data from this sample.

There is certainly evidence that Chinese farmers do not value
education highly, preferring to keep their children home to work,
especially girls who are often viewed as not worth wasting money
on. Pepper writes how 'people who work the land and have never
been educated tend not to grasp the advantages of sending their
children to school'. They will not do so voluntarily 'unless the
benefits can be seen in clear and simple terms to outweigh the
costs which invariably include some fees, income foregone and
loss of parental control' (1990:75). She also mentions rising
tuition costs as well as location with some schools being too far
away in isolated areas. Whilst in some areas of China it is poverty
which keeps children at home, the profit motive may also be a
deterrent. The implementation of economic reforms meant that
farmers could grow produce for sale in newly established markets
and also develop sideline businesses. The prospect of making
money renewed the emphasis on the family as an income-earning

unit and involving all family members in this process prematurely ended some children's education.

Some farmers during the reform decade did have their expectations raised. One survey of 'peasant families' showed that 90 per cent hoped that their children could leave the countryside (Thogersen, 1990:45). Whilst traditionally not encouraging education, rural families may have increasingly desired a different way of life for their offspring but looking at the figures, many were not linking an improved way of life with going to school.

Rosen points out inequalities in expenditure between urban and rural regions where there are 'poorer salaries, facilities and educational materials' (*op. cit*:86). The conditions for rural schools may deter teachers from working in such regions and some may go only under the duress of the state assignment. The lack of free choice about place of work may reduce the motivation of rural school teachers and some may concentrate their energies instead on trying to leave the countryside. Disgruntled teachers further exacerbate the difficulties facing rural pupils and convince them that education is not a worthwhile pursuit.

The 'black pathway' of higher education (Hooper, 1991:265) acts as a form of social closure based on credentialism, separating those who can from those who cannot enter this group. The social and economic rewards which may accrue from this experience, as well as social status, are also a means of further distinguishing between the different social strata within the youth group. In the 1980s, tertiary education was viewed as an effective route to high social position because the attainment of a university place was usually linked to a white collar job in the state sector upon graduation with the associated intellectual status. 'University entrance is the prize, one that provides an "iron rice bowl", since university graduates are assigned jobs by the state. Once a position is allocated, an individual is virtually assured of retaining his job until retirement' (Rosen, 1984:74). White writes of the 'intense pressure' for such jobs, 'especially from young people emerging from a highly academic, competitive and elitist educational system' who hold the 'tantalising hope for an "iron rice bowl" in the state sector' (1983:277).

By the mid-1980s, however, this link was being eroded with fewer prospects of secure employment for graduates. The government was planning to move away from 'arranged marriage' to 'free love' (ZGQN, 1988 5:27) and end the link between higher education and state allocation of jobs. Although this assignment system was often criticised for its shortcomings and lack of choice for graduates it did at least provide work for most people but in the emerging free market context, this was threatened. At the outset of the reform years, Deng's generation were expecting suitable rewards for their educational endeavours and many young people remained eager to join the educated elite. By the end of the period under review, they were not assured of jobs after graduation and this contributed to the perceived educational crisis, to be discussed in the next chapter.

Before the link between higher education and 'iron rice bowls' was threatened, those young people with educational aspirations faced several main hurdles. The main one, presuming they had a successful secondary education, was the college entrance examination system which can be seen as a form of elite recruitment, paralleling the Imperial Examinations and the associated exclusivity has clear implications for the perception of this group as an elite, being part of a social closure process. The exams not only determine who enters into the *qingnian zhishi fenzi* category but contribute to the formation of perceptions about the group by other sections of society as well as helping to shape the expectations of those entering it.

This system also exacerbated inequalities of gender, class and region. The examinations probably did little to help aspiring women and non-Han youth. Official policy expressed commitment to promoting equal opportunities but practical problems confound the legacy of discriminatory practices against females and China's 55 ethnic minorities. Even in the changed post 1976 climate, there remained many impediments for ethnic minority youth hoping to become *qingnian zhishi fenzi* because of the 'significant gaps between the educational accomplishments of China's national minorities and that of the Han majority group. This is true with regard to a variety of dimensions of education and levels of schooling . . . ' (Postiglione, 1992:315).

Disappointed candidates can resit and in the meantime be situated on the margins of educated youth. Some try again under pressure from teachers and parents who might be prepared to pay for special revision classes. In the 1980s an increasing number of institutions as well as private individuals offered such services for first-time failures or for those who required additional tutoring or cramming. During 1988, I had the chance to lecture one such group of young hopefuls. They were mostly under 20 and their parents were paying in order to help them pass on their second or, for some, third attempt. The popularity of these classes can be seen as a result of reinstating the unified entrance examinations and the importance of these for entering the 'new elite'.

Retaking the examinations can be tedious and embarrassing. Once past the normal age for college entrance, even if only by a year or two, candidates may feel too old, having failed to make the transition at the officially appointed time. Age gradations have become more rigid with fewer mature students studying at the undergraduate level. There is a clear divide between secondary and tertiary education and college and students are supposed to transfer at the correct age. With the entrance examinations the main route into higher education, middle school graduates accustomed to taking academic tests have an additional advantage. Older youth faced diminished opportunities in the post 1977 situation and the official maximum age limit for university entrance was set at 25, thus formalising the preference for younger educated youth. Another factor working against later examination attempts is the implication of an extended period of dependence upon the parents. Young people may not be able to look for work and consider leaving home if they are revising lessons.

Overall, then, intellectual status is associated with higher education, and in the period under review, the college entrance examinations. Only relatively small numbers of young people could be successful, thus perpetuating an elite status, but this has been questionable over the years, as will be shown in the next part of this discussion. Past legacies have helped to shape them as an insecure elite with problems and frustrations, raising the question of whether they exist more in despair than privilege, (Tournebise and Macdonald, *op. cit.*). The status frustrations of youth are possibly exacerbated in the case of young intellectuals as they experience additional years of full-time education and, in the communist era, the vagaries of political policies. The shared identity of young intellectuals is emphasised, it can be noted, by the processes they have to go through to enter this social group and social cohesion is mazimized as a result. This has been both encouraged and attacked by the communist authorities as will be shown below.

TREATMENT OF YOUNG INTELLECTUALS

The intelligentsia have been considered as a social stratum within Chinese socialism, different from the 'peasants' and 'workers', and their chequered fortunes have been excellently described by, for example, Kelly (1990) and Goldman *et al.* (1987). They have a contradictory inheritance: '*le respect confucéen pour les lettres et la persistance d'une hostilité maoist au savoir*' (Tournebise and Macdonald, 1987:46); that is, the Confucian respect for study and the Maoist hostility towards knowledge. Although educated youth have traditionally had elite status, they, like their senior counterparts of 'mental labourers', have been subjected to different CCP policy decisions.

The existence of elites has been problematic for the communists who intended to equalise society and avoid the rise of a technocratic 'new class' (Djilas, 1957). The elite status, however, has proven difficult to separate from the identity of young intellectuals who have attempted to show themselves as an elite by stressing the importance of their credentials and possession of various types of knowledge and training. Other groups may be seen as inadequately trained or unqualified to undertake social duties traditionally fulfilled by the intellectuals whose strong sense of historical and social role need to be expressed behaviourally as well as verbally.

The potential for antagonism between the different youth sub-groups has always existed because of different evaluations of their respective social positions and roles. Lessening the gap between mental and manual work (*zhubu xiaomie naoli he tili laodong de chabie*) was formerly a stated policy of the Mao regime but proved difficult to realise as a social project. The emphasis upon this, however, was not always the same, with mental work being more highly valued and rewarded during certain times over the communist decades depending upon the prevailing factions within the Party leadership. Periods of allowing young intellectuals to pursue academic training contrasted markedly to those when they were forced to leave the cities and expend their energies in trying to become the 'first generation of educated peasants in the motherland' (RMRB, 22 Aug. 1957:17).

The persistent divide between the largely urban-based educated youth and rural youth was highlighted during the *xia xiang* movements. The implications of rural relocation included the eventual demise of the educated youth category because they would become 'proletarian intellectuals' by putting down roots in the countryside where they would receive a truly socialist rather than 'bourgeois' education. To work on the 'agricultural battlefront' was proclaimed the 'most glorious thing' (SCMP 1603, 1957:15). Publicity given to this policy illustrated the type of ideological work (*sixiang gongzuo*) necessary to convince urban youth that going to the countryside and abandoning their educational ambitions was a patriotic thing to do. But there was a great degree of compulsion and pressure put upon city youth to relocate.

On the other hand, young intellectuals had possibilities for elite status within political organisations such as the CYL. This is not to say that they have traditionally had privileged access to power and influence within the sphere of politics: the CCP has at times been more likely to exclude intellectuals from its upper echelons. The inherent distrust of those with academic backgrounds has already been raised. It is the case, however, that educated youth were more likely to dominate the CYL. Rosen writes of how the CYL has been an organisation 'whose primary functions have always been political socialization and party recruitment' (1985:267). Although officially described as 'a mass organisation of advanced youth' (FBIS CR 390, 1983:22), in proportional terms, students are the bulk of its membership. In 1956, 57.3 per cent of university students were in the CYL but this had risen to 86.9 per cent in 1988 (Rosen, 1993: 326). This elitism is also a characteristic of CCP recruitment procedures for which CYL membership is usually a prerequisite because it is 'the recruiting ground for the Party' (Rai, 1991:185).

Entry into the League depended on education, class background and 'correct' political practice. Acceptance conferred 'increased prestige and enhanced one's prospects for social mobility: CYL membership was taken into account in university entrance and job assignment decisions' (Rosen, 1985:267). This was not so much the case by the late 1980s. Rosen notes how rising League membership figures 'have been concurrent with the decline of the organization's relevance to the lives of the students. This contrasts sharply with the 1950s and 1960s when joining the CYL was hotly contested and membership was an important indicator of upward mobility' (1993:325). It remains an elite organisation, however, contributing to the distinctions between educated youth and less educated youth.

Young intellectuals, especially students, were expected to participate in the political campaigns of the Mao era, such as the 'Hundred Flowers' campaign (1957–8) and the Cultural Revolution. They were presented with negative models to publicly revile, in contrast to the official role models (*hao bangyang*) they were supposed to emulate (Sheridan, 1968). Students had a particularly prominent role in seeking out the 'poisonous weeds' amongst the staff at their educational institutions. The participation in the public meting out of punishments could become violent (Wu, 1993). Some were over-zealous in the seeking out of 'rightists', finding them amongst non-targeted groups. Official limits were occasionally ignored and youth spontaneously attempted to redefine their activities in their own terms. Red Guard factions who challenged the authority of their elders have already been referred to.

Education was linked to the goal of political conformity in terms of both its organisation and content. Pupils who violently beat their teachers had been educated totally under communism and told constantly that they were the 'revolutionary successors'. The Cultural Revolution probably appeared as an opportunity to really express their revolutionary potential even though it was orchestrated largely by the leadership and involved punishing older members of their own social category.

At other times, young intellectuals were treated as 'red and expert' (*you hong you zhuan*) and had to emulate this model instead. This combination was considered appropriate for modern educated youth although it was a remnant from former times, especially the late 1950s. Editorials proclaimed 'Let them be both red and expert' (SCMP 1772, 1958:1). This part of the official discourse addressed the potential rise of a 'new class' or technocratic elite. 'University students still under the influence of the bourgeois ideology . . . lack experience of class struggles . . . A small number of them have been severely poisoned' (SCMP, 1575, 1957:3). They were advised to 'follow the instructions of the Party and Mao and strive to remould themselves as "red and expert" intellectual elements of the working class' (ECMM 170, 1959:25). Similarly, there were exhortations not only to possess scientific and technological skills but also 'great aspirations and lofty ideals' (FBIS CR 329, 1982:33).

The model appeared as 'expert' and innovative in terms of their specialities but politically passive. On the one hand the country needed its intellectuals for economic and technological development, but sections of the CCP had a disdain for academics which was a significant factor throughout the reform decade. Certain figures were more favourably inclined towards intellectuals, such as Zhou Enlai, who recognised their contribution to China's modernisation drive. There are various labels for the factions whose existence is usually denied by the CCP leadership. Some of the most frequently used ones of the 1950s and 1960s describing those in favour of economic reforms were the 'pragmatists' or 'modernisers', 'technocrats' and 'developmentalists'. Dittmer (1987) also describes the modernisers, among whom he lists Deng Xiaoping, Liu Shaoqi and Zhou Enlai, as 'managerialists' (*op. cit*:6). They were likely to be labelled as 'revisionists' during the Cultural Revolution by those in favour of political 'struggle'.

There is also the distinction in the more recent period between the 'hardliners' or 'leftists' and 'liberalisers' or 'reformers.' The first group includes those who accept policies based upon Maoist principles, with stricter political controls over economic and social life. The latter could include, once again, Deng and former Party, Secretary Hu Yaobang. Deng, however, could also be described as a 'hardliner' in the political sense given his record on democratic reforms. Chang (1988) believes that 'factional conflicts' will continue into the future because Deng's reform programme will take decades to achieve and during this time, different interest groups would be apparent.

The existence of factions, as well as the potential for people to move between them according to the existing status quo, adds to the changeability and looseness within the official discourse which provides young intellectuals with opportunities to negotiate their position as well as for risk taking, depending upon which faction has the upper hand. Young intellectuals can be expected to favour those CCP leaders who emphasise education and its personnel and vice versa. There would be similar interests between these groups. Additionally, young people do not merely accept the official messages but select and modify them according to their circumstances and examples will be discussed in this book.

White (1981) noted how educational policies were positively affected when the developmentalists were in ascendancy with an emphasis on technical expertise. This reaffirms the links between intellectuals and Party factions with the position of the former being contingent to some extent upon the latter. This factor of political patronage remains important in the treatment of the intelligentsia as a whole, as well as the youthful section under examination here. It will be shown that as long as young intellectuals in the late 1980s had the support of certain leadership figures, they were to some extent protected but once this was lost, their situation was not so secure.

This review of the official discourse of educated youth, incorporating key historical as well as cultural, social and political features of youth and intellectuals, provides the context for the emergence of Deng's generation of young intellectuals. It must be remembered that it was not fixed but subject to changes. Whilst distinctions between mental and manual labour are not always clear cut, for example, it is argued here that young intellectuals in the 1980s remained an elite group largely because of their participation in higher education which is a kind of social closure based on credentialism. Membership of the CYL is also an important factor. Social closure, as already indicated, may help to maximise rewards and include the dual acts of keeping certain people in the desired group and keeping others out. Such processes are largely the result of traditional and official practices in China with junior members of the intelligentsia placed in a situation of dependency.

The maximisation of market potential is part of this, with young intellectuals trying to realise the exchange value of their relatively scarce educational credentials or to 'cash in' in order to acquire favourable symbolic prestige, material rewards and access to political power or influence. The next chapter will explore the initial hopes placed on higher education which were subsequently unfulfilled, creating widening disparities between the expectations and actual experience. Alternative strategies developed by members of the reform generation for dealing with these disparities which emerged as significant during the fieldwork will be analysed as will the contradictions of the generation that arose from having 'one foot in history and the other striding towards the future' (Luo, 1995:558). The educational sphere will be examined first because, as already emphasised, higher education is a key part of the identity of this social group and is what distinguished Deng's generation of young intellectuals from other youthful social categories.

3 From Educational Crazes to Educational Crises

The ways in which the key generation-shaping events contributed to the main educational trends and attitudes will be addressed in this chapter. The reinstatement of the entrance examination system led first to exam 'fever', a higher education 'craze' and 'diploma fever' at the time when Deng Xiaoping's star was rising. The official emphasis on education in general, and science and technology in particular, helped to popularise the 'four modernisations'[1] early in the decade and the open door policy of increasing contacts with other countries, particularly western ones, was also a feature of the new regime. The chances to study overseas increased as a result of the shifts in policy and many young intellectuals joined the 'going abroad tide' (*chuguo chao*). What began as a 'new dawn', however, became a familiar, premature sunset and by the late 1980s there was despair and pessimism. The growing educational crisis seemed to reach a turning point in 1988 with the devaluation of knowledge a major 'hot topic' (*redian*) amongst young intellectuals. Poor rewards for academic careers seemed particularly disappointing after the initial expectations of higher education.

FROM THE REVIVAL OF OLD DREAMS TO AN EDUCATIONAL NIGHTMARE

The Policy Setting

Higher education had been disrupted throughout the previous decade but policy changes were instigated even before Mao's death with moves to restore exams and a degree of competition based on merit rather than politically motivated class labels. The Ministry of Education, later renamed the State Education Commission (SEC) was restored in 1975, a decision related to the pro-modernising faction. The adoption of the four modernisations programme also occured in the same year, indicating that the technocrats were gaining the upper hand. In Shirk's view previous socialist 'virtuocratic' principles were subordinated to the meritocratic ones of the Party modernisers with the shift 'initiated by Deng and the leaders allied with him who believe that virtuocracy produced economic disaster' (Shirk, 1982:86). Education was the first to receive attention, being subject to more pragmatic policies before the economy was dealt with.

The introduction of the responsibility system in the country-side, for example, came after the restoration of college entrance examinations (Wang, 1989; Griffin, 1984). Gardner writes that it was the 'severity of China's educational difficulties' which necessit-tated early changes 'well before other economic and political reforms' (1989:223). Pepper makes the point that changes in the education sector 'did not need to await the Third Plenum. By that time, almost all the decisions necessary to recreate the regular education system in its pre-1966 state had already been announced, and implementation was well under way' (1990:71). These early reforms increased optimism amongst young people holding educational aspirations with Deng's envisaged role for science and technology necessitating 'special attention to educa-tion' (Rai, 1991:41).

In practical terms, the exams were intended to remedy the shortage of suitably trained intellectuals. 'An adequate supply of qualified personnel is the key to success in China's modernization programme. Only a sound and efficient educational system can ensure this' (CD, 24 May 1985:4). The decision at the end of 1978 to restrict rural assignments and their subsequent abandon-ment assured the continuity of the education reforms. Previous policies were criticised for wasting talent in the pursuit of political goals. 'China shifted abruptly back to a system that makes educational excellence the filter for career access' (Rozman, 1981:393). After several 'battles' it was claimed that 'respecting knowledge and useful persons (*rencai*) has become the tendency of our time' (ZGQN, 1988 1:6). The policy shifts were pitched in terms of national needs with a large group of scientific personnel envisaged to compensate for the losses caused by the Cultural Revolution. The educated elite were exhorted to make their contribution and this had the effect of raising expectations about their subsequent position and role in Chinese society which was central to the identity of Deng's generation.

Other policy decisions made at this time reaffirmed the com-mitment to education and the rise of credentialism. The 'Outline

Programme for National Education 1978–85' proposed curriculum changes, a return to more formal education, emphasis on examinations at all levels and the reopening of key point schools. This last decision was, according to Thogersen, 'an unmistakeable signal that more attention should be paid to the education of the elite' (1990:77). Tertiary education was expanded by increasing the number of establishments from 404 in 1977 to 704 in 1981 and student numbers rose from 625,000 to 1,279,000. (Gardner, 1989:223). The better universities were designated as key points and could recruit the brightest students.

1981 saw the decision to award academic degrees. Graduates who had 'fulfilled all the requirements of a four-year curriculum and had been approved for graduation would receive the bachelor's degree' (Du, 1992:81). Before this period, diplomas were awarded but no higher degrees and this policy shift added to the growing 'diploma craze' with educational criteria increasingly replacing the former political ones. Later in the decade this 'diploma effect' was considered as 'unfortunate' in one commentary entitled 'Rise and Fall of the Diploma' (CD, 24 Jan. 1991:3). The 'clammering for the "little red passport" which seemed to be the only access up the career ladder' was in sharp contrast to the previous clammerings around Mao's 'little red book' of essential quotations.

With the granting of degrees, students could consider once more having educational careers. The expansion of postgraduate study was quite rapid with only 226 postgraduates in the whole of China in 1977 rising to over 37,000 by 1983. (Gardner:223). The 'diploma disease' (Dore, 1976) phenomenon spread to young Chinese intellectuals who had been temporarily excluded until the reform decade. After this time, they grasped the significance of academic credentials and it became part of their generational identity. The assessment and evaluation of these credentials was a continual process throughout the reform decade.

The possibility of training outside China was also introduced and the seeds of the 'going abroad tide' sown at the start of the reform decade. For nearly 20 years, the government had sent only a few scholars overseas and during the 1950s they went mainly went to the USSR. Even that destination was eliminated after the two countries ended their relationship in 1959. The post 1976 leadership expressed a need to gain scientific and technological knowledge from advanced countries if China was to 'catch

up' with the West. Apart from importing this through foreign
teachers and equipment, students could go abroad. This could
have been facilitated by the degree system because Chinese
graduates would have comparable qualifications to present to
foreign universities rather than a nondescript diploma.

Taken together, these policy shifts clearly helped to shape the
expectations of those attempting to enter higher education at the
start of the reform decade and the rising generation of young
intellectuals defined itself in these terms.

The Educational Crazes

The first examination sittings were seen as a 'symbol of a new
dawn' for a generation who had 'suffered through the nightmare
years' (ZGQN, 1988 1:2). Chinese youth had a chance to become
useful persons in society and rushed to examination centres to
register their candidacy but the 5.7 million applicants far outnumbered available places, (Cleverley, 1985). Rozman gives the
figure of 1,020,000 enrolments in 1979, and this was after nearly
200 new higher education institutions had been established.
(1981:425) In 1977, the competition was intense with demand far
outstripping supply. 'Examination fever' spread quickly through
work units where older educated youth were employed which
further overloaded the system and probably exacerbated the
failure rate.

The selection process involved standardised measures with
graded test scores replacing the previous practice of giving
priority to class background and political activism. The younger
sections of the generation looked optimistically to the future
but there was a degree of frustration for their seniors when
comparing themselves to junior counterparts. The exam fever
was evident amongst an increasingly smaller group of people after
the initial surge of candidates and social closure based upon
credentialism became more evident. The natural decrease was
assisted by a screening process so that by 1983 there were 1.67
million candidates with only 360,000 being successful (Hooper,
1985a). Given the increasing numbers of young people in the
population, tertiary education was set to remain a privilege.

Entering the competition itself was not always straightforward
with a lack of facilities, especially in rural regions, inhibiting
academically ambitious youth. Subsequent protests by older,

rusticated youth who returned without permission to cities like Beijing and Shanghai, notably in 1978 and 1979, illustrated the problem, (Brodsgaard, 1981; Gold 1980). There were further protests in June 1985. Around 300 former Beijing students travelled from Shaanxi province to the capital and staged a sit-in demonstration outside the city hall, demanding the right to return. They felt they had made their contribution to the nation but the authorities would not accept their pleas. They were a reminder of the existence of the many former urban-educated youth who could never return to their homes and for whom sitting the entrance examinations was an unfulfilled dream.

Some city youths also had problems. The required time off from work for lessons was not always forthcoming. Other older youths with families were also disadvantaged and these factors created social and personal difficulties for those who had caught the examination fever. There were also those who had married in the countryside and experienced problems in fulfilling educational ambitions. According to Liu, a 'great majority of these were female students who had married local boys' (1991:29). They were no longer considered as educated youth because they had already made the transition into adulthood. Rural marriage had automatically changed their social status: they were 'peasants' like their spouses and as a result, excluded from urban relocation. Liu believes this accounts for many divorces after 1977 when married people tried to regain their educated youth status and city residency.

Those who could not enter the exams received worn-out ideological consolations about making their contribution in other ways. The most important thing was having a 'red heart' in order to assist socialist reconstruction. This may not have ameliorated the disappointment caused by the narrowing of employment and status prospects facing those without higher education. The 1980s had brought new dreams but not everyone could hold onto them. A large number of candidates were going to be disappointed, perhaps for the second time in their relatively short lifetimes. Rozman put the ratio of aspirants to successes at something like 20 to 1 with 'a highly elitist tertiary system' restored (1981:426). The exams became not only a major strategy of action but also part of the identity of this generation. Younger candidates also faced increasing competition. In the early 1980s, an estimated 3 million lower secondary school graduates from approximately 13 million progressed to senior secondary schools and from these, only around 300,000–350,000 went to university. Competition was 'relentless' (Rosen, 1984:74).

An important implication of educational reform was the anticipation of an improved social position for intellectuals and recognition of their important social role. They were no longer to be included in the lowly 'stinking ninth category' and young intellectuals expected changes in their socio-economic position as part of the wider process of 'restratification' occurring in the post 1976 context. They were promised 'better conditions for their work, including more research funds and equipment, research assistants and contact with foreign scholars . . . those who make outstanding contributions are being promised access to better housing, among other 'perks' (Whyte, 1981:321). The extent to which these aims were realised will be examined but to begin with the outlook was positive.

The most senior interviewees, Qiu, at 31, Gao and Zhou, both 28, realised very quickly that the examinations would have an important effect on their lives. They had all suffered disruptions in their education but the chance to enter higher education was not so much a new dream but the revival of previous aspirations and ambitions. These respondents had originally expected to continue with education because of parent and teacher expectations and gaining academic qualifications was an accepted goal. As with other members of their generation, they had particular reasons for pursuing educational goals.

They were illustrative of their intra-generational unit in viewing higher education as a strategy for obtaining advantageous life chances in their populous and relatively poor nation. For those who had not avoided rural relocation, the examination offered hope not only of resuming education but also of transferring back to the cities. Gao, Zhou and Qiu had intended to return to their homes and Zhou claimed that entering university was a good way out of the countryside. The realities of life in China made this all the more necessary. They had seen the conditions in the rural areas and realised that without qualifications, they would be unable to move. These respondents already valued higher education for the extrinsic rewards it could bring. Few other ways existed for gaining access to scarce material rewards and advantages at that time.

Qiu had been forced to suspend his studies because from 1975 to 1977 he was a 'peasant, a peasant in the countryside', assigned to Anhui province. He managed to move from the farm to a factory in a small town and such a move was not uncommon towards the end of the Cultural Revolution. 'There was great competition for this work. People fought and bribed their way into these jobs', wrote Liu (1991:28). With the implementation of educational reforms, the situation became more fluid with the higher education 'escape route' from the countryside for those suitably qualified.

Qiu's hopes and ambitions were revived by educational reforms. 'In 1977, I met a chance, the method of entrance of the university was reformed. The government held the national examination and I was selected. The people who got the good mark entered university. So at last I was lucky. Without this reform, without this change, maybe I was a worker until now.' Qiu described as 'unfortunate' the experience of having his education halted. 'All my dreams were broken, broken. To be true, at that time I never dreamed of entering university or college. I was only third grade in elementary school. I didn't know how I could graduate from elementary school, from middle school. No-one could know.'

It was a similar case for Gao. 'Certainly the examination system for the university returning is the background I think. Without that, maybe I'm a peasant in the countryside now. I couldn't sit here and talk you', claimed Gao. He could not go to university when graduating from middle school. 'You know at that time our examinations system had not been restored (*huifu*) so I had to stop my study and find some job to do in 1976. In 1977 our examination system came back and I returned to middle school, to review the lessons and try to pass the examination.' After ten months he was successful. 'I passed it and entered the training college, to become a college student and then I carried on my studies without a stop.' He was fortunate, like his colleague Zhou whose education was interrupted for only a year.

Gao, Qiu and Zhou were among the first few millions to sit these examinations and wanted to 'try, just try', as Gao explained, not believing himself capable of passing after his spell in the countryside. Other young people had been similarly sidetracked during the 1970s but we can consider next what exactly Deng's generation hoped to gain by following the 'black pathway' of higher education.

The Expected Outcomes of Higher Education

Asking respondents about the reasons for entering university made them think back to their earlier youth, especially their teenage years. These could then be compared to the subsequent evaluation of higher education and the prospects it offered, that is the actual outcomes. In making this comparison between their motivations and subsequent evaluations, senior sample members clearly had more to recount. The youngest interviewees had just one year's experience of university life whilst others could look back to the late 1970s when they began university. The disparities in length of educational experience will be taken into consideration since it has already been noted that higher education appeared to be more taken for granted amongst the younger respondents whose opinions were still being shaped by contemporary events.

A number of advantages were envisaged, such as training, making contact with foreigners, self-discipline and social experience. Issues of social position, material rewards, status and influence were emphasised. Instrumental motivations were frequently mentioned with the aims of obtaining secure employment, higher salaries, a good standard of living and a high social status. Expressive motivations were less frequently articulated, with education rarely described as a worthwhile activity in its own right, irrespective of where it led in terms of career, salaries and status.

Six interviewees linked higher education to obtaining a 'better job' and others saw it as offering a 'good future'. A degree was important for being assigned to a 'good' work unit in an urban area, that is an 'iron rice bowl'. Rural assignments were undesirable. Although the situation was changing, as Jiang pointed out, it used to be the case that 'if you couldn't enter college, you couldn't get a job'. He compared the socio-economic climate of the late 1980s to that of the early 1980s when he was applying for university, with the increased likelihood in the contemporary period of finding a good job without a degree. His entry into university was due to his desire to learn technical skills such as computing, viewed as a more practical subject and a better qualification to offer on the employment market.

Hua was also interested in gaining a good job as well as knowledge, and this had led him to resit the examinations after initial failure. Another young teacher, Yang, also failed but never resat. He attended instead a Normal College (*shifan daxue*) for middle school teacher training. He recounted his disappointment about not attending university and how it had negatively affected his life. His ultimate objective was to continue studying and gain more academic rather than vocational qualifications. He still held the 'dream' of having a degree to his name.

The postgraduate Guo had considered attending a professional or vocational institute, thinking it could be useful to learn a trade but chose university instead. 'I thought it might be a better future to go to university.' When he was about to graduate from middle school, there were increasing numbers of vocational institutions and this was becoming a viable alternative. They tended to have, however, lower status. Guo's doubt about the wisdom of his decision led him to question his ultimate course of action.

The desire for more knowledge was given as the main reason by eight interviewees. Wen, a 20 year old English student, referred to the quotation that 'knowledge is power', but this was not her main reason for entry into higher education. It appeared that as with other respondents, it was parental encouragement and their plans for her future which played a key role. A good job was considered important not only for improving material benefits but also for the social rewards it could bring, such as enhanced social position (*shehui diwei*), status and influence. Further study had been clearly linked to better employment prospects and, therefore, recognised as a route of social mobility early in the reform decade. Those in the sample who had been upwardly socially mobile were successful largely as a result of education.

Another respondent at the younger end of the age range, 20 year old Gu, also linked education to social mobility through credentialism. He gave a mixture of reasons but said that he wanted to improve his social status. 'With a family like mine (that is, father a worker, mother a housewife) it's difficult to get a good job without college education.' The social stratification dimension was evident in other responses which further supported the view that educational level was dependent to some extent upon social class in spite of the stated meritocratic principles. There was certainly the desire to have more influence in society as a result of acquiring more knowledge. Wen's comment, therefore, about knowledge and power is significant in this respect. Replies were occasionally expanded by slogans, and were a reminder of the many ideological messages respondents had been subjected to throughout their lives. These offered clues to the different layers of expectations around certain issues as well as indications of the disparities between official messages and actual experience.

Only Yu and Liu cited as a major motivation their desire to 'contribute' or 'devote' something to the country. This patriotic type of response conformed to the official models but they were in the minority. Most people were more concerned with improving social position and status. It was felt that being a student looked good to other people and would lead to improvements in social standing. 'The family will be proud to have a university student', said Zhen. 'Students being able to go to university was a kind of good student [*sic*] in all the people's eyes.' This was a similar opinion to that of another young woman, Chen, who felt her neighbours respected her family because all the children had gained university places.

These ideas would have been attacked during the Cultural Revolution, but by the early 1980s, instrumentalism was more prevalent than socialist ideology. Respondents were not immediately recognisable as 'reformers with ideals' as expressed in the communist rhetoric but appeared as sensible youths taking a recommended route. A high degree of compatibility between their ideas and those of parents and teachers, appeared to be the formula for educational success. Families and teachers expected good results and higher education offered better prospects than seeking employment at the end of secondary education. It was admitted by the authorities that those entrants from 'bourgeois' backgrounds were more successful than the workers and peasant which is a 'familiar phenomenon of most educational systems' (Gardner, 1989:223).

Many respondents mentioned parental values and preference for higher education, which can be considered part of the cultural inheritance factor. According to Hua, 'Intellectuals definitely want their children to go to college because they think the more knowledge the better. Children of intellectuals usually go to college so parents encourage and support them.' We can also consider the situation of a 'typical' key middle school student such as Wang. His parents wanted him to enter a prestigious university and it appeared as a 'natural progression from a good middle school' with 'everybody' taking this course of action. Zhen described how her parents helped her so she could be successful. 'They were very keen and encouraged me all the time before I went to the university. When I was a middle school student, they even did not want me to do housework, to save my time, and review my lessons so that I could to university.'

Zhang cited the 'influence of the teacher'. The school ethos is important, particularly in the case of key point schools which sought to maximise university entrance amongst pupils. Wang expressed it in this way: 'I think at that time we didn't have any hesitation to go to university. We even didn't have any idea of quitting school unless we were unlucky to not be qualified for entrance of a certain university.' He had internalised the pro-education values of both his parents and teachers and this appeared to be the norm at his school where maximum entry into universities was the goal. The peer group was also cited as an important source of influence, indicating the shared social and cultural background amongst educated youth. Jiang referred to the shared 'dream' of pupils at middle school of going to university.

Overall, instrumental attitudes predominated with ideological values taking a secondary place, and this also seemed to affect the choice of subject area. It is useful to explore briefly the links between expectations and the specialisms studied because these provide a basis for the major trends of thought as well as some of the variations. It also enables deeper layers of expectations about obtaining academic qualification to be brought to the surface.

The Importance of Subject Area

As with the decision to pursue education, subject choices reflected external variables as well as personal ambitions nurtured by the respondents. There was evidence that official messages concerning the desirability of science and technology expertise had been internalised. The high profile given to these meant that there was optimism amongst those studying science and technology – '*like*' -- courses rather than those on the '*wenke*' side and the possibility of an emerging new technocratic elite was indicated which influenced the aspirations of young people at the time.

Respondents had experienced varying amounts of choice because of the external pressures and limitations. Zhang, who graduated in 1984, said that there was little choice to begin with and he was assigned to study electric thermal power. 'It's according to the marks in the examination', he said. Some people were channelled into a particular discipline by parents and teachers and admitted to having little idea about what their major might entail. Others took up available places on courses because their marks were not high enough to take their preferences. Others who were 'good at' or interested in a particular subject at school wanted to follow it through to university.

Examining parental preferences reveals motivations other than the purely academic or professional with strong indications of economic and political pragmatism. Qiu, who specialised in dentistry, said that he hardly knew anything about the subject but his parents encouraged him to select medically oriented studies. They thought that everybody needed doctors and dentists so this was a good profession to enter. This was just after the Cultural Revolution and qualifying in medicine may have offered some security. They were concerned about possible future anti-rightist campaigns and this was a general cause of anxiety for intellectuals, many of whom had already suffered. They may have been attempting to steer their children away from areas which could be negatively evaluated. It also had the prospect of desirable urban residency and Qiu had, indeed, finished up in Shanghai.

Qiu decided to pursue an academic course on the advice of his parents as being less likely to result in personal 'trouble'. The intellectual status was present but if there was anything like a repeat of the Cultural Revolution, then he would be relatively immune from criticism. It appeared as a safe option and contributed to his expectations of improved prospects for intellectuals with a scientific background at the beginning of the reform period. Goldman (1992) writes of this relative safety awarded to the scientific community at this time and how they were largely exempted from continuing political campaigns against intellectuals in the 1980s. Possible links with foreign scientific communities and overseas study periods were also appealing. Goldman writes that such links actually increased the degree of 'protection' for scientists in this period, with astrophysicist Professor Fang Lizhi[2] being a good example. Although he was eventually blamed for causing student unrest and purged from the Party, he had years of relative freedom to make speeches critical of the Chinese system of government.

There was also a similar combination of political and economic pragmatism in the reasoning of Sun's parents. 'My parents insisted I study science because during the Cultural Revolution people in the arts were tortured more. My parents thought scientists could be more useful.' Science and technology appeared as less tainted by 'bourgeois liberalism' in the eyes of the older generation who feared anti-intellectual campaigns. Sun did not, however, follow her parents' wishes and took English instead. She was just about to leave China and had a positive evaluation of higher education. For her, it had created an opportunity to join the *chuguo chao*.

Xiu also chose medicine because of her parents, saying that the 'traditional thinking was that education and medicine would provide a good job'. Her own ideas 'didn't count much in my life', and she succumbed to external pressures in contrast to Sun who went against her parents. Xiu was more of a conformist who claimed that 'most children in China are dependent upon their parents' decisions'. Lu also said that his family had encouraged him to study medicine.

Another set of expectations were expressed by Jiang, also on the *like* side, who had an instrumental attitude and studied computers at university. He considered himself fortunate to have the chance to follow his ambitions and his desire for good employment prospects had been met. This led him to positively evaluate higher education. The specific branch of knowledge or expertise gained seemed to be a significant variable which could improve or further depress the social position of individual members of educated youth. Jiang was one of the few who could 'use their knowledge and technology to make money'. He stated that the social position for young intellectuals was not low but 'about middle', with the situation changing 'not for the better, not for the worse'. He felt that young intellectuals could alter their position if they wanted to in spite of their common problems. It was easier for him to find well-paid work, to 'look around' as he put it, feeling that he had some control over his own social position.

This view was not widely shared by others and Jiang could be viewed as part of the technocratic elite within the intelligentsia. His subject area probably mediated the evaluation process, leading to a less pessimistic view about the main trends in the social position of intellectuals. This point was upheld by Qiu who said that most young intellectuals could not show their ability unless they had education in something like computers. The small size of this sample, however, means that the influence of subject area on the evaluation of social position is indicative rather than conclusive.

Guo had also wanted to be part of the scientific 'revolution' but had to accept a place to study zoology. 'It's not according to my will. I wanted to study genetics but failed.' His disappointment indicated a hierarchy of specialisms with genetics being superior to zoology. This represents a further refinement of expectations and how they were linked to the emerging social divisions in Chinese society. Entering higher education was the general aim, with more specific ones being related to the choice of subject. On the *like* side, some subjects were seen as better than others and these evaluations influenced respondents' choices. Guo's expectations had been largely unrealised and he was actively trying to improve his position by studying abroad.

Liu considered physics but said 'I'm not good at physics so I can't enter the physics department. I was good at English and maths. I thought computer science was suitable so I chose it.' It is significant that Liu chose a subject with a modern image and central to technological innovation of the contemporary era. Some respondents selected English, however, believing this would offer opportunities related to the open door policy. Wen and Lili, for example, studied English partly because they hoped to go abroad to study but had later realised that their initial objectives were not easy to achieve. Most interviewees expressed some disappointment with their prospects and their subsequent evaluations of the higher education will be analysed in terms of a perceived impending or existing educational crisis.

Shifting Evaluations of Higher Education

The data indicated that ten years after it had began the examination 'fever' had cooled down but education generally had become a 'hot topic' and in a sense considered as a social problem. Its value was being questioned, both privately as well as publicly with articles frequently appearing in the press. Some colleges were selling diplomas in order to receive extra money and they were no longer 'colourful kites flying high in the sky' (CD, 24 Jan. 1991:3). Nor were people surprised as they used to be by the fact that ' . . . a pedlar selling eggs can achieve a better standard of living than a college graduate. Knowledge is seen as being virtually useless' (CD, *op. cit*). The ongoing debate about the devaluation of knowledge and qualifications was in large part the expression of the frustration caused by growing disparities between initial expectations and subsequent realities.

There were many indications of dismay with the actual experience of higher education as well as with its outcomes. The process of social closure through credentialism appeared to be flawed with educated youth not always appearing as an elite group. There were criticisms about the courses offered, teaching styles, textbooks, curriculum, living conditions and social life on campuses. 'After graduation from high school I thought universities were mysterious but when I came here I found it was just so-so', was Zhao's opinion. This view was very critical of one of Beijing's most prestigious universities. His teachers may have given him unrealistic expectations as, indeed, may have been the case with other interviewees.

The disparities between expectations and experiences were distributed across the age range. Negative evaluations also emerged from both sides of the *liko/wonko* divide although scientists were more likely to more satisfied with their progress. In terms of the gender dimension, there were also comparable expressions of disappointment. Outright dissatisfaction with the experience of higher education was expressed by seven interviewees, four of them women.

There was not enough practical instruction, according to Zhou who complained that teachers emphasised knowledge more than talent. They were not encouraged to think for themselves, the lessons were as 'dull as dead water' with few opportunities to experience real life. This meant that they ill-prepared for post-university life and could find it difficult to know how to behave. Zhang criticised the emphasis on book learning and in his opinion, more practical technology teaching was also required. Lu was generally satisfied but stated that the teachers 'talk for too long. They can't make people think about the subject.' This didactic method was acceptable for some subjects such as his own, medicine, where large amounts of information had to be memorised, but for others it made the educational situation 'uncomfortable'.

Apart from being discouraged from thinking for themselves, others subscribed to Zhou's view that students had little chance to learn about society. Wen complained that 'College life doesn't teach us much' and was supported by her classmate, Lili who felt their education was too limited. The textbooks were 'out of date' and like older intellectuals, the books belonged 'to the 1950s'. There was a strong sense of identification with the 1980s but they considered education to be lagging behind the times. Although they were supposed to assist in China's reconstruction, the resources were deemed unsuitable.

Wen and Lili also felt that campus life was somewhat restricted. These views were shared by Guo who complained that 'I just think it's not quite good. They teach outdated things. Teachers are not good enough.' Like Wen and Lili, he felt that campuses should be livelier places because 'students need entertainment, need activities'. Another woman, Zhen, was disappointed not only with her own education but for the country as a whole. In her view, funding was too low as well as teachers' salaries. She believed that deteriorating conditions led many people to abandon education and this situation was 'not very good.' Her own education had been acceptable, providing her with career opportunities. After her first degree in engineering she was able to take special English training classes. She admitted that this was quite 'unusual' and probably contributed to her feeling of relative satisfaction, but she was worried about general educational problems in China.

These disappointments did not, however, mean that they had learned nothing because they valued quite highly their own educational capabilities and achievements. Perhaps this generation had learned many important things outside their classrooms but certainly they felt they knew a lot more than their senior counterparts with several students comparing their own level of knowledge and capabilities favourably to that of their teachers. Wang thought that 'In some ways I'm more masterful than my teachers. They are not so qualified, a serious problem I think. For example, we can speak English very well, can learn in different ways, to listen to the "Voice of America" and so on but our teachers can't. We are better informed.' He drew clear comparisons between the generations, linking the differences to the outcomes of official policies.

The older generation was viewed as deficient in the areas of science and technology. Younger people possessed the necessary skills and had, according to Wen 'grasped new knowledge fitting into the new tide'. Embedded in such replies were implicit criticisms of older intellectuals whose knowledge was claimed to be obsolete. Links were made between this superior knowledge and *gaige kaifang* policies which allowed new ideas to enter China and young intellectuals were very receptive to these.

Those who expressed more favourable views of higher education included medical graduates Lu and Xiu. The nature of their specialism may have caused the relatively positive evaluation because they saw it was of use for society as well as for themselves. Looking at the characteristics of the other relatively satisfied respondents, Hua, Sun and Jiang, further underlines the fact that certain sections of educated youth fared better than others in the reform decade. Hua was studying English, like Wen and Lili, but was noticeably more optimistic about the prospects. He felt that studying English had given him a chance to meet foreign teachers and that other subjects were 'not as good'. Zhen felt her English had improved her own position. It also assisted in the attempt to go overseas to study, as will be discussed.

According to Sun, higher education was 'very essential for any person ... especially people like me who didn't really study during the elementary school time because of the chaos'. She felt she had 'really realised' herself as a result of studying. Similarly, Lu felt that it was 'very important for young people. You get the key, we say in China. You can open the door of knowledge so higher education is much better for the young people.' Lu himself had found the 'key' of going abroad to study through higher education. He also mentioned other aspects such as learning to get along with other people, essential in crowded student dormitories where there is little privacy. This, he claimed, was 'basic social experience' to be gained before entering the society and is in contrast to criticisms of students not being able to learn social knowledge at college. It is also similar to the findings of the 'Roots' survey where some respondents felt themselves more 'adaptable' due to their university experience.

In spite of an underlying sense of pessimism, there remained a degree of confidence in higher education. It still incurred social advantages which made it worthwhile pursuing but change was considered necessary. This general view is explicable given the fact that they had already committed themselves to this route. Some regrets and concerns were expressed but mostly it was

considered the recommended course of action although in need
of improvement to make it more suitable for their generation.

Gao, for example, saw higher education as 'the most important
thing for China'. He had always felt 'lucky' to be at college and
not disappointed because only very few could be there. 'There
are 800 million people in the countryside and many of them are
illiterate', he pointed out. 'Higher education is the most important thing if any country wants to be advanced'. This outlook was
not solely oriented towards his own personal development but
that of the nation and was clearly affected by his having to
postpone his studies. Zhou also expressed a positive view in
general rather than personal terms, saying it was something
'essential' although he criticised the actual conditions at the end
of the reform decade.

Xiu felt that it was preferable to enter a college, whatever
education one receives. 'In university we can form our basic
qualities, it doesn't matter which speciality we choose. It is
necessary to receive such education no matter what.' She also
mentioned the importance for the nation which could improve its
'quality' through having highly educated people. Yu saw higher
education as the 'best way to improve society and the civilisation
of human beings'. Four people mentioned the national benefits of
higher education but personal concerns tended to predominate.

Those about to take up jobs expressed anxieties. The informant
Chu, for example, felt he may have made a mistake in choosing
the 'black pathway'. One of his classmates at middle school had
ripped up his acceptance to university, preferring instead to move
directly into a job. 'Perhaps he was right', Chu mused, having not
yet been assigned suitable employment. Four years of study had
not brought about the opportunities he had expected and he felt
worse off than his former classmate.

After a decade of reforms, it may have been more promising to
follow the occupational rather than academic route. Intellectuals
were no longer openly persecuted as before but were, instead,
beset by economic problems, and this situation could have been
rerouting young people away from colleges. It was recognised
that higher education did not always hold the 'key' and the
reform programme meant that other means of attaining high
incomes and social status were becoming necessary. Business was
the most frequently mentioned method as well as having good
guanxi or personal connections. With the value of higher educa-

tion being reassessed, the social position of educated youth would also be subject to change, as will be discussed next.

THE SOCIAL POSITION AND SOCIAL ROLE OF INTELLECTUALS

'People are not starving', remarked Jiang, as a rejoinder that the situation was not as bad as some may have felt but actual experiences generally fell far short of expectations. By 1988, it seemed that reforms were failing to improve the social position of intellectuals which was perceived to be in relative decline. Some felt that it was 'too difficult' to describe their social position and tended to focus on two aspects, these being economic and status issues with only a minority of respondents raising the question of political influence. There were few attempts to quantify statements in terms of figures for economic renumeration in order to substantiate their claims. This may have been considered unnecessary given the prevailing socio-economic context of the study and the publicity given to the educational 'crisis' in China. It was not the intention to prove whether the decline was real or imagined but to analyse the prevailing perception of downward social mobility.

Those already employed made a direct link between education and social position, expressing some dismay that they were not getting the rewards they had expected. Zhen stated that she never realised 'things were getting worse' when she entered higher education. Deng felt that 'the situation has become worse'. Another informant during a discussion was more specific, claiming that 'Compared with earlier, in the 1950s, now Chinese intellectuals' salary is low.' Usually, as with claims of receiving 'poor treatment', there was an absence of precise definitions of the historical period the present one was being compared to. The frequent use of 'nowadays' and 'recently' indicated that the decline was linked to reforms.

'I think this problem is caused by reform. Many problems occurred in reform. In the future our government may solve this problem', claimed Zhang. He distinguished between the economic and status elements of social position believing that before the reforms, the political position of young intellectuals was lower but not their economic situation. In the 1980s, their financial position was worse than before. This outcome had neither been expected nor desired. The lack of improvements was also attributed by Qiu and Xiu to problems of the reforms. Gu felt that young intellectuals had 'no good treatment, no high salary and also are worse off than others in many other fields'. The lack of fit between the economic rewards and the level of esteem was similarly summed up by Zhang: 'Most people want to go to university but most of them can't. But those who do go to universities or colleges, when they graduate, their social position is high but their salary is not high enough.'

Xiu's view in many ways encapsulated general opinions about social position. 'After the college entrance examinations were restored, the status of intellectuals has been increased a lot in people's minds. But in the recent years the status of the intellectuals has the trend of going down in the shock wave of reform and open policy.' First, there had been expectations of better prospects; then subsequent disappointment that reforms had not brought the desired rewards. The social position of young intellectuals according to the majority of respondents was low or 'not as good as it should be', even 'unfair'. Wang felt that 'They should have done better than they have'.

Xiu's statement referred to the links between higher education and social position; the uncertain outcomes of the restructuring of the social stratification system, and the importance of the relative evaluation of social position, such as comparisons with other social groups. Even if evidence for a rise rather than a decline in living standards and status levels for young intellectuals had been forthcoming, their situation could still have been viewed critically if comparisons were made to other social groups whose progress had outstripped their own. Social position is, after all, relative, and cannot be considered in isolation.

Xiu attributed the decline to the 'reverse phenomenon' (*ti nao dao gua*). 'This is a special term in the newspapers. These words simply mean the more knowledge one has, the higher education one receives, the less one earns. Many people who have made a lot of effort and studied very hard can't earn as much as those who are very poorly educated. Therefore, they begin to waver in their thought.' The situation facing young intellectuals appeared to be the as opposite of what had been anticipated and this was one of the main complaints. The post-Mao government had strongly hinted that academic qualifications would be highly valued and lead to higher social position. Wealth, however, was entering into the equation as economic reforms led to the growth of a small yet symbolically important private sector.

Qiu observed that 'Nowadays the money is very important in Chinese people's minds. So most people judge the social status of others by the money they have. Chinese people are extremely short of money and in the future five or ten years, this situation won't be changed.' He also saw a link between the relative scarcity of both wealth and status, indicating that if people generally were better off, then money might not be such an important factor in determining social position. It was only because a small proportion of the population were growing wealthy that money was becoming a major source of social differentiation, possibly displacing academic qualifications.

Xiu felt that it was difficult to evaluate social position in this period of social change, frequently referred to as an historic 'turning point' which had given rise to a 'clash of values' (*Weiding Gao*, 1988 8:26) as old ways were replaced by newer ones. The process of restratification was incomplete and their emergent social position remained unclear. In this context, some respondents adopted a 'wait and see' attitude to discover whether wealth, expertise or 'redness' was going to be the major determinant of social position in the future. The official commitment to raising the position of intellectuals both in economic and status terms was not always supported by policy shifts. Contradictory messages and unintended consequences of the 'turmoil' of reform were reflected in the position of young intellectuals compared to other social groups.

The situation of the *getihu* appeared to represent the other half of the equation in the 'reverse phenomenon'. With fewer qualifications but perceived as earning more than the intellectuals, they were seen as the ones benefiting from reforms. By exercising individual initiative, taking risks and developing economic skills in the burgeoning private sector, they were symbolic of the social change facilitated by economic reform. According to popular belief, they were making vast sums of money and becoming China's own *nouveau riche.*Young *getihu* could be successful without higher education. This is an important issue because it relates to the self-evaluation of Deng's generation who appeared to be left behind. The youth aspect is a significant point: they may have been part of the same generation but were contrasting generational units. The rise of the stereotyped 'rich' *getihu* countered young intellectuals' perceived decline with some dismay that this group of low social rank appeared to be doing so well. Young intellectuals were finding that they were unable to move into the social position they felt was theirs.

Guo discussed a case cited in the media of a university professor's three children. The eldest two were graduates and had academic jobs but the youngest, a daughter, left education after senior middle school. 'The highest paid is the girl because she works as a *getihu* . . . so it's the complete reverse.' He blamed the government, saying 'they always think that the intellectuals should have a higher position but actually they did not give them enough money, so their economic position is not high'. *Getihu* were referred to as 'pedlars' by Jiang. Five interviewees, including Guo, cited them when comparing social position. The perceived relative wealth of this group who 'make a fortune overnight' as Wen put it, was often brought up in discussions. Lili claimed that business people have 'a lot of money' but intellectuals, on the other hand, 'are not rich as they have no way to make a fortune, though they can write articles. It is difficult to get them published though'. Even if they did, the financial renumeration was not very high.

Unfavourable evaluations of *getihu* were to some extent the unanticipated consequence of earlier government propaganda. By reading about examples of educational failures who established profitable business ventures, young intellectuals had become increasingly aware that money could be made and influence gained without pursuing higher education. The original intention may have been to placate those unable to enter university with the message that there were other ways to make a living. This type of reasoning, however, exacerbated the devaluation of the knowledge process and by implication, the downgrading of intellectuals. There was later a change in the policy of advertising such success stories and more was made of the need to recognise educational experience and qualifications. However, even with the subsequent playing down, of the successes of relatively uneducated people, this perception prevailed.

All stereotypes have their limitations. The idea that most *getihu* lacked education was not a proven fact. Not all of them were rich, a term used as loosely by the respondents as by the government, and young *getihu* were themselves subject to the vagaries of official policies. The problem facing the CCP was how to publicly evaluate successful entrepreneurs without further alienating the rest of the population, especially those excluded from the money-making process. From the evidence here, it appeared that they had not found a satisfactory solution. Young intellectuals were so concerned about *getihu* because their position was intricately tied up with their own.

Chen, however, suggested that the traditional esteem awarded to educated people remained intact because 'they have talents, they do much important work for the country'. She recounted her own situation: 'I live in an apartment with several families, just ordinary people, very common. They just do labour work so my family is special in that area. I have three elder brothers, we are all university students. So they (the workers) respect our family very much, they are very polite.' She noted, however, that in terms of financial considerations 'the treatment is not good', and concluded that if people valued money highly, they would neither desire nor respect college education. Wen noted that young intellectuals still had a more 'stable' life than the entrepreneurs because the state provided their medical and welfare facilities. *Getihu* did not receive these benefits even if their salaries were higher which was an important consideration. 'They have no assurances when they are ill and will have to spend a lot.'

There was a common view that whilst the economic position for intellectuals was relatively low, in terms of social status they remained at a comparatively high level, which was the opposite of young entrepreneurs. Lili said that 'They have a high economic position but their social status is low while the young intellectuals have little money but high social status. This is really frustrating.' It was also probably frustrating for many of these entrepreneurs who wished to increase their social status. It appeared almost as a consolation for those on the point of entering intellectual occupations or having already undertaken such employment that members of society were still prepared to award them a certain degree of respect even if they were inadequately rewarded in financial terms.

'Although the pedlars make a lot of money the people still look down on them', remarked Yu, whilst Wen felt that 'Entrepreneurs are rich and living a comfortable life but their social status is low'. Young people who go into the money business don't think too much about being educated', said Sun, who drew a clear division between her own social group and other young people. She also said 'all my friends are relatively educated people'. This emphasised that they represented different social classes, with a degree of antagonism between them and did not mix socially. This was the accepted norm in her opinion.

Zhen reinforced this view, claiming to 'disguise' her educational background when in the company of *getihu* because her middle school friends who had taken up jobs rather than higher education tended to shun her. 'They think you are in the other world', was how she described this different peer group attitude. She felt that qualifications did make a difference to career possibilities and that educated people had more opportunities. 'If you are not very well educated then you cannot get a good job or you cannot go abroad, take exams etc. So, in this sense, educated youth has really got a high position.' She claimed that for those who went into hotels, business, or small shops, education meant something but it was not 'too serious'.

Other workers in the expanding service sector such as taxi drivers and staff in the luxury joint venture hotels were perceived as earning excessive sums of money. This comparison usually included the much-quoted reference to waitresses in hotels earning more than university professors (FEER, 1988:6). Certainly in terms of financial renumeration, this sample felt relatively deprived but still believed they had a higher, if insecure, social position. According to Xiu 'in people's minds' the status of educated youth was not low and it was only in the area of salaries that intellectuals were 'poorly treated'.

Others made comparisons with 'peasants' and 'workers'. Yu remarked that the situation for those in the countryside was 'worse' and that 'most Chinese people, especially peasants, don't have much money'. Yang, another young teacher, commented critically on rural life. 'Comparatively, things are worse in the countryside. People generally cannot satisfy themselves. So they give up their jobs and move.' He cited low salaries and poor conditions as problems which deter graduates from settling there. Young intellectuals were not keen to be assigned as teachers in rural areas and this was partly related to the traditional preference for urban residence noted earlier. The countryside held few attractions for educated people who feared a decline in their social position upon leaving the cities. Even if some farmers had benefited financially from the rural reforms, their situation was still unenviable. This is in line with many of the discussions in the media about the problems of rural teachers due to inadequate renumeration, living conditions and social status (CD, 4 Oct. 1984:3). Compared to his counterparts in urban areas Yang felt he was in a lower position and wished to change this.

There were also negative implications for children of the 'entrepreneur' farmers because of the tendency for them to be taken out of school early. Official statistics for primary and middle school 'dropouts' between 1980 and 1987 were set at 30 million with the numbers rising rapidly in rural regions (CD, 7 Dec. 1988:3). In Hubei Province alone, close to 1.5 million students aged between seven and twelve had left school in 1987. A survey of nine provinces found 15 per cent of six to 14 year olds were not in school in cities compared to 25 per cent in the country (Pepper, 1990:90).

Guo made the comparison with 'workers' in cities instead. 'You know that in the newspapers we are always discussing this problem because some workers have more pay than intellectuals.' Workers were ranked highly in terms of political features in the previous decade but intellectuals had been promised higher status. In the restructuring of the social hierarchy, such comments indicated that workers were faring better than expected with the lack of social progress made by 'mental workers' disappointing. Both the urban and rural stratification hierarchies were seen to be in a state of flux and young intellectuals were unsure exactly where they would eventually be ranked.

Zhen's description summed this up with her generation viewed as the 'victims of the reforms'. Compared to the previous decades of communism, when things were 'quiet and smooth, although our living standard is low', the 1980s brought greater inequalities. 'Some people can make millions but our salaries on the one hand are just a little, it is not equal. As reform goes on, people think this difference will get bigger. The rich are becoming richer, the poor poorer. We can do nothing, simply wait.' She was one of several who also cited this adverse situation as the major source of motivation for those going abroad. If there was 'no hope' in China, then perhaps it lay elsewhere.

Similarly, Qiu believed that 'The status of intellectual youth will remain lower than other youth for at least ten years. Only very few can use their knowledge and technology to make money.' Pessimism about the future was not unusual with other

interviewees referring to a 'long period of time' needed to raise
the situation of young intellectuals. Most of them felt they could
do little apart from be patient.

The problems were not caused, however, by reforms alone.
Two respondents cited 'tradition' as partly responsible for the low
position of intellectuals. Yu said that 'In our country, the intellectuals' position is not only a social problem but a historical one'.
Yang echoed this, stating 'It has a history of many years'. There
are parallels with the contemporary period when undergraduates
hoped to be assigned to 'iron rice bowl' jobs but it was only at
certain points that the situation for intellectuals was satisfactory.
Being educated was not enough to attain high social position. 'I
hope it will become better but it's only my hope', said Qiu. They
could only stand back and evaluate the recent past, especially
their own experiences and project contemporary trends into the
future. Zhen was also pessimistic. 'Most young people do not see
hope in the future', she declared.

Another more traditional reason for young intellectuals' relatively low social position was the seniority system or *lunzi peibei*.
Respondents saw this as a significant factor distinguishing them
from more senior intellectuals and bringing in the generational
dimension. At any one time, young people may feel relatively
disadvantaged when compared to older colleagues but it was
clear that in the views of the sample, Deng's generation felt
themselves superior to their elders. Wen discussed this point,
saying that in China at that time 'juvenilization' (*qingnianhua*) was
being advocated. 'Now it's possible for young intellectuals to
become high ranking officials. Many leaders have resigned, so
that the young can have better opportunities, to bring their
talents into full play.' There had been some resignations of older
CCP leaders from the Long March generation it was true but
still, as Lili countered, it was hard for young people to get ahead.
'There are relatively fewer young people in high positions as the
young first must be appreciated by their elders before they can
get a high position. We still have the system of assigning people.
It's not easy to get good positions.' They were confident about
their own abilities and desired role even though they saw
themselves as downwardly socially mobile.

Corruption was also a problem. Even during the Cultural
Revolution university entry was not always based strictly on
'redness' with the use of *guanxi* prevalent as well as tendencies for

'favoritism and backdoor deals' (Shirk, 1982:188). Qiu stated that 'Those who could go to university or college did not need to take the examination, only by having some relationship with some people in power they would be lucky enough to enter a university.' Qiu described how his family had 'no relationships' although they could have found some if they had wanted to. His parents were described as 'good communists' and thus 'never, never were willing to go by the back door to find some old friends, or ask some old friends to help. They always asked us to try by ourselves. So, at that time I never dreamed of entering university. It was absolutely impossible.'

For him, the corruption engendered by these practices had seriously undermined the workings of the system supposedly based on political merit and in the contemporary period, that of educational merit. The use of *guanxi wang* continued to influence university entry after 1977. This also affected their perceived social role.

Social role can be viewed as the active expression of social position and respondents clearly wanted to show they were an elite even if in reality they were slipping down the social scale. The notion of playing a 'leading' role in national development and even being indispensable because they were the only social group deemed capable of fulfilling this key role came across strongly. There was a related stance of developmentalism with young intellectuals depicted as modernisers, paralleling to some extent the official discourse. This included positive evaluations of their knowledge, skills and abilities as well as more traditional ideas about their historical role in Chinese society as pioneers, with links to the 'May Fourth' ideal.

There was a patriotic strand, with respondents reiterating the notion of having historical duties to perform. A typical view was expressed by Chen. 'They are the most important role because if the country wants to develop into a more modern society – stronger, richer, they [*sic*] need the educational group to support them and to do things for the country.' Similarly Liu declared that 'They should be the main force. It's their responsibility.' These statements reinforce the impression of this generation as possessing high levels of self-confidence and self-importance but being held back by their elders.

Young intellectuals were described as an 'advanced force', 'pioneers' of reform and 'planners'. By playing a 'more important role in the reform', with the government 'adopting young peoples' ideas', their position would improve and the country as a whole would benefit. Without their contributions, the reform programme would, according to Gu, be 'caught in a crisis'. Self-confident Wang believed that young intellectuals could 'open their minds, speak out, speak straight' and tell the leaders what they thought. He felt that they could 'produce the spiritual atmosphere for ordinary people to realise the necessity of reform both political and economic'. They were portrayed as possessing attributes lacking in the masses and it was their social duty to promote (*tuidong*) ideas and encourage others to play their particular roles. This is further evidence of their self-confidence and desire not only to occupy a certain social position but to enact it, in fairly traditional ways, and to manifest in behavioural terms who they were and what their position signified.

Once again, however, there was ambivalence and selectivity about the importance of traditional ideas. Whilst stressing their traditional role on the one hand, they also pointed to the negative influences and problems created for young intellectuals by the persistence of traditional cultural values and thought, as referred to by Gao. 'Some can't forget the old ideas and especially the cultural factors – *wenhua de yinsu* – because of the long history of China.'

It was claimed that young intellectuals could compare Chinese and western cultures more objectively than their senior counterparts. They believed themselves capable and knowledgeable enough to offer solutions to China's problems if the situation arose and seemed to be waiting for an opportunity to carry out this role. Wang insisted that 'Only the intellectuals can devise a plan to avoid some consequences [of reform]'. Respondents often described themselves as a frustrated generation in search of ways of fulfilling their role without coming into conflict with the older generation. Zhang said 'Young intellectuals are usually looked down on as youth by older people'. They were expected to be patient and wait their turn to take over the running of the country and its institutions but this generation was not so keen to wait as their predecessors. They had accepted their official role as pioneers of reform and wanted to express this as soon as possible

Consequently, higher education as a strategy and a form of social closure was called into question with the possible need for other strategies to secure the better outcomes more in line with their expectations. Intellectuals were seeking other means of signifying that they were an elite group.

A poster campaign at Beijing University in April 1988 also indicated that young intellectuals were feeling worse off after ten years of reform. The immediate context of this campaign was the NPC and the Chinese People's Political Consultative Committee Conference (CPPCC) (25 March to 13 April). This short-lived protest was not solely about higher education and the related social position of intellectuals as it contained some more overtly political issues. The devaluation of knowledge was, however, a strong theme.

Another set of posters, also at *Beida* two months later, appeared as more spontaneous, triggered by the violent death of a postgraduate student during a brawl. The themes and messages at the beginning of June were similar but there was more of an emphasis on politics. Nathan writes how these protests raised the by now standard issues of freedom of speech, human rights and democracy. Discussing the inherent problems of the reform programme and Chinese society may be considered as a coping strategy and the April campaign will be considered in this light.

THE APRIL POSTER CAMPAIGN

This appeared as an extension of the education debates, and poster writers wanted representatives at the ongoing NPC to consider the crisis, demanding action to improve the situation of intellectuals. They were taking up the call for 'dialogue' made at the NPC, described as one of the most open ever held. Some sessions were publicised through the media in an atmosphere of relative liberalism. Guo referred to this openness which indicated to him that some things had changed. 'We can know something about what is happening in China. In the past we couldn't say if the NPC will be held in Beijing or not. At the end of the Congress, the radio said during so and so time, the Congress will be opened and passed some policies. The people knew nothing about it. Now people know more and more things about it and can discuss it openly to some degree. During the Congress meeting, everybody was talking about this.'

The government appeared to encourage the debate, allowing criticisms of the reforms to be aired alongside praise for the positive achievements of *gaige kaifang* policies. As a critical atmosphere developed within intellectual circles, this debate sometimes stretched the limits of official tolerance. Unlike the arguments within the Great Hall of the People, the posters were illegal but were allowed for more than a week. The *dazibao* raised the main concerns of the changing evaluation of higher education in 1980s China.

The campaign began on 5 April with an 'open letter' pinned up on the university's main noticeboards which immediately attracted the attention of students and staff first at *Beida* then from elsewhere. Education was described as 'backward' and the conditions for those involved in it as 'miserable', in line with comments made elsewhere. More posters quickly appeared. The majority were critical of policies which were seen to impoverish intellectuals whilst street pedlars were becoming 'rich'. Some posters expressed anger that little had been done to prevent the disparities.

Corruption was seen as a particularly serious problem which contradicted meritocratic principles. If the trend of using non-academic means to obtain success was set to continue, then the value of knowledge would decline even further. Degrees and diplomas could not be traded for anything in the market place. There was the desire for more emphasis upon merit which would lead to highly qualified people being rewarded rather than destined for 'miserable' conditions. 'Intellectuals cannot be silenced any longer', read one poster which was almost a rallying call to action, similar to posters in previous movements throughout the century. Some were signed, whilst some writers remained anonymous. There was, however, no immediate action taken by the university nor by the public security bureau to remove the posters or apprehend any of their authors.

When visiting the poster site on 7 April I saw crowds of students and teachers reading and discussing the posters. Some were making notes with others recording the texts using hand-held tape recorders. The main noticeboard area was mostly but not completely taken up with *dazibao*. Announcements of forthcoming films and dances were mixed up with the calls for government action on the education crisis. During the next few days, more posters appeared. Some of the original ones were pasted over by the following day, 8 Friday but there was no obvious attempt to pull any of them down. The message of one ended with a regret that there was no other way for young intellectuals to get in touch with the Party leaders. Posters were not a satisfactory medium, but without free speech they had no other recourse. This sort of message articulated the frustration felt with official media as well as with the situation for intellectuals.

Criticisms were also made about the recent appointment of Li Peng as Premier. Although he could be considered a relatively young technocrat (aged 59 in 1988), Li was unpopular. Many considered him to be untalented, dull and not qualified to hold such high office. He was seen as a supreme example of *guanxi*, being the adopted son of Zhou Enlai and it was suggested that he used this relationship to promote his political career. Li Peng was viewed as an unsuitable leader at a time when problems with reforms were seen as multiplying. The posters articulated the view that feelings of hopelessness amongst the young intelligentsia would intensify.

One poster called for a demonstration outside the Great Hall of the People to attract the attention of the NPC delegates and demand that they act rather than just talk. A demonstration would have made the situation more serious and increased the likelihood of intervention by the authorities who had, up to this point, not interfered directly. There were rumours at *Beida* that some teachers would stage a demonstration but there was no clear evidence one was being organised. In the event, a small group of young teachers did stage a 'shoeshine' protest in Tiananmen Square. By mimicking small-scale street 'capitalists' and offering their services to the delegates, they were vividly illustrating their angry response to one suggested solution to the crisis of funding higher education: the 'doing business tide'. This protest did not escalate into anything more serious.

Members of Deng's generation, from younger to older, had seen the educational revival and all of their expectations had been affected. They were in a sense united in their initial optimism but by 1988 this had become shared pessimism. Any signs of combined protest action and radical action was a cause of concern for officials and the university attempted to contain this expression of discontent. On the Saturday evening (9 April) they tried to distract attention from the posters by a number of officially sanctioned entertainments. Leisurely diversion appeared as the official strategy for avoiding student disturbances. Young people questioned at this time believed that to be the case. Judging from a visit to the unusually lively *Beida* campus that Saturday evening, this strategy could be said to have had some effect.

Several dances were arranged in student refectories and a few small bars selling soft drinks and beer were doing a brisk trade. It was a warm Spring evening and many young people were strolling around the campus. The dances had attracted many outsiders and the noticeboard area which had been a source of interest in the daytime was largely neglected as dusk fell. Posters calling for improvements in the living standards of intellectuals became the backdrop for an evening of 'disco and break dancing'. These western imports were permissible, unlike 'bourgeois' democracy, still labelled as unsuitable for China. These aspects of the unofficial youth culture were encouraged, as long as they diverted young people's attention away from the educational crisis.

The posters and the dancing parties appeared to be contradictory phenomena but there was a link. With more personal freedom, improved pay and conditions and enhanced social status, then there would be more opportunities for intellectuals to enjoy themselves. The enthusiastic crowds at the dances, which included middle aged as well as young intellectuals were an indication of some of the desires expressed in the *dazibao*.

This apparent contradiction was discussed officially, although the context was different (ZGQN, 1988.8:5). Differences of opinion between young people and educational 'experts' recorded during a debate in a Special Economic Zone (SEZ) in January 1988 had links to the April events. The so-called 'Shekou Storm' (Luo, 1995) occurred when the CYL branch in Shekou invited the experts to meet young people and the former expressed disappointment with the latter. Young people did not appear to be fully devoting themselves to opening up new fields in the reforms, it was claimed, with many of them appearing as 'gold rushers'. The article reported that 'today our slogan should be to open up new fields and to sacrifice oneself for the reform'. The notion of opening up new fields, encapsulated in the expression '*jiwang kailai*', was popular during the 1950s and 1960s when work in outlying territories would have involved self-sacrifice.

This slogan seemed to have been revived in a minor way during 1988, also appearing in an article about a speech of CYL Secretary Song Defu to commemorate 'May Fourth' (RMRB, 14 May 1988:2). One young participant in the Shekou debate said that opening up new fields and enjoying oneself were not contradictory with wanting to make money and lead a good life being compatible with the reform programme. The notion of self-sacrifice was not acceptable to the 1980s generation who were more conscious of their own individuality and keen to preserve their own self-worth rather than dedicate themselves to the 'masses'.

In crowded *Beida* dormitories, I spoke with students about the posters, their lives and other key issues of the time. The dormitories were the setting of discussions described as 'bedroom conferences.' (Wang, 1989:234). Sitting on old bunk beds amongst piles of clothes, bedding and books, it was suggested that 'to know *Beida* students is to know students throughout China'. They were considered a special group, being an elite in one sense but sharing common characteristics with their colleagues elsewhere as they faced similar problems. Much of the evening's entertainment, they informed me, had been organised by the CYL or the official Students' Union. It was difficult to arrange unofficial gatherings other than of those provided by such authorised organisations and this reflected the lack of freedom discussed in some of the *dazibao*.

All the students I spoke to were CYL members. A branch official said that membership was 'important' but it appeared that its main function was to provide social gatherings and activities for, students such as that evening's entertainment. The role and function of the CYL in the contemporary context is an important theme investigated in more detail in Chapter 5. The young official was eager for me to sample the dances arranged that night and he arranged free entry into these, not only for myself but also the other students from the dormitory, using his *guanxi*. This access to dances and 'bedroom conferences' was an added advantage for the research and provided some close contact with the young people being investigated. Although concerned about the pressing issues of the day, they also wanted to enjoy themselves.

After the weekend, it was not clear whether the poster protest would quietly die out or be taken further but there appeared little desire to extend the campaign. The weather helped to resolve the situation. Very strong winds and a dust storm deterred many people from going outside on the following Monday and left most of the posters in tatters. The short poster campaign was over but had made some relevant points in line with the issues raised at the NPC sessions and elsewhere. It also represented a continuation of the small-scale, localised protests which had occured throughout the reform period.

Several students on another Beijing campus viewed the posters as a 'normal' occurrence for *Beida* with its tradition of outspokenness. Some informants were dismissive and did not attach any importance to the posters although they also expressed concern about the crisis in education. Some were, however, set to go abroad to study and probably wished to distance themselves from such activities. Being critical of *Beida* activists did not necessarily mean they had no sympathy with their views and the difference between active and passive support will be investigated later.

Overall, the posters reflected the general concerns about the educational crisis. Going abroad could also be viewed as part of the increasing trend towards materialism and 'looking towards money'. The 'Roots' survey uncovered similar worries and attitudes. The poster writers, therefore, can be viewed as more than a vocal minority. The spontaneity of the poster campaign was questioned, with its timing coinciding with the NPC. Other student movements, such as the 1986–7 demonstrations, have also been attributed to leadership factions rather than grassroots feelings and actions. There may have been an element of manipulation, either by the pro-reformers or by more conservative CCP officials who wanted to bring the reform programme into disrepute by causing a disturbance. This is difficult to prove, but the link between intellectual movements and leadership factions is to be borne in mind.

The theme of perceived social decline was raised again during the next poster campaign in June, as were more overtly political demands for increased democracy and freedom of speech. Writing posters may have helped to air some of the problems facing young intellectuals but growing numbers were seeking another way of improving their social and economic position by leaving China.

The going abroad tide was, as already stated, made possible by the open door policy. Officially, overseas study was to benefit the nation but unofficially it had quickly become viewed as a temporary, perhaps permanent, way of avoiding the problems in China. The dismay of young intellectuals, well-documented in this work, can be viewed as the context for the adoption of this strategy.

THE 'CHUGUO CHAO'

The reform policies not only allowed intellectuals to travel but actually encouraged them to seek western knowledge and increasing numbers started to go abroad. SEC Director, Lie Tieying, said that students were sent abroad to 'absorb the advanced science and technology like bees' (ZGQN, *Bao*, 18 Nov. 1988:1). The reforms needed skilled personnel for their success and some of these needed training outside China. The two were to some extent mutually dependent: the going abroad tide depended to some extent on the continuation of the reform programme and vice versa.

During 1988, publicity concerning the *chuguo chao* emphasised its associated problems such as the increasing numbers involved, and this in turn reflected the educational crisis. Members of other social groups were also attempting to go abroad in this period but it was young intellectuals more than any others who were linked to this trend. It can be seen as another characteristic of the 1980s generation although, historically speaking, it was nothing new. Earlier generations of Chinese chose to go overseas to seek a better life either in the short or long term. During previous decades, however, opportunities for overseas travel were extremely limited due to the relatively 'closed door' policy of the Mao regime and destinations tended to be restricted to other socialist countries. After 1978, 36,800 Chinese students were sent overseas, the equivalent to five times the total sent in the 28 years from 1949–77.

It was not the case, however, that restrictions were suddenly lifted nor was it easy to find ways of leaving China, but after 1979 it was certainly more feasible and not long after the 'rush' into higher education, the trickle of people applying for places at foreign universities became a flood. The associated procedures and requirements were becoming familiar even to those not planning such a course of action. Even by 1980, the numbers were 'unprecedented' and this was perceived as 'unimaginable' before the open door policy (FBIS CR, 4, Nov. 1985:42). By the mid-1980s, the 'tide' was being referred to as a 'boom' (CD, 26, Nov. 1984:3). After 1978, 36,800 Chinese students were sent overseas, the equivalent to five times the total sent in the 28 years from 1949–77 and this was described as 'hordes of young scholars' (FBIS CR 112, 1985:115). They went to 76 countries and regions. There were also 8000 '*sifei liuxuesheng*', that is self-financing students who went without state financial assistance (*China Information*, 1991:980).

It is acceptable that in any country at a particular point in time, a certain proportion of young intellectuals go abroad and this trend is not in itself unusual, as Hua pointed out. 'It's not just the Chinese who want to improve their living standard. It's a common hope of all sorts of people. There are so many people who have emigrated to the USA, for example. They're not only from China. There have been five generations of going abroad. Every one devotes more to this country.' It appeared, however, that the 1980s trend was a lot 'deeper' than past movements. 'Some people even become foreigners with black hair and black eyes', one article stated, indicating that going abroad was a subterfuge for emigration (GMRB, 22 Feb. 1988:1).

Poor housing and research facilities, unsatisfying jobs which did not match higher qualifications and few opportunities to use their skills and knowledge were cited as the prospects for talented young intellectuals.[3] It was suggested that if they found more satisfying and rewarding employment abroad, this was a loss for China but understandable for the individuals concerned. An example was given of a young musician whose situation in China was 'oppressive'. He lived in a small, dark room separated from his wife who was assigned to work elsewhere. Although given some recognition for his skills, he was not awarded the title of associate professor at his institute. Eventually he accepted a place offered to him at an American university because he could not 'put his talents into full play'. (GMRB, 24 Feb. 1988:4). It was implied that he had been driven away and others were adopting the same strategy.

China had limited resources for education and those at the upper end of the system were recipients of greater investment than primary and secondary levels (FEER, 1 June, 1988:6). Young intellectuals were expected to provide some sort of return for this investment by doing something beneficial to the 'motherland'.

This could not be the case if overseas students failed to return or did nothing useful upon their return. The subsequent lack of trained personnel would detrimentally affect China's efforts to catch up with the West. A high proportion of non-returnees would further deplete the ranks of intellectuals in China which had already suffered losses due to the various anti-rightist campaigns. The reforms would be jeopardised rather than assisted if too many of the country's brightest people became in the strict sense 'emigrants' rather than temporary absentees. It also involved calculated risks for the students because they were unsure of the outcome of their endeavours.

Some of the publicity focused on the problems for the nation rather than the drawbacks for individuals with descriptions of shortages of suitably qualified personnel in various work units. One article epitomised this concern. 'In some scientific research units, only 60 year old instructors who are on a temporary work basis are left to do the work' (FBIS CR, 6 June, 1986:65). The high rates of non-returnees was considered as the main problem of the going abroad tide. Figures suggested that Chinese students were reluctant to return once their stay had elapsed and being 'detained' (*zhi liu*) was common.

Official statistics stated that up to 1985, 16,500 students had returned (*China Information*, 1991:981). This is similar to the FEER article (*op. cit*:33) claiming that out of 50,000 or so scholars who had been sent since 1978, 20,000 had returned, or less than half of the total sent by the state. From the self-financing category, 'virtually no-one' had returned. One unofficial source within the SEC said that around 80 per cent of those sent since the late 1970s had failed to return. Although figures vary between the sources and across the different categories, it is clear that China was experiencing its own brain drain which was causing increasing concern for the authorities.

The shortage of personnel was not the only problem. Many students and graduates were spending so much time trying to find 'connections' in order to go abroad that they were not concentrating on their work. Guo complained about the amount of time and effort this involved which distracted him from his studies. Kwong also noted that 'They tried their best to leave, and how to do it was the major topic of conversation when the young gathered' (1994:260). This was certainly true during my own fieldwork period and frequent contacts with educated youth.

Sometimes questions concerning overseas universities, funding, examinations and so on seemed endless and I began to dread the TOEFL[4] examination and 'going abroad' being mentioned during conversations. TOEFL was the most common test of proficiency taken by those intending to go to the USA. Liu referred to the 'many people taking TOEFL exams. Sometimes they even drop classes to do this. They write many letters to the US universities.'

Respondents trying to obtain study places and scholarships often consulted me as well as any other foreigners to hand. It is a possibility that they agreed to be interviewed in the hope that they could gain some *guanxi*. Cultivating relationships with foreigners was viewed as a useful strategy by some people. I should also admit that I had to use *guanxi* to some extent early in the fieldwork to obtain the interview sample (Appendix). No-one asked directly for help but there were many indirect requests as well as the seeking of advice. I made it clear from the outset that I could only assist in a practical way, that there would be no special privileges or favours, and that I could not offer financial assistance.

Overseas study was certainly an ambition which figured very strongly amongst the sample and the question was put to interviewees as well as informants during informal discussions of why young intellectuals were expending their energies on it. It emerged as an issue to which they had all given a lot of consideration when evaluating their own situation and prospects in China. The nature of the sample partly accounts for this trend but when considering the growing numbers leaving the country, they were perhaps not so untypical.

The main categories of responses related to educational training and qualifications, social and economic status with some acknowledgement of the official notion of contributing to China's development. Mostly respondents put self-development first with national development linked to that. Going abroad appeared as an attempt to rectify the disparities between what they had originally expected to gain from higher education and the actual rewards. It could also be viewed as a form of escape from the social problems affecting young intellectuals, such as the devaluation of knowledge phenomenon. In this sense, the *chuguo chao* was not only an expression of the discontent felt by Deng's generation but an ongoing strategy of action, involving adaptive behaviour to alleviate or avoid the problems of the contemporary period. The educational motivations will be considered first as these appeared, perhaps unsurprisingly, as the most important.

The Desire for Additional Education and Training

Although the reform programme had provided more educational opportunities, it seemed that the ambitions nurtured by the post-Mao government could not be met within China. The educationally oriented replies focused on China's shortcomings rather than recent achievements and young intellectuals looked to the West for the further opportunities which would lessen the disparities between expectations and rewards.

Ten interviewees referred to gaining advanced qualifications, studying foreign technology and furthering their skills. Others mentioned improving personal abilities and achievements which can also be linked to education. A fairly typical comment here came from Lili who said that it was 'necessary to go abroad if we want to learn new things'. Older and younger members of the sample shared similar views. Lili believed that academic conditions were better outside China and young intellectuals could do well. According to Qiu 'Most of them want to learn, study advanced knowledge and technology and have success in their careers'. This was an important point because of the previous stated concern that they could have little success careerwise in China due to the various impediments. With perceptions of being blocked in their work, looking overseas offered some hope.

The situation in China was usually described as unsatisfactory for conducting research and obtaining the latest knowledge and techniques. Educational facilities, as well as conditions in general, were assumed to be better overseas. Wen claimed that 'Most of them go abroad for study because the standard of education and the level of knowledge and equipment in the western countries is much more advanced. They can further their research work.' China was not 'modern' nor the state of knowledge and technology. 'We're lagging behind. We'll go abroad to learn new things', claimed Lu who was about to leave China. Jiang said that 'Generally speaking our research conditions are very poor. If I want to do something, I first must ask for financial aid. It's very hard to get so usually many people do nothing. They do not like to spend the whole day doing nothing so think maybe they can go abroad and study something there.' Wen also said that 'In China we don't have such good conditions for the intellectuals to go about their research'.

Judging from these responses, they could only go so far in their studies in China and then ran into impediments. The only way to overcome them was to leave because it was difficult to do anything worthwhile, either for themselves or for the nation. If young intellectuals wanted to progress in their field they were impelled to seek a way of going abroad. Their own progress was related to the nation's because the knowledge and skills they gained might be used on their return. This line of thinking was also linked to the 'leading role' theme mentioned earlier. Individual motivations contained patriotic elements but the former tended to be prioritised and it could have been the case that fulfilling their own careers might push out the patriotic elements, as will be discussed in a later section.

Chen thought that going abroad would help those with unfulfilled ambitions. 'It provides them with more chance to study and do things. In China some people can't do what they like to do but when abroad, the society is more open, you can do what you like.' Chen did not elaborate on what sort of things could be done so easily abroad. There were freedoms, it was implied, that could not be sampled without going overseas. The comparison may appear as idealistic, lacking an informed view on the problems facing students in other countries, such as finance. The main point, however, is that this was a typical expression of intellectual frustration. For the participants, the *chuguo chao* was a strategy aimed at bringing about the completion of the higher education process begun in their own country but considered as incomplete. They may have been mistaken, for example, to believe that research facilities were better in the West but the issue is that they had positive images which sharply contrasted with the negative ones of China.

According to Chen, when overseas, 'If you want to get a degree, you can find a way'. Similarly, Liu said that 'They think that if they can go abroad, they will make achievements, greater achievements than in China'. The range of knowledge and skills available abroad was also mentioned in positive terms and it was not only a question of the qualifications but experience. 'They go abroad mainly to strengthen their abilities' was a typical comment here made by Lu. Eight interviewees referred to young intellectuals having opportunities outside China to develop themselves. Consequently, these highly educated people were probably not untypical in believing that gaining more education was the key reason for the *chuguo chao*, just as it was largely their main reason for going to university in the first place. They remained strongly commited to higher education, which was the focal aspect of efforts to find a suitable strategy to improve their situation.

Xiu claimed 'They go abroad not for a comfortable life but to learn more things'. This might appear as paradoxical in some ways because respondents had described earlier the devaluation of knowledge and how it was no longer a main source of upward social mobility. The question is raised of why the aim of gaining more education was given as a major reason. This predominant concern had at least two possible causes. One is that although educational orientations were cited as a main reason, it could have been that there were other motives for leaving China, such as to make money or to emigrate. Alternatively, the desire for foreign academic qualifications may have been based on the hope that the recipients would be taken more seriously and treated with more respect on returning to China. This moves the analysis into the area of social position and role, closely linked to level of educational qualifications and experience.

Improving Socio-Economic Position

Elements of pragmatism entered into the discussion very early on because respondents were aware of what foreign study could lead to upon return to China and what it might do for those who stayed away. The concern about declining social position has already been analysed and reemerged in the replies. According to Li 'They want to learn new ideas and new knowledge and they are also concerned with their future treatment in China. The last point is very important.' Lili also expressed anticipation of higher status accompanying foreign study experience. 'When they return to China with more advanced knowledge they will be more appreciated by their leaders.'

Disappointment gave rise to a transferral of frustrated ambitions on to overseas higher education where it was anticipated that better conditions would bring about the professional success and rewards denied to them in China. If the Chinese authorities did not acknowledge the worth of their existing credentials by paying better salaries, for example, then their holders felt they would gain something of more marketable value with foreign higher degrees. If they decided to stay away, then foreign qualifications would be more useful than their original Chinese ones. In this sense going abroad could be viewed as a double-edged strategy for improving their situation not only in China but possibly overseas should they fail to return.

Other data supported this pragmatic view with comments about personal advancement, both in career and social status terms. 'As far as I know, some people really want to, can learn something and then they come back and have a better job, a better position', claimed Yang. Guo, himself trying to find a way out, claimed that 'You know, a foreigner is always respected by Chinese all over China. They can get the facilities and good treatment but if you are Chinese you can't. So, if you come back from other countries, from abroad, you can get higher positions and social status will rise.' This implied that an association with 'foreignness' was valuable and to be respected. It was not necessarily the case that the study experience was inherently better but not being conducted in China could lead to more rewards. This negative view of Chinese education, it can be argued, was part of a wider dismissal of Chinese things occurring in the 1980s amongst young intellectuals in their search for alternatives. It was hoped that some of the desirable characteristics of foreigners would be theirs as a result of studying overseas.

Official messages about the importance of developing the potential of young intellectuals appeared as empty promises with frequent expressions of being held back, similar to ones described elsewhere in this book. Gao summarised this feeling. 'They're discontented so far, maybe just because of this reason: frustration.' Zhen also believed that going abroad was a way of overcoming frustration and other negative feelings associated with this.

A related factor in these discussions was the economic aspects and these are clearly linked to perceptions of social status. Nearly half of the interviewees, for example, cited poor wages and conditions as major reasons for going abroad. Gao felt that the second main reason for the *chuguo chao* was that the intellectual's standard of living was too low. In other replies, it was assumed that on returning to China, their experience overseas would enable them to have an improved economic position or the 'better treatment' they desired.

The economic aspect was cited by some respondents as the primary cause whilst others regarded it as secondary. Qiu said that 'The second reason is they want to make money'. For him, this was an important factor but learning advanced knowledge was the main goal. He said that 'After one year or more abroad, they can bring back all the utilities like TV, fridge etc. They can live better in China. Otherwise you have to save money from the salary, it's a very limited salary to buy all of these things.' In Zhen's view, overseas students 'make a lot of money and they bring the money back to China. Maybe it seems a little in other countries but if you bring the money here it is really a lot.'

The goal of 'making money' implied that for some would-be overseas students, educational ambitions were an excuse for doing something which they found hard to do in China. Opportunities for earning money were restricted but they believed that it was easier overseas, as Qiu certainly felt. 'Abroad, there are a lot of chances to make money, not like in China. Nearly no chance to make extra money.' They wanted to 'live a good life', remarked Liu. Similarly, Yu said that 'Maybe some people heard that in the West people could get money easily and when they get enough money they go back to our country. Then they can live a very good life.'

In the short term, it was recognised that many young intellectuals wanted to make money and to take home some consumer durables. Six interviewees referred to materialistic motivations along the lines of Jiang's comment about going abroad 'not just for study, maybe for money, to buy a colour television, something like that'. Qiu explained that some overseas scholars planned to save money by spending as little of their allowances as possible and perhaps having part-time jobs or sharing accommodation, thereby cutting down on their outgoings. 'Even if they don't find a job, they can save from the allowance or can have a lot of people living in one room. A lot of people coming back to China tell us about this.' Such strategies could enable overseas students to buy those consumer durables difficult to obtain in China without foreign currency or the right social connections. These materialistic motivations once again seem in contrast to

educational ones and are another aspect of the social changes in
China brought about by the reforms.

Chinese people were becoming increasingly materialistic in the
changed economic climate where there was more advertising and
awareness of market forces. Consumer goods were no longer
being produced according to a centralised plan in order to satisfy
basic needs but to make profits and notions of socialist frugality
were on the decline throughout the 1980s. People were more
conscious of material possessions, viewing them to some extent as
indicators of socio-economic position. If intellectuals in China
were relatively worse off, as this sample had indicated, they could
not afford these items. Apart from feeling relatively deprived for
not owning, for example, a colour TV, this would also be a sign
of relatively low social position. Consumer durables were required not only for practical use but also as signifiers of wealth
and status. Intellectuals wanted to be conspicuous consumers of
these goods, just as their *getihu* counterparts were seen to be.

Going abroad to earn money for buying consumer goods,
therefore, was part of another trend in China related to economic
reform. In the pre 1978 era, people were encouraged to manifest
their 'redness' by doing good deeds. In the 1980s being a socialist
consumer was becoming important with its manifestation increasingly viewed in materialistic rather than ideological terms. Zhou
believed that there were people who wanted to go abroad in
order to 'modernise their own family by buying a refrigerator,
TV etc. We are poor but we're sure we can change it. We haven't
lost hope to change conditions.'

Several respondents, however, did not feel this was the main
reason for the trend. Other, less self-centred motivations were
described but patriotic considerations appeared as a weak source
of motivation. Only a few respondents discussed the prospect of
returnees bringing back their new knowledge and skills to be used
for the benefit of the nation rather than just for personal gain.
The idea that intellectuals went abroad to learn things for China
was the main thrust of official pronouncements on overseas study
and this also relates to the fact that most overseas students were
sent by the government in some form or another. In a sense, they
were bound to the state to give back some of what they had been
given.

According to respondents, placing the nation's needs above
individual gain was not commonplace. 'Some really want to do

something for society, to improve it', remarked Zhou. He described the situation as 'complex' and it was not easy to separate out the individual from social interests. 'Since 1949, society has been built up with conflicts between the system and ideas', he continued. This resulted in many young intellectuals wanting to leave although their commitment to the nation remained strong. They wished to serve society in some way, as they had been encouraged to do and there were elements of traditional thinking here as well although most interviewees wanted to leave for some time mostly for their own benefit.

Hua expressed traditionalist sentiments. 'I was raised in China so I am accustomed to Chinese ways. I think perhaps the foreigners have the same feelings. I remember a British novelist said that when one is in a foreign country, he should try to learn the foreign ways without forgetting his motherland, not forgetting your own roots. That is the best way.' Lu similarly said that Chinese people would like to die in the 'motherland'. The inherent contradiction of being 'modernisation successors' was apparent with a feeling that the country had failed them in some key aspects. The *chuguo chao* represented both the successes and failures of the reform period. A total rejection of the country was out of the question for these young people who had been brought up to be patriotic and view their own careers as ultimately related to the national good. They had not abandoned completely their historical role and were reluctant to use the word 'emigration'. It was believed that even if people did not return, they could contribute something to China by making achievements elsewhere. Overseas Chinese who had become famous scientists or businessmen were considered worthy models because they were still Chinese even if they had never set foot on the mainland.

Gu echoed the official line in this response. 'I think they want to learn more and contribute more to the country. If they can go abroad they'll surely do something good for China.' They could only make their contribution, however, if they returned at some point and many were not doing so. The patriotic link between the individual and society was also discussed by Lu. 'China is still very backward so when people have the chance to go abroad and study in the advanced countries, they can learn a lot of experiences and knowledge which will be used for the construction of the country when they return.' It was not clear from these responses what they would feel if they were unable to do something worthwhile upon returning with their higher qualifications.

As one of those about to go abroad, Lu believed that most people would return to 'serve our country. This is something praised by our Chairman Mao Zedong.' This last comment referred to the previous era and it appeared that he was reading a well-rehearsed script. He continued, however, to say that there were 'two kinds of problems. One is the young people want to grasp these unknown things, the other is our country needs this unknown knowledge. When the two are put together, it's very likely for people to have the desire of going abroad. In my view when we look at this phenomenon we should connect the interest of the individual with the needs of our country.'

In this logic, motivations which appeared as orientated towards the individual can be viewed as socially beneficial. It was also implied that more freedom for overseas travel was advisable for China's developmentalist policies. Obtaining advanced technology and skills was stressed after 1978 because this was necessary for China's modernisation. Another relatively conservative respondent expressed this patriotic theme by drawing a clear relationship between the *chuguo chao* and the reform programme. According to Zhao 'Going abroad is in accordance with the demand of reform. It's a result of reform and open policy.' This can be compared to earlier generations whose going abroad, usually to the USSR or other communist countries, was linked to socialist reconstruction.

Sun disagreed and believed that even when students did consider doing something for the nation on their return, the idea got 'thinner' after living abroad for a few years. 'It just happens naturally', she said. Additionally, those who returned, inspired by patriotic duty, were likely to be disappointed in her view. 'I hear several people say that when they were abroad they didn't think anything about being very comfortable. As soon as they came back to China, they regret it, wished they did not come back.' Judging from the sample data, there was little support for the notion of going abroad to benefit the nation. Self-interest predominated along with pragmatic views rather than notions of social duty. Whether political considerations were important sources of motivations will be discussed in Chapter 5.

There was certainly a generational consciousness about this trend as a potential or actual ambition with a sharing of information and perceptions. Those who did leave and come back, for example, were an important source of information, as were relatives who remained on the outside. 'Their relatives and classmates. Their friends go abroad, come back and tell them about it', said Gao. 'I have a friend, she went abroad', began Lili, saying that from her letters she can gain clear ideas about what it is like outside China. The growing numbers of overseas students meant that more people had access to first-hand accounts of life in the West, with all of its possibilities and problems. This seemed to further excite those wishing to join the *chuguo chao*.

Xiu said that she knew many people who were studying abroad or were preparing to go, like herself. 'At the end of the 1970s quite a lot of people went abroad.' From this group, however, she heard negative views because they said life there 'was not much better than in China . . . here they belong to the elite group but can only do some odd job abroad'. Clearly these reports were not considered to be applicable to her own hopes of improving her socio-economic position.

It was certainly more acceptable to have overseas links and throughout the reform period there had been relaxations on the regulations allowing visits by *huaqiao*, or overseas Chinese. In the past, those with relatives living abroad were more likely to be viewed as 'rightists' and could have suffered because of these family ties. This was changing in the 1980s and Lili referred to such families as 'prestigious families' in China. She believed that 'Children in these families have been influenced by western ideas at a very early age. China hasn't modernised yet and can't provide these people with a proper environment. It's understandable for them to go abroad. Another case is that some families have relatives abroad so they'll send some to study abroad.'

Most potential *liuxuesheng*, however, were going because of their own disappointments and frustrations in China. The desire for a fresh start and new opportunities was just as influential in shaping their views as concrete information about other places. The mixture of hopes and desires, anxieties and ambitions may have set them on a path which was a shared 'dream' remaining at the end of the reform decade. Not everyone, however, could see this as a possibility and there were other 'crazes' which distinguished Deng's generation from others and these will be considered in the next chapter.

4 Generational Fads and Feelings

This chapter examines the shift from educational to economic and entertainment 'crazes', exploring trends in leisure and life-styles as well as attitudes. Disillusionment with education predisposed young intellectuals to be more economically active whilst retaining sufficient motivation to stay on the 'black pathway'. The *jingshang re* will be analysed as will ways in which money was spent on the growing diversity of leisure activities in the 1980s; these will be viewed as elements of both the official and unofficial youth cultures. There was some merging of trends within the popular culture sphere and the implications of these trends will be discussed. My own observations were consistent with those of other commentators who, when considering the students in particular, noticed several main groups in terms of leisure activities.[1] Fads for pop songs and films will be included and how these reflected other trends will be discussed. Analysis of data about respected people in Chinese society indicated that Deng's generation were searching for alternative role models with a 'no more heroes' syndrome emerging. The popularity of the '*He Shang*' series will be considered in the light of key generational features and this will set the context for the trends of the decade as well as for the following chapter on the political nature of the generation.

THE IMPORTANCE OF THE '*HE SHANG*' CRAZE

Much has already been written about '*He Shang*', the six-part television programme shown first of all in June, then again in August 1988. The aim here is not to reiterate the conclusions about its importance in the immediate pre-Tiananmen period but to note its relevance as a generational marker in terms of attitudinal shifts and ideological explorations. It became a classic text of the late 1980s, moving quickly into print from the TV series and it achieved something like cult status amongst Deng's generation. In many ways it was the outcome of a decade of

116

ideological shifts, the product of both cooperation between generations of intellectuals as well as conflict because ultimately the authors supported the pro-reformist faction. It appealed to and, indeed, was assisted by those who wanted to extend such policies.

In addressing the question of why Chinese civilization declined during the previous centuries whilst the West prospered, criticisms were made of Chinese traditions which kept the nation backward and denied the prospect of true democratisation (Su, 1988). The authors, themselves young intellectuals, criticised China's insularity and located the faults of present-day China in its lengthy history and oppressive culture. *He Shang* emphasised the need for more fundamental reforms apart from economic ones and also made a plea for the value of intellectuals to be recognised because if they were held back then so was the nation. The controversy caused by the programme ensured the spread of a widespread debate and the '*He Shang* effect' extended far beyond its immediate audience. Young intellectuals, already questioning many aspects of Chinese culture and society, seized this debate.

I was first alerted to the programme by several interviewees who told me of its importance and others subsequently pointed out the many media articles on the programme, its authors and its main points. A number of informants were asked about the series during focused discussions and most, but not all, agreed with its main messages. One young man said that 'Young educated people especially liked this programme. It criticises traditional ideas, culture and weaknesses. It is against conservative ideas, and feudalism. It criticised the Great Wall and what it stood for. It held back development rather than invading armies.'

Another informant pointed out that the leaders of China 'preach modernisation but can't get rid of traditional ideas'. It was very negative about Chinese culture and this is why some older Party leaders and officials were 'angry, very angry when they watched *He Shang*. One of the senior leaders wanted to forbid this programme.' Respondents generally agreed with the programme's thesis that China's past stifled the present and there was a contrast drawn between backward and stagnant China and the developed, free and prosperous West which also featured in the series. One point made by informants was its ability to compare China with other countries in the present period. 'Chinese leaders always compare with the past in China. Even now, they talk about our progress since Liberation, since the Cultural Revolution and so on. But China is still backward in the world. The old people are too conservative and can't accept new ideas.' Informants referred to comparisons with near neighbours such as Japan and Taiwan who had become modernised and affluent, leaving China behind. *He Shang* seemed to have located some of the reasons for this in China's own culture and history.

Such ideas were not new but the freedom with which they were allowed to be disseminated appeared as an indication either of a degree of change or a crisis point being reached in terms of the alienation of Chinese intellectuals. Discussion of the oppressive nature of Chinese tradition can be found in the earlier underground journals of the 'Democracy Wall' period (Nathan, 1990). At that time it was not possible to widely publicise such views which were part of the illegal activities of rusticated youth without access to official media unlike the privileged authors of *He Shang*, some of whom had experienced that previous outbreak of dissent. The freedom to broadcast such ideas and views was not indicative, however, of any great opening up to free speech or political change compared with a decade before although this appeared to be the case.

In fact, as Kelly (1990) points out, their privilege was the result of one of the traditions being criticised, that is, political patronage, a specific form of *guanxi*. Without the help and even protection of some key CCP officials, they could not have been so outspoken. This phenomenon was seen as an unwelcome cultural legacy but, ironically, it was the context young intellectuals had to work within. Those with important social contacts were more likely to be able to speak freely than those without and this offered a degree of protection should their messages be critical of the regime. This was the case with other leading intellectuals of the 1980s as well as the *He Shang* authors. It seemed as if 'The more independent their words, the more popular such thinkers seemed to become among intellectuals' (Nathan, 1990:110).

He Shang can be viewed as selective modernity and tradition in action with the authors marking out elements of the past to be consigned to the dustbin of history along with some aspects of modern society also unsuitable for the present. Making these points is not meant as a criticism of the writers but a recognition of the often contradictory parameters they had to contend with.

There was very little legal entitlement to free speech and any such outbursts of dissent have to be viewed as part of the way Chinese communism worked in the 1980s, with political patronage rather than autonomy prevailing. *He Shang* put forward a lot of challenges not only to the regime but also in cultural and ideological terms, yet it relied on that same sense of patriotism laid down by that very system (Kelly, *op. cit.*). One informant noted this in his comments about the programme, saying that it was not only one big 'complaining session' but a 'high class' one at that. Other people lower down the social hierarchy without the patronage of key CCP leaders may not have been able to complain so freely.

The Zhao Ziyang faction probably needed the intellectuals for support due to internal Party struggles and the series helped to play out in a public manner some of the conflicts over ideology and policies. Some senior Party leaders castigated the programme and its creators for their negative analysis of Chinese culture and society and its implicit challenge to their ruling orthodoxy although Zhao sanctioned its broadcast in the first place and suppressed an early attack on it (Jenner, 1992:17). When it was reshown in August, there were some revisions which toned down the commentary but its popularity amongst intellectuals, especially younger ones, remained strong and it was a 'hot topic' for many months.

There was some feeling that the messages were not new but the way they were put across was significant. Some respondents, however, did not agree with the tone of the arguments, believing that the authors may have been overly critical of China's history and some people pointed out some positive elements of the nation's long history. Not everything was bad or worthless from the past and respondents were keen to salvage the good aspects for the present period. 'It is dangerous to reject everything in the past', warned one person, mentioning that this may be symptomatic of a generation gap. But traditional culture, it was often acknowledged, is 'bad sometimes' and needed to be changed. Considering the prospects of combining China's past and western capitalism, however, another informant warned that 'In China the worst thing will be for feudalism and capitalism and dictatorship of the proletariat to be together. This will be the worst situation in the world.' There was also some agreement that the traditional idea of following one person and one body of thought as in the 'old days', was wrong. More democracy was needed, following this line of argument.

One respondent was more critical, saying that *He Shang* offered few suggestions or ideas to remedy China's ills apart from adopting full-scale capitalism. *He Shang* had certainly, however, given people and the government a 'stir' and that was a good thing in their eyes. It summarised many of the contradictions of the reform era which young intellectuals were only too well aware of.

Against the background of questionable economic reform and intellectual decline, there was an ongoing 'business craze' which many of Deng's generation were involved in, as will be discussed next.

THE 'ECONOMIC FEVER'

The economic changes had made a big impact not only on people's living standards but also on their ways of thinking. 'Looking towards money' (*xiang qian kan*) and materialism could not be avoided once the profit motive had been allowed to thrive even if the changes were made in the name of 'Chinese style socialism' (*Zhongguo tese de zhuyi*). Economic changes at first appeared to reinforce those in the educational sector with the previous emphasis on political campaigns giving way to economic pragmatism. Allowing elements of the free market economy (the term capitalism was always avoided) first of all in agricultural then in industrial enterprises transformed many regions of China. So-called 'rich peasants' emerged in rural areas because of the responsibility system and sideline businesses although such stereotypes must be treated cautiously, as previously discussed. There were sections of society who could and did make a lot of money because of the reforms but there remained areas where people were very poor.

It became more common throughout the 1980s to see farmers selling their products in the market places, providing more varieties of produce as the decade progressed. Gao felt that 'The normal people's daily lives, their living standard is higher than before. If you go to the countryside you can see the peasants' lives improved a lot. Most people have improved standards, the open door policy brings such a result.' Attempts to change the economy accompanied the demise of 'redness.' Competition was viewed as preferable to the stagnation caused by egalitarianism. Just as students were to compete for places at key point schools and colleges, so farmers and businesses had to compete for trade and profits.

The media concentrated on the successes and praised those who took risks and helped to create jobs and wealth for others. One article, for example, made links with a past generation of Chinese who had flourished overseas and raised the notion of 'Chineseness' itself which was another discussion topic of the 1980s. When praising farmers who had successfully turned their hand to business, the writer indicated that a talent for making money was part of the Chinese identity. 'The achievements of enterprising farmers over the past five or six years have been beyond everybody's expectations. They have shown such business acumen that I am convinced the coolie-turned-millionaires among the Chinese overseas are but a chip off the old block' (CD, 4 Oct. 1984:4). Discussing the use of surplus rural labour in the newly established rural businesses, the writer also noted positively that 'After the new rural policies were introduced in late 1978 the dream of getting rich was no longer pie in the sky'.

Rich people were formerly despised under communism but were now almost glorified as socialist heroes. According to Rosenbaum 'Admiring accounts of wealthy entrepreneurs contributing to China's new prosperity conveyed the impression that "to be wealthy is glorious" ' (1992:13). This had major implications for the acceptance of official ideology by young intellectuals with new economic models indicating that it was acceptable to make money and unacceptable to be financially dependent and poor. Deng Xiaoping's favoured expression was frequently cited to justify the changed policies, that is, 'it doesn't matter what colour the cat as long as it catches the mouse'.[2] This was largely supported early on but by the late 1980s there was anxiety about the widening income and wealth gaps with intellectuals seeing themselves as losers in this cat-and-mouse game. The moves towards privatisation encouraged the business craze amongst young people although not everyone was rushing out to find ways of making money. Some were forced to seek alternatives because changes in government policies reduced the value of their income and to some extent necessitated institutions and individuals joining the business trend in any way they could.

Main Reasons for 'Doing Business'

The *jingshang re* was clearly related to the economic features of the generation which was maturing when economic reform was being prioritised. The demise of the 'iron rice bowl' also added to the necessity to develop business acumen early on with students no longer assured of job assignments at the end of their university careers. Wang stated quite unequivocally that his generation would be 'more adventurous', and it was 'impossible to imagine the old generation of educated intellectuals running their own shops. We want to. Life in business and trade is more adventurous. We will be more commercialised.' He also felt that they would be 'more influenced by economic benefits, more concerned for himself than others such as the motherland, and the state. These are not so important.' This reflects the trend towards this generation being less self-sacrificing than their predecessors. Kwong also observed that the young were not willing to serve the country in the same way as their predecessors' (1994:259). Being involved in the economic fever gave them a degree of individual autonomy.

The business tide can be viewed on several layers, from the institution down to individual lecturers and students with clear links between them. If, for example, a university was attempting to foster a business-like environment, then this would encourage personnel to seek their own ways of making money. The institution can be viewed as a source of influence for the students as well as for the staff. There was also peer group influence because if some students were seen to be earning money, then their classmates might be encouraged to do the same. There was sharing of ideas and inspirations as well as practical knowledge about where to seek part-time jobs, how much to charge, where to find goods for sale and resale and so on.

The main impetus for these developments came from official policies of promoting economic self-sufficiency. Language institutes were well placed with the growing demand for foreign languages, especially English. Short courses were offered which utilised some of the expertise of language teachers in profitable ways. Fee paying students were not difficult to find and the large classes I taught certainly added to the coffers of previously run-down language institutes. These types of enterprise activities were praised because they appeared to embody the pragmatic spirit of the reform decade.

The fact that increasing numbers of academics had second jobs in order to boost their income was not lost on their students. Lili remarked that 'Some people who have very low salaries, such as the teachers, try to do some part-time job beside their own occupations so they can make more money to meet their consumption'. On the one hand it was enterprising but on the other it could cause stress with the inability to carry out either job effectively. Stories appeared of some middle school teachers being forced to sell tea and eggs during break times to raise funds. This was seen as an unsuitable activity for academics and raised serious questions about the state's commitment to higher education. It was difficult to halt this trend, however, because the leadership was committed to extending economic reforms and making higher education more self-financing. Without bonuses to supplement the fixed salaries, teaching positions offered little else but security of tenure. Some intellectuals had only their knowledge to offer in the market place and if this was not in areas such as computing or foreign languages, then its value was low.

Students chose to do business if they could find a way to participate. This can be viewed as another strategy for overcoming some of the disparities between their expectations and their actual experiences. They were initially encouraged to do so mainly to improve their economic position but also to gain first-hand experience of society. They were frequently accused of having unrealistic expectations because of their sheltered campus lives and did not know the social realities. Those whose English level was good were well placed as they could give private lessons as home tutors (Cherrington, 1988b). In the early months of 1988, many trees and lamp-posts in the capital, for example, were adorned with small posters advertising coaching in various subjects, especially English. The interviewee Li described how she took care of herself financially. 'Many students now do a paid job. They no longer rely totally on their parents and families. I am a home tutor. I have to arrange my time carefully so that it doesn't interfere too much with my studies.' These aspects of economic independence and astuteness emerged as a common characteristic of the sample linked to govenment policy shifts. Some students attempted to develop themselves as successful young entrepreneurs simultaneously to being scholars.

There were peer group models to follow with many young intellectuals taking the 'doing business' trend to the extreme by abandoning their low-paid 'iron rice bowls'. Entering business-oriented occupations seemed to be a strategy for intellectuals dissatisfied by their conditions and salaries. The benefits of the service sector might have been more appealing, especially in terms of remuneration and working environment. Going to a brand new, joint venture hotel, for example, appeared attractive after the run-down conditions of some educational establishments. One informant gave the example of a colleague who transferred into the service sector. She was warned that in the long run, hotel work did not have much security but it did offer immediate material benefits.

Another informant told me about his brother who had graduated from a prestigious university. Although 'very clever', he was continually held back at work and denied promotion. 'So, he changed his job. Now he's a businessman. He's the manager and very rich.' By moving out of education this young man improved his financial and material situation. The informant was proud to announce that 'At noon in my dormitory I got my father's letter which said that my brother will go to Japan for business'. This opportunity for overseas travel was highly valued, further adding to the apparent benefits of 'doing business'. It also indicated that this trend was an alternative way of going abroad and this was an added incentive for gaining business experience whilst still within education. Both frequently involved finding and developing good *guanxi*.

It must be remembered that many students had to rely on their parents who, as intellectuals themselves, may have been increasingly hard-pressed. By taking on a job, students could not only help their families but gain some independence. At first, this was seen as beneficial because the students could be more self-supporting and gain social skills outside university. In an era when employment prospects for graduates were uncertain, business experience may have been a useful back-up. Even the CYL became involved in this trend, encouraging branches to set up small-scale businesses to help raise funds (ZGQN, *Bao*, 16 July 1988:15). There were, therefore, a number of interrelated strands behind the 'doing business' trend and the presence of more than one would increase the likelihood of adopting this as a strategy. The risks involved, however, may have acted as deterrents.

Inhibiting Factors

Not all universities and colleges, as well as their staff and students, were equally involved in business activities. Some could not participate even if they had been encouraged to do so by official messages and the economic necessities of their situation. Personnel in less prestigious institutions or in departments with limited practical applications were largely excluded from the accumulation of extra funds. They began to feel increasingly pressurised by an inflationary spiral on the one hand and the state encouraging self-sufficiency on the other. So it was with the students inside these institutions. The relatively healthy financial situation of the model colleges was often quite different from the reality facing less well-off counterparts. Many humanities and arts faculties would be relatively badly placed, becoming less attractive to both students and staff whilst the more scientific and technological ones had more opportunities. The geographical placing of institutions was also significant with those close to financial and business centres more likely to find a market for their services than those in China's hinterlands.

One deterrent was the government's own later change of mind. The SEC, for example, called upon provincial education departments and universities in October 1988 to curtail participation in business activities (CD, 7 Oct. 1988:3). Students were expected to be 'hardworking and thrifty', earning only limited amounts to help meet their expenses or to gain some practical skills. Such activities were not meant to distract them from their studies or promote a 'get rich quick' ideology. The business fever was viewed as detrimental to academic study with tiredness and truancy appearing as related trends but by this time it had already become endemic. Many students struggling on small scholarships had, indeed, become the economic generation and were more responsible for their financial affairs.

There was also some backlash due to the traditional image of the scholar, set apart from mundane, everyday matters, being too rapidly eroded with little difference between young students and their *getihu* counterparts. Social values were changing in the reform decade but conservatives wanted to retain some of the old values and aspects of the social hierarchy. Xiu criticised the student 'business fever' for diverting attention away from studying and towards making money. In this respect, she mirrored the concerns of officials who were concerned about students spending too much of their time and efforts on money-making activities.

Another deterrent was the association of doing business with criminal activity. The distinction between the official promotion of financial autonomy and the unofficial one of people finding illicit ways of exchanging goods and services was not always clear and this brings the discussion back to the issue of corruption. Officials at all levels had access to scarce goods and resources because of their *guanxi* and could abuse their position to make extra money. This become a key issue in the late 1980s and was a significant factor in transforming the generation into a politically active one. It was known that senior Party leaders were using their position to help family and friends and this was raised during the 1989 student movement.

According to Yang 'Corruption is much worse than it was. Much worse. Some high officials earn money illegally so the other people, I mean the officers at the lower level, they do not have any fear because the high authorities are doing the same things. It's very bad. Although the government has tried to solve the problem they have not been successful.' The association of doing business with corruption could act as a deterrent. Respondents had ambivalent views about the use of *guanxi wang*, criticising them on the one hand but having to depend on them to some extent because that was how a lot of things got done. Some posters in April and June 1988 cited corruption of this type as an endemic problem which had to be dealt with, from the top layers of society downwards.

Some respondents had gained various chances by the 'back-door' (*houmen*) and were actively seeking social connections. Certainly business activities were facilitated by having useful *guanxi* in order to obtain goods to sell, for example. In many spheres of life *guanxi* were important and although respondents were critical of this, they perceived themselves as being able to do very little about it. It was the case that 'if you can't beat them, join them', in many ways as with other trends of the 1980s. There were too many people 'looking towards money' which possibly encouraged corrupt dealings and this emphasis on money was a negative result of the reforms.

Hua, for example, said that 'After 1978 it turned too quickly, selfishness became people's goal, their aim in life, to struggle for themselves. To struggle for oneself is important but we cannot ignore other people's interests.' Gao similarly was depressed by these developments. He thought that 'looking towards money' was the 'biggest problem'. For him, 'The success of reform lies in the sacrifice of one or two generations but which generation is willing to sacrifice themselves? I can't say. This generation is not willing to sacrifice themselves. They only find a method to make money for themselves. They don't care about the next generation. They discard the valuable tradition.' He was showing himself to be an older member of the generation with these comments, a person who had known some sacrifice already due to the Cultural Revolution, but this was an unpopular idea in the 1980s and young people were 'impatient' to get the rewards of reforms in their lifetime, not their children's. This attitude, however, had been encouraged by the authorities in their early enthusiasm for individual initiative and entrepreneurialism.

Chinese social life was changing in the reform period, perhaps for the worse, because of the emphasis on money. Materialism and increased opportunities for corruption were viewed as significant forces depressing young intellectuals and denying them their perceived proper place at the head of society.

Overall, there were factors both encouraging and discouraging young, and not so young, intellectuals from taking part in this trend but many still did and sometimes the consequences were to further depress the state of education with increasing numbers leaving the teaching profession, for example. The government's own shifts in official statements probably did little to deter people because of the reform context with its emphasis on economic pragmatism rather than socialist egalitarianism. There were other ways of trying to resolve some of the problems, however, at least on a temporary basis and these will be discussed next.

THE 'STUDYING ENGLISH' CRAZE

This was obviously linked with the going abroad trend previously discussed. The enthusiam for learning foreign languages, particularly English, can be seen as lying somewhere between leisure and education. For many, the aim was to pass an examination such as TOEFL in order to qualify for going abroad but for others, knowledge of English could open up forms of literature and philosophy as well as the ability to communicate directly with the increasing numbers of foreigners entering China. As many would-be overseas scholars were considering western countries, particularly the USA, proficiency in English was a necessity. It was also vital for those who wished to read books and watch films coming into the country, as well as other cultural items, without having to rely on translations. Other languages were popular but English was the favourite.

In the reform period, language skills were emerging as necessities for implementing the four modernisations with English in particular a means of accessing technological and scientific knowledge. This shift had signalled the official approval of learning English with the 'craze' developing rapidly as a result. Whilst the official agenda for this trend may have been the pursuit of advanced knowledge, those who took part in it may have had different ideas. The need to get high TOEFL scores was uppermost in people's minds as well as in other tests set by overseas bodies.

The numbers of TOEFL candidates in Beijing, for example, increased from only 285 when the examination was first held in 1981 to 2500 in 1983 and 8000 by 1985. In 1987, an estimated 26,000 people applied (GMRB, 22 Feb. 1988:4). The figures remained high in the early 1990s with a trend for increasing numbers of younger students at senior middle school taking this and other tests to go abroad, (Rosen, 1993:329). Test centres were opened in other major cities throughout the 1980s. I saw the growth of popularity for this examination as students skipped classes or tried to study surreptiously during class time. There were entry procedures to follow and hundreds of people would queue outside the appointed offices just to get hold of the application forms in time. They also had to pay the test fee in dollars and foreign teachers were frequently asked to exchange Chinese currency to enable them to do so. Failing that, they had to resort to the black market. It was a lengthy task with a high risk of failure because of the hurdles at each level, let alone the demand for good pass scores which required learning much vocabulary.

There was the strong possibility that inadequate scores would be the result first time around. Those who were unsuccessful often tried to resit even though the procedure was complicated as well as expensive.Trying to find other ways of going abroad was also an option. It seemed that even those who could not pass

TOEFL or failed to find a place at an overseas university did not abandon the idea of going abroad altogether. Further study may have been planned. Renewed attempts to find the right *guanxi*, both at home and abroad as well as ways around the official regulations were all tactics cited as possibilities. It was hoped that it would all become easier in years to come. Being patient and making the best of the situation in China, for the time being at least, was another way of coping for those who had exhausted every possibility.

In order to assist with the preparations for the tests many young people 'sharpened their language skills at every opportunity' (Kwong, 1994:259). During the fieldwork period I frequently spent Sunday mornings at the local English Corner in Beijing and whilst travelling around the country at other times found similar gatherings for those wishing to practice their language skills. Even on very cold days, with below freezing temperatures, young people and older youth milled around hoping to find a foreigner to converse with or just to talk with each other. Not all those attending English Corners were students. In fact, from casual observation on a number of occasions, most participants appeared to be from other sections of youth, such as *getihu* who were self-taught English speakers with little or no formal training. They found the English Corners particularly useful places for practising what they learnt. It was possibly the case that younger students who had been exposed more to English at school and university might not have valued the English Corners as much as their senior counterparts.

Attending these gatherings could be an exhausting experience, especially if there was only one or two foreigners around to talk with the scores of young people wishing to put forward their questions about the language, foreign countries, television programmes and other innumerable topics. These extended across a wide and diverse range, with questions about English grammar or vocabulary intermingling with those about politics, although these were usually raised in an indirect manner. There was always the possibility of police 'spies' attending these gatherings who were not there to learn English. Questions about Mrs Thatcher were common and often led into other political topics. There had been much publicity about her perceived political strength in China and she was admired for this as well as being compared with Deng Xiaoping.

Football, pop music and other subjects were covered often in a volley of questions that was sometimes overwhelming. Answering such questions from many young people, with crowds gathered around just to listen as well as talk, gave insights into the enthusiasm of this generation and their desire to know more about the outside world. Their frustrations and disappointments were also raised during these ad hoc discussions. Other opportunities to practise language skills were seized upon when coming across foreigners on trains and buses. At times it appeared as if everyone was learning English or taking TOEFL.

For those not involved in the English craze, there were other means of trying to improve one's life and lifestyle.

ENTERTAINMENT AND LEISURE: AN UNOFFICIAL YOUTH SUBCULTURE?

Pursuing various leisure activities can be considered as offering an alternative way of solving some of the problems facing young intellectuals and providing an escape route, albeit on a temporary basis. They wanted to enjoy themselves and forget the contradictions of their privileged yet difficult position. The reforms had led to greater diversity in the range of leisure pursuits available, especially in the cities, which can be linked to the general increase in consumerism in Chinese society. There was, additionally, some relaxation of rules and social mores about what young people could do in their free time.

These developments were usually endorsed by the authorities because they indicated that China was becoming a developed society with higher standards of living. By the mid-1980s, for example, fashion consciousness had been officially approved. One article began 'She strolls down the street wearing fashionable boots, stylish pants and a lightweight down jacket . . . She even sports a touch of makeup.' (BR, 18 Feb. 1985:7). According to the China Youth News, the 'new life' for young people included fashion, comfort, good food and entertainment, (BR, *op. cit.*). It did appear that 'Young Chinese seek more colourful life' (CD, 7 Jan. 1985:3).

The respondent Lili remarked on this, stating that you could see the changes brought about by reforms on individual appearance. 'From the individual perspective, there are many changes in their appearances. In the past, people were only dressed in blue and black, two very dim colours. Now people wear clothes in all sorts of colours.' Her friend Wen agreed, saying that 'People now choose what they wear. They have become more casual in dress.' In this sense, fashion and entertainment were parts of an official, rather than unofficial subcultural development but it will be shown that certain elements were less acceptable to the authorities. It was diverse rather than monolithic.

The choice of leisure activities was affected by several major factors. Availability of entertainments, their proximity and level of provision were clearly important as was, indeed, cost. Some activities would be out of reach because they were prohibitively expensive. Keeping up with the latest fashions could also prove difficult for those living on fixed, low incomes such as student scholarships. Earning extra money for buying fashionable clothes, for example, might have been necessary at this time. The influence of the peer group was very important at this stage of their lives with possible conflict between peers, parents and official bodies. This conflict can be seen in the first 'craze' to be addressed.

Escape into Love

There was a serious side to romantic and sexual relationships, which were still frowned upon for young people by the authorities. Before the 1980s, it was difficult for romance to thrive given the socialist morality which stressed political rather than personal relationships. Privacy was a rare commodity given the way the state organised itself right down to the local level through its various organisations. Students and their young teachers living in crowded dormitories could hardly find privacy and were relatively easy to survey, with their '*banzhuren*', an official minder, keeping an eye on them. Relationships had to be conducted in the proper manner, at least publicly, and students were discouraged from 'talking love'.

Although in the 1980s it was rare to see any physical signs of romantic liaisons, they did take place but young people had to be careful. That many were giving in to 'temptation' was evident in the official concern expressed about these issues but by the middle of the decade the authorities were finding it increasingly difficult to control the morality of youth. Trying to gain personal space and pleasure through relationships was an alternative to more officially accepted means. Things did become more open and public displays of affection more common but still infrequent amongst students. It remained risky to be found in the wrong dormitory outside official visiting hours but finding boyfriends and girlfriends was something attractive and natural which was once firmly denied to them for as long as possible.

The uncertainties of the reform programme probably exacerbated any relationship problems young people encountered and they were ill-prepared to deal with them because of a lack of suitable channels of help early on in the decade. Later, some were set up as personal life became more permissible and the authorites recognised the need for some less formal means of communication. Respondents cited examples of 'love suicides' from the media where students had killed themselves because of failed relationships. One young woman told me of a colleague who had 'gone mad' after a failed relationship. These may have been extreme examples but show the seriousness of the romance craze if it turned sour.

The aim of finding a suitable partner at university may have been more important for young women than for their male counterparts because of changing gender expectations and stereotypes. There was a noted shift back to ideas of traditional femininity rather than feminism and it was clear that having a university education was not enough to secure a job. Seven of the eight female interviewees were asked about problems facing women, with the general view being that there were additional difficulties. Their experiences of inequalities were seen as resulting from what at first sight appear to be two opposite forces; persistence of traditional thought and practices on the one hand, and the consequences of reform on the other. Closer examination shows similarities between these forces with elements of reform causing something of a revival in what can be described as 'feudal thinking'. Females were seen to be victims of discrimination, especially in job assignments after graduation as well as in obtaining opportunities for promotion and going abroad.

Six females immediately identified the job problem. 'When we are assigned, many units do not want to accept females', said Liu, echoing a common remark. Sun had also experienced discrimination in employment and believed that 'Female students graduating from college have a hard time to find any job'.

Undergraduates had yet to experience this for themselves but knew of the situation from older friends and teachers. These educated young women were frustrated because they had positive ideas about their talents and capabilities yet they faced a 'struggle' to find work, whilst some of their less capable male classmates would have more chances.

Li felt that some educated women were oblivious to the social reality and not fully aware of the extent of inequality. Being in higher education probably gave them a sense of security with the illusion of equal opportunities dependent upon academic attainments rather than gender. They were still confident but 'once they enter the society they find discrimination at once', she said. Considering her own position, she believed that 'In the future, first of all there is trouble for me to find a good job. I think I will meet with difficulties because according to the present situation the female college graduates have much more difficulty than the male ones.'

Wen shared this view: 'Nowadays, many enterprises don't want female graduates for the reason that it's troublesome to have women'. This was thought partly due to women's entitlement to maternity leave which was a problem for companies in the era of economic change. As enterprises were increasingly required to make profits and streamline production, reducing numbers of female employees was seen as a money-saving exercise because there would be less maternity leave to finance. Zhen believed that 'If you are child-bearing age, 25 to 30, they will probably not allow you to work in that unit'. This reaffirms the idea that employers were reluctant to accept females, regardless of their qualifications and this was a source of relative deprivation acutely felt by the female sample members.

One of the major causes was that 'the social thinking always regards women as inferior to men', commented Li. Sun also mentioned that in a 'feudal' society like China 'women have in history always been looked down on'. In spite of 40 years of communism during which equality between the sexes had been official policy, these young women felt that strong elements of 'feudal' thinking persisted. According to Wen 'Women are not supposed to be not too capable and even if they are, they are still considered as inferior to men'. The reform programme was not seen as helpful in this respect and Zhen suggested that the situation could become even worse. 'Originally, before reform, we had a slogan, men and women are equal which means they get equal jobs and equal pay. Now the problem (of inequality) is popping up.' Sun was unsure, saying that 'After reforms it will get better but it's hard to say'.

The prospect of discrimination added to an already hostile environment which may have dampened young women's enthusiasm for study. Some may have preferred to spend their college lives looking for a partner rather than studying if they thought they were going to be unable to secure a satisfactory job and would have to rely on a man. It reflected to some extent the failure of reforms to provide sufficient opportunities for graduates of both sexes and was indicative of the devaluation of knowledge already referred to. The problem was that females could suffer more than the males as a result of romantic encounters and face harsher criticism because of sexual double standards. There were also the associated problems of possible pregnancy and sexually transmitted diseases.

The authorities were aware of growing trends in so-called 'unhealthy' behaviour and frequently blamed the open door policies, these being unwelcome imports rather than home-grown problems. Young people were perceived by their patronizing elders as particularly vulnerable to such temptations. The implication was that China was relatively free of such immoral behaviour before the 1980s and it was part of the risk of opening its doors to the outside world. China did not want these so-called 'flies and pests' and there were regular attempts to try to decrease its influence, such as the 1983 'anti-spiritual pollution' campaign (*wei jingshen wuran yundong*). This involved the authorities at all levels trying to clamp down on what was viewed as 'yellow' material, such as pornography and excessive 'bourgeois liberalism'. In some places dancing was forbidden as well as foreign films and fashions. Sexual liasions between unmarried youth were also criticised.

The communist authorities were, in fact, trying to monitor cultural changes, a task which they had begun before 1949 with some success. In the 1980s, there was a sudden and enormous input from overseas, as well as from closer neighbours such as Hong Kong and Taiwan and it was no longer feasible to control what young people were doing in their spare time. Technological changes also made many attempts redundant with cassettes, videos and fax machines available for the dissemination of various cultural items. Whilst controls may have had some effects, along with punishments meted out for those considered to be guilty of 'polluting' Chinese socialism, they were of decreasing importance. Videos may have been destroyed but they could be replaced. By 1984, the campaign was revoked because there was a danger of it becoming too far-reaching and thus threatening the reform programme itself.

There was antagonism between the economic aspects of reform and those within the cultural sphere. The reform-minded leadership's plan to maintain economic change without influencing too much elsewhere was wishful thinking. Their conservative colleagues, not entirely convinced of the necessity of reform, could easily seize on undesirable social behaviour as evidence of mistakes by the reformers and this struggle was never far from the surface. It partly explains some of the shifts of the decade. Young intellectuals were at the middle of this contradiction, on the one hand being told to 'emancipate their minds' in terms of reform but at the same time to stay on the 'socialist road'. They were not only watching fashions but also the leadership factions throughout the decade.

'Falling in love', then, had its serious side as did the other crazes. For those who wanted to find someone of the opposite sex to enjoy themselves with, going to dances became popular, as will be discussed next as part of the rapid diversification of youth subcultural trends.

Quickstepping into the Contemporary Era

Holding dance parties became increasingly common from the mid-1980s onwards in a wide variety of settings. Macartney writes how 'Dancing gave students an opportunity to meet members of the opposite sex in an atmosphere of freedom from social constrictions they had never before encountered' (1990:4). Dancing was previously viewed as 'bourgeois' behaviour because of its links with western settlements in China, especially coastal cities like Shanghai. It remained a risky activity even in the early 1980s, being severely curtailed during the anti-spiritual pollution campaign but was officially rehabilitated after some key CCP leaders, significantly wearing western-style suits, danced at celebrations towards the end of 1984. This signalled that it was once more acceptable to two-step, tango and disco and the 'dance craze' swept campuses during the Christmas and New Year period which I witnessed for myself.

Prior to this, official parties or 'meetings' as they were usually called, were allowed with some dancing but it was very restrained and was generally called to an abrupt end by 9.00pm. By the end of 1984, the students were organising their own dance parties usually in classrooms or sometimes in dormitories at every possible chance. It was also feasible then to celebrate Christmas as a time of festivities which was a marked change from previous policy. Dances were usually organised by the class as a group, with their peer group identity strong and reflected in the use of their own designated classroom, if they had one. Outsiders were not particularly welcome unless invited as guests by class members to make up the numbers and balance out any imbalances in the sex ratio.

They were every enthusastic and decorated the classrooms as best as possible to make them less formal and cold. They put up sheets of coloured paper and there were usually fancy messages chalked up on the blackboard welcoming everybody. Borrowed cassette players and much copied tapes were played, with a mixture of slightly dated western pop and more recent Hong Kong and Taiwan imports. The older style, ballroom dance music was often preferred to begin with, such as the two-step, where couples could go through their carefully rehearsed routines. If there were not enough members of the opposite sex available to dance with, then classmates of the same sex would do because the young people did not wish to miss out on any dance time. At first I excused myself from this dancing but I found that learning the basic steps enabled me to participate more fully in the 'dance craze'. I was frequently requested to demonstrate disco and breakdancing techniques but my efforts with the latter often fell short of their expectations. Disco was more part of my generational identity. By 1988 dancing was a well-established leisure activity for students.

They usually used the classrooms, canteens and other communal areas partly out of convenience but also because they did not have the money to attend the new dancehalls and discos springing up in the big cities. These were more for the wealthier *getihu* who could afford the cover charges and over-priced drinks. The atmosphere in the commerical dancehalls was in marked contrast to the makeshift ones in the classrooms. Established to earn profit in the changed economic climate of the 1980s, these places attracted not only legal but sometimes illicit trade and some became known as 'pick-up' places for prostitutes. Blackmarket money changers and others who operated on the margins of society would also be present because they had money 'to burn'. I saw young *getihu* do this literally several times to show off in front of students. Foreign tourists and business people would also be welcome with their foreign currency, and such places thrived in the large cities as a result of the open door policy. The fact that young intellectuals were largely excluded reiterates the distance between the different sections of youth which added to resentments and misunderstandings.

At the do-it-yourself classroom dances there were usually soft drinks brought along by the students themselves. I hardly ever saw alcohol at these gatherings but drinking parties were also becoming popular on campuses and the '*jiu pai*' have already been mentioned. There were more bars on campuses but they were more likely to be found at colleges where there were foreign teachers and/or students. Frequently these attracted outsiders, not all of them welcome. It was the dancing and to some extent the chance to mix freely with the opposite sex which seemed to be the main appeal of the classroom dance parties.

Although self-organised, there was still a degree of formal regimentation about these events with a programme sometimes opening the proceedings, perhaps with some games or performances by participants, such as singing, telling a story, joke and so on. There was frequently a good deal of pressure put upon people to perform but shy, nervous types found this embarrassing. I went to some parties where older educated youth became extremely animated when shouting at those who declined to perform and there were insights as to what it must have been like at 'struggle sessions' during the Cultural Revolution. Even in having pleasure, there were reminders of the past with group pressure to conform to 'having fun'. Another area of leisure also had its more serious aspects, as will be shown in the discussion on the construction and consumption of pop music in the 1980s.

Pop Music: a 'Knife' or a 'Double-edged Sword'?

This question refers to a discussion of pop music in contemporary China by Jones (1992) who sees it as 'less a mere adjunct to leisure than a battlefield on which ideological struggle is waged'. This, of course, can be the case with almost anything in the highly politicised Chinese context but the ways in which pop music 'struggles' occurred in the 1980s will be related to my own observations.

I saw how young intellectuals and other youth were attempting to eke out personal space and express themselves in ways independent of Party organisations and pop music did provide a medium as well as a message. Whilst some of the lyrics were extremely meaningful and perhaps subversive if 'read' by audiences in particular ways, thus representing part of an unofficial subculture, there were factors of the official youth culture coexisting with them, especially the aim of making pop music a profitable industry. This would be what Jones identifies as *tongsu yinyue* or 'officially sanctioned' pop music as opposed to *yaogun yinyue* or underground rock music (*op. cit*:3). The latter was denied access to the national, state-run media.

At the same time, pop music was consumed for pleasure and it can be stated simply at the outset that singing was very popular amongst students as they attempted to escape from some of the depressing realities of their lives. They often wanted to sing and dance without caring too much about ideology but for fun, and that should not be omitted from the equation. Pop music can be either conformist or rebellious and even a bit of both at the same time; as Jones claimed, 'the knife cuts in many ways' (*op. cit*:3).

Communal singing was part of their childhood and early youth experience but the communist songs were rapidly replaced by others which expressed their own generational identity. A range of music and songs was listened to with some words learned by heart and such songs could be sung as a group activity during class time, at parties or when out together on visits to parks and other excursions. This range became noticeably more diverse as the decade progressed because of increasing contacts with the outside world and the fact that China was becoming part of the international market not only for industrial goods and services but cultural items such as popular music which found a mass market in China. There were plenty of willing consumers, especially amongst youth.

British and American songs were popular early on in the decade, with songs like 'Country Roads' (John Denver) learnt by heart when I was first in China. I remember very well listening to many renditions of 'West Virginia, that's the place where I belong' whilst in Zhenjiang and could not quite understand why this particular song had managed to become so well known. Whenever I hear it now I think of that small town in the middle of China back in the early days of reform but when I think of my later experiences in China, I only recall Chinese pop songs. Probably there was very little choice to begin with and any tapes were readily seized upon and copied over and over again. I'm sure that my own cassette collection worked its way around China in a number of ways after being borrowed by students and young teachers. There was probably a desire to practise or improve English skills for those studying the language as well as an enthusiasm and even desperation for anything new, something different to listen to as well as to learn new words. Many young people stuck with their old favourites for some years. These included Christmas songs which could be heard all year round in some restaurants and hotels.

An important factor affecting accessibility and availability to new material was region. Large cities like Guangzhou and Shanghai were more likely to have recent imports than smaller towns, like the one I first lived in and also these cities had links with Hong Kong and Taiwan through social and family networks, probably more so than the more conservative and politically dominated Beijing. Shanghai people were always trying to convince me that they were more cosmopolitan than their counterparts in the capital, more open-minded and modern because of their historical background and position as an entrepot. Not all of the links were positive in terms of socialist morality, being more likely to be labelled as 'bourgeois' but the flair for doing business and trade was definitely promoted earlier in the decade in such a city and pop music was part of this. Guangzhou had the added advantage of geographical proximity to Hong Kong and new materials could easily slip across the border.

By 1984, there was already an interest in pop music from Hong Kong and Taiwan. These brands of pop music could be readily promoted by their record companies, as well as being more easily pirated, and presented few language problems. They were Chinese in the wider sense and part of an increasingly influential '*Gangtai*'[3] popular culture, as Gold (1993) refers to it. Young mainlanders could identify with the 'Chineseness' of these pop stars (*juxing*) especially as China attempted to move closer in economic terms to Hong Kong. These stars represented more than just pop music but lifestyles and ideals to look towards so they were keenly followed. Through popular cultural means, pop music in particular, there were some aspects of 'redefining the essence of what it means to be a "modern" Chinese at the end of the twentieth century and popularizing a new language for expressing individual sentiments' (Gold, 1993:907). In the official communist songs, there was little room for individuality because it was the 'masses' that counted the most but the new generation had, as already pointed out, a greater sense of self-importance. Foreign popular music, a relatively new genre, was becoming a means of expressing relatively new feelings and identities. Romance and love were part of this.

Pop music also made links which mirrored to some extent those occurring within the economy but perhaps were not happening so quickly in the political sphere. Whilst there were increased official contacts with Taiwan in the 1980s, for example, young people were enjoying much more of a cultural exchange than their elders through listening to pop music and 'worshipping' pop stars from there. Shambaugh makes the point that for the under-40s generation, it was not Deng Xiaoping who ruled China 'but Taiwan's popular singer Deng Lijun (Teresa Teng)' (1993:659). Shambaugh, in making a distinction between 'inner China' (the PRC) and 'outer China' (Taiwan and Hong Kong), stresses the impact of the latter on the former in terms of lifestyles and fashions, and remarks on the forging of new links (*op. cit*:658). This was facilitated by technological change with increasing numbers of cassette players, videos and faxes in China. It is also important to note that the international aspects of pop music were not lost on many of its fans. They were aware, for example, that other Chinese youth would be listening in London, Los Angeles and Sydney to the *Gangtai* pop stars so it represented not only a link between the component parts of 'Greater China' (Shambaugh, *op. cit.*) but almost a global one.

China had been more or less shut off to the outside, including to overseas Chinese, for a long time but the 1980s saw all that alter and there was a sense of reuniting distant groups of Chinese not through high culture but popular cultural means. There may have been a breaking down of barriers although I would not over-emphasise this, but certainly the sense of a shared identity was extending beyond the borders of mainland China. I would argue that by the time of the pro-democracy campaign in 1989, there was a sufficiently well-developed sense of a cross-border generational identity that helped to bring many Hong Kong students into China to support the students there or to give money to their cause. There was also the noticeable participation of a popular Taiwanese pop star, Hou Dejian[4], in the final stages of this movement. It was certainly not pop music alone that did this but it was one contributing factor because it was increasingly a part of this concept of 'Greater China'. Chinese communities all over the world were united by grief after the Tiananmen massacre but perhaps young people more so because of their generational links, albeit from a distance, and some of this was expressed through the sentiments and words of pop songs.

As a result, then, of the economic and related cultural developments of the 1980s, there was more choice for young people in terms of youth culture because they had at their disposal elements of a rapidly expanding 'eastern' as well as western popular culture and could select, mix and match what they wanted to listen to and emulate in terms of fashions and behaviour. Later in the decade, there were home-grown pop stars to add to the mix. Again, this was affected by availability and region but increasingly even in the small cities, there was access to *Gangtai* as well as English language pop music. I saw this for myself as I travelled around China. In the mid-1980s, it was the private businesses, an important sector of the changing economy, that were more likely to promote the *Gangtai* culture as it appeared more modern in all senses and definitely fashionable. Small, private shops newly opened in the town where I first lived blasted out such pop music from morning till night in the hope of attracting attention and custom. Privately owned restaurants would do likewise. Sometimes the copies were obviously far removed from the originals and the sound quality left a lot to be desired but nevertheless it was worth playing, in the eyes of the *getihu* owners.

Love songs based on *Gangtai* models began to compete for popularity with disco and 'energy' (*jinge*) songs that were more inspired by the mainstream pop music of Europe and North America (Jones, 1992:17). All this added to the cacophony on the streets of the main towns. There were also 'jail songs' (*qiuge*) whose lyrical scope was limited to the laments of youthful convicts and rusticated urban youth of the Cultural Revolution. Although produced as part of the state-owned network, their lyrics were often indirect criticisms of the regime and this gave them a degree of popularity. They were unofficially adopted by the *getihu*, supposedly as symbolic of their 'marginalization and disillusionment' (Jones:45).

Young intellectual audiences were both advantaged and disadvantaged in this process of selecting from what was available and putting together their own youth sub-cultural variations. Financially they were probably worse off than many of their *getihu* counterparts but because of living in urban areas, had access to different materials and those with language skills could follow English language pop songs more readily. I would argue that they were self-conscious and critical in what they chose to accept and reject in terms of constructing their own subcultural identity and this matched their behaviour in other areas such as ideological and political explorations.

There were definite links, for example, between the 'roots-seeking' phase when intellectuals were trying to discern what was the true nature of the Chinese identity after the enormous shifts of the reform decade, and several popular music phenomena. 'Roots seeking' involved critical examination of Chinese culture and tradition in order to find a suitable essence upon which to build a viable modern identity. This again evokes the process of selective modernity previously mentioned, and a link can be made with the *He Shang* series. Jones goes so far as to state that the ideologies and self-perceptions of both student activists and rock musicians in 1989 were clearly indebted to the 'cultural self reflection' of River Elegy. These developments were present also in popular music with a mixture of the past and the present taking place particularly after mid-decade when problems with reforms were becoming more obvious.

There was a brief 'craze' in 1987, for example, for the television version of the Chinese classic 'The Dream of the Red Mansion' (*Hong Lou Meng*). The series, viewed by millions often on newly acquired television sets, was very popular as it retained the original story but packaged in such a way as to be suitable for mass consumption and entertainment. In some ways, it 'soap opera-ized' the classic.[5] There were criticisms as well as praise for such ventures but its popularity was facilitated, it can be argued, by the music and songs accompanying the series which were classical in style but sung by popular stars of the time. Cassettes of the soundtrack sold well and it appealed to young intellectuals because it was a modern phenomenon with an intellectual basis. It was something traditionally Chinese to be proud of in the face of all the competing imports.

There may have been indirect political references in the programmes but many people bought the cassettes because they thought the songs and music were good. Although it was not strictly 'pop' music, it was packaged and sold as such. The interaction between media is also important because this intensified as the decade developed, as elsewhere in the world, with film soundtracks, television shows and pop songs being closely intertwined, often with one promoting the other. This is nothing new, and Jones points out that in China, cinema has served as the 'principal medium for the dissemination of pop music since the 1920s' (*op. cit*:9). The level of sophistication of this media mix, however, increased in the 1980s because of technology and the introduction of a market economy.

There was another fad for the '*Xibei Feng*' (Northwest Wind) in the following year and this was 'a style that fused the folk music of North West China with disco and rock rhythms' (Jones:55). It quickly gained widespread popularity by combining the old with the new in an acceptable fashion for consumers, particularly discerning young intellectuals who sought something they could feel patriotic and proud about, again being selective about tradition and modernity.

By the key year of 1988, the pop music cultural mix was in place and the potential for the ideological battles which could accordingly be played out, as Jones implied, as well as the commercial battles for sales. It did seem that there was a merging of trends within the pop music genre and this meant that youthful audiences could read it in different ways along the anti/pro-establishment continuum. This is possibly what Jones means by 'negotiated content' (*op. cit*:52). China had its own pop stars by this time, like Cui Jian who had a unique and sometimes confrontational style which went beyond emulating *Gangtai* stars. He became something of a hero for young intellectuals and as such a dangerous person to the state.

My own students and informants were part of all this subcultural activity. Whenever we were out together, on excursions to local parks for example, we sang songs in vogue at that time. The students played them at parties and other gatherings and were happy to teach me Chinese pop songs such as those from the *Xibei Feng* which they took as part of their generational identity. Some songs specifically made references to the generations, such as 'What's the 90s gonna bring?' (*Jiushi Niandai zenmeyang*) by Xie Chengqiang.[6] Along with their fondness for dancing, pop songs can be viewed as generational accessories. Both younger and older parts of the generation were enthusiastic about pop music trends although the younger ones had more time and money to dedicate to them. This pop music was, however, basically '*tongsu*' or conformist and could be criticised for its simplistic fusion of modernity and feudalism.

One popular '*Gangtai*' song was '*Genzhe ganjue zou*' ('Go with your feelings') by a Taiwanese star. According to Gold, it was 'used to sum up the extremely volatile situation of Spring 1989' (1993:907) but was popular before that. The idea of 'going with your feelings' and 'grasping your dreams' as the song suggests must have appeared attractive to students and other Chinese youth who had few choices about where they were going in life, facing state job assignments for example, and they were trying to carve out a small piece of personal space and choice whenever possible. Another popular song considered vexing questions about life, whether it is best to go or stay, whether the sun in the sky is brighter than moonlight reflected on the water and so on.[7] The answer to all these questions was '*wo bu zhidao*' that is, 'I don't know'. That just about summed up many young intellectuals attitudes at that insecure time. They didn't know what was going to happen or what to do for the best in a changing society.

Another extremely popular song, much discussed since 1989, was Cui Jian's '*Yiwu suoyou*' which became known as the 'students' anthem' because the lyrics were about the 'one who had nothing'. The hero in this song pleads with his girlfriend to go with him, to love him even though he has nothing to offer apart from his freedom. Many students identified with the character in this song and the sentiments behind the words. 'We too have nothing, not even the freedom he sings of which we would like', I was told. It was frequently sang during the protests of 1989 but had been around since 1986.

A group of students presented me with a collection of the most popular songs at the beginning of 1989 as a going away gift and a reminder of our time together. The collection also served, unexpectedly, as a reminder of the tumultuous times to follow. There were both *Xibei* and *Gangtai* songs that I had come to know off by heart because of the students' patient tutoring. When I returned to China in 1990, these songs were still popular and some had graduated to video and were available at the increasing numbers of *karaoke* outlets in the major cities for commercial entertainment purposes. Yet there were still subversive elements to some of them, especially ones like '*Yiwu suoyou*'.

Several other popular songs came from an award-winning film of 1988, *Hong Gaoliang* (Red Sorghum) which developed something of a cult status amongst students. Jones (*op. cit*:55) also makes the links between this and the *Xibei Feng* as well as *He Shang*. Films and cinema will be considered as another part of the generational identity. As the interviewee Lili pointed out, films, books, newspapers and periodicals, had all become very popular in the 1980s, showing more freedom in the exchange of ideas.

The Films of a Generation

Generally speaking, watching films was a popular activity although it was done increasingly in smaller audiences later in the decade with cinema attendances in decline. Different types of films became available throughout the 1980s due to the open door policy although not all of them were 'legal', as already mentioned. I was warned by officials when I first arrived in China, not long after the 'anti-spiritual pollution' campaign, not to assist anyone in the distribution of 'yellow' or pornographic materials.

Going to the cinema was relatively cheap in the early 1980s so it was popular for students and there was very little else to do. Living in crowded dormitories with a dull routine and only a few leisure activities, students were pleased to go even to a cold and dank cinema to watch something for a bit of escapism. Sometimes films were shown on campus and attracted large numbers. It often did not matter what was shown because it was something to do. Some were comedies whilst others contained more serious political messages. The 'new ideology' of reform encouraged films with elements of consumerism. I remember one film in 1984 made in Guangzhou about the burgeoning, glamourous Chinese fashion world. It told the story of a group of entrepreneurs overcoming the odds to make a successful business and was very pro-reform. After being transported temporarily to a world of glamour and nice clothes the audience trooped out into the rain, most of them wearing the old Mao tunics and dark overalls so typical of Chinese communism, with hardly a splash of colour.

The generational notion comes up once more when considering film makers in the post-Mao period. The so-called 'fifth generation' of the 1980s includes Chen Kaige whose best known films include 'Yellow Earth' and 'The Big Parade'. His colleague Zhang Yimou is particularly known for 'Raise the Red Lantern' and 'Ju Dou' (Rayns, 1992). Their films addressed some of the key social, political and ideological problems of the 1980s as best they could without going beyond the official limits, although these were shifting and unclear. There was a reassessment of the Cultural Revolution period in some of their films just as there was in society in general in the early 1980s and some of them won international acclaim for their efforts. The Chinese authorities were usually slower to give them credit because there were some subversive elements to their films, a point not lost on young intellectual audiences. Apart from possible political problems, there were very definite financial constraints in the reform era as state-owned studios suffered cutbacks. Large-scale communist propaganda films were no longer required and the market was changing. Frequently film makers had to look to foreigners for funding for new ventures and it was not easy for them to compete.

Aside from more intellectual offerings, however, many young people enjoyed foreign films which were part of the *Gangtai* culture, made in Hong Kong and Taiwan. Kung-fu films were popular and Chinese film studios churned out such productions in order to make money. These were also a combination of the old and the new with stories of Shaolin monks in historical periods overcoming evil through their martial arts skills. Watching the expertise of the actors was pleasurable for students, who were often powerless and even quite weak physically. I noticed that there were occasional fads for learning martial arts amongst students, possibly inspired by such films.

Western films were increasingly allowed on general release in China, intensifying the diversity of the cinema in the 1980s just as with pop music. Young people enjoyed watching them for several reasons, not only for escapism but to gain some knowledge about life in the USA or elsewhere. Of course some of the

images could be distorted but they entered the popular consciousness and probably contributed to the going abroad tide. The
interviewee Liu claimed that there was some such effect of
watching 'American movies'. She said that 'I've seen a lot of
American movies, around 20. Every weekend on campus there
are about three or four American movies'. This was in 1988.
According to Lili, 'After reform started, we learned through
magazines and TV many things about the foreign countries. I get
the American ideas from magazines and newspapers, and also see
which American films which have a large circulation in China'.

Young intellectuals had their favourites, and certainly the
previously mentioned *Hong Gaoliang*, directed by Zhang Yimou,
was one which tied in with other aspects of their generational
identity. It brought together 'roots seeking' and modernity as well
as national identity. The film depicted 'peasants' during the
anti-Japanese struggle and apart from very serious parts also had
comic elements with popular songs such as '*Meimei, ni dadan de
wang qian zou*' ('Sister, Go Bravely Forward'). As Jones noted, the
song is 'to be shouted, and its popularity lay in the fact that
listeners were gratified by shouting along' (*op. cit*:57). It also
apparently 'indirectly inspired' one of the creators of River Elegy,
thus with yet another link in trends and explorations.

Not all young intellectuals were spending all their time singing,
dancing, watching films or playing around with the opposite sex.
Many remained studious but there were plenty of distractions.
Some other key activities will be discussed next.

Reading and Other Pastimes

Reading falls between education and entertainment and Deng's
generation were reading widely and eclectically. Some students
were following reading lists more self-orientated than those set by
their lecturers and were keenly reading an increasingly diverse
range of books. Those with English skills bought and borrowed
imported and pirated books which were available and often quite
cheap in the '*neibu*' sections of bookstores. These were for internal
consumption only and not supposed to be seen by foreigners who
would recognise the lack of copyright permission.

From time to time there would be 'crazes' for the works of
foreign writers such as Nietzsche or Alvin Toffler which would run
their course and die out. It appeared that young intellectuals were

picking up ideas, becoming interested in works that were once forbidden to them, then dropping them again quite quickly in favour of something new. There was an element of exploration and selection going on amongst Deng's generation, especially the younger members. Western philosophy, politics, social comment-ary and so on were permitted reading material and they were working their way around them, often in such crazes which would also attract media attention. I was sometimes asked for my views about particular philosophers and writers during class discussions and at the English Corners. It was often the case that reading foreign writers was part of the self-education process many young intellectuals were conducting to supplement their university courses.

Their own reading was probably more interesting to them than that set by lecturers which was often viewed as out of date. There was a potentially subversive element to this otherwise laudable effort to improve their own levels and types of knowledge. There could be a craze for writings which were critical of the Chinese system of politics, for example. Gao mentioned his reading of western political works and how important these were for provid-ing information to young Chinese intellectuals. Popularity of such works could indicate trouble for the authorities amongst their well-read young intelligentsia.

They also read a variety of newspapers and magazines. Liu said she did not believe that Chinese newspapers were very useful because they were 'boring' and sometimes 'do not tell the truth'. She read the *China Daily*, the English language newspaper and also *Reference News* (*Can Kao Xiaoxi*). Yu said that some people found infomation by reading stories about the West in newpapers and magazines. There had been an increasing numbers of publications available in China, both Chinese and foreign, which greatly expanded the range of information about life in other countries.

Other popular activities involved the playing of various games such as bridge and mahjong and I often saw students busy with their preferred pastimes in the dormitories. Bridge was popular because it was relatively new to China and considered as an intellectual pursuit. There was also an association with Deng Xiaoping whose passion for bridge playing was widely publicised. Such games would have been forbidden previously because of bourgeois connotations.

This survey of the main activities of Deng's generation indicates strongly their search for self-identity and knowledge and this is also suggested in their ideas about figures of respect in past and present Chinese society, to be discussed next.

A 'NO MORE HEROES' SYNDROME? CHANGING ROLE MODELS

The interviewees were asked to consider who, if anyone, they used to consider worthy of respect and who occupied that place in the contemporary period. The retrospection involved a matter of only a few years for some whereas for the older respondents it may have been more than ten years. The citing of different people could be partly attributed to the age span of the sample but shifting expectations are also partly responsible. The relative success of political socialisation in its promotion of conformity to real life as well as the model heroes also has to be considered. If there were similar references to model heroes, for example, this could be indicative of success for the authorities in promoting the official discourse. Shifts in the patterns of awarding respect for other people in society can be viewed as linked to the changing expectations as society was transformed by reforms.

Other intellectuals, both those known personally by respondents and those outside their own spheres of interaction, were considered important when asked to remember anybody they had respected. Some respondents referred to people they knew rather than notable people in society. Li, for example, cited her boyfriend along with her parents which was a very personal response. Others mentioned groups such as teachers and scientists rather than individuals in contrast to those who referred to outstanding people or model heroes. These variations, it can be argued, show respondents as possessing their own criteria for awarding respect, not always in line with the official ones. The criteria were more individually than socially inspired. On the level of social interaction, young people had received the help and support of parents, teachers and friends and chose to respect these real people.

Variations can also be attributed to the replacement of Maosim by Dengism. As with the evaluation of social position, ideas of respect were in a state of flux because socialist values had been called into question. It was perhaps no longer clear who they should respect, either past or present. Lu pointed to the 'disappearance of individual worship' in the contemporary context. 'Though some people still have such things, it's gradually disappeared. What people are pursuing now is facts and truth. In the past people only worshipped individuals but now they'll never do that'.

Past Models and Respected People

Lu had referred to the personality cults that frequently accompany totalitarian leaders such as Mao but when recalling the past, only five respondents mentioned him although his political presence and influence had been overwhelming across the decades.

Even during his lifetime, Mao's reputation went through peaks and troughs and it further declined after his death with an official reassessment of his policies. It was admitted that he had made mistakes and was viewed as losing his ability later in life to 'do things reasonably' according to Zhang who was at middle school when he died. There is an indication of political resocialisation occuring with Mao judged in the light of the contemporary context rather than the previous one. Zhang claimed that in the past people had only 'respected Mao because of the propaganda. If we knew what he was, we wouldn't respect him anymore'. He compared him to the first American president. 'Washington made a good foundation for the USA but Mao didn't for China', he said. Taking the analogy further he described how a state, like a building, needs a good base. 'If the foundation is better, the building is good. But a bad foundation leads to a bad building. We need to reform because the foundation is poor but maybe we have already built ten or twenty floors.' He blamed Mao for many of the contemporary problems in China.

The status of Mao had been keenly discussed at Beijing University. Outside the library where the young Mao had worked, was a large statue of him, typical of those that had once graced most campuses in the 1960s and 1970s. Many had already been removed but the one at *Beida* remained, perhaps because of these special links. In mid-April 1988, however, not long after the poster campaign, this statue was suddenly removed. Some young people were angry about this. They claimed not to be in favour of a personality cult around the past leader but noted his special association with the university. The statue was 'ugly' and an unhappy reminder of the past but they felt that its sudden removal was disrespectful. For others, it was not so much the statue being taken away that was at issue but the manner of its departure: overnight and secretive. 'Bedroom conferences' were held about this event and its implications yet students were unwilling to air their opinions too openly.

Putting interview responses and the statue incident together, there are mixed messages about Mao. He was no longer revered but it was not clear exactly how young people should evaluate him in the reform period when many of his policies were being overturned. This reevaluation was also referred to by Qiu. He had respected Mao when he was at elementary and middle school. After the Cultural Revolution, however, 'I changed, I changed with a lot of people because I know a lot more things. In the past the propaganda made a big effect on us, especially in a family like mine'. His parents were communists but his experience of Maoist policies and subsequent changes in the official evaluation of these caused an attitudinal shift in terms of the former leader. Generally speaking, ideas and ways of thinking had changed, as Gao explained.

> Ideas changed a lot. You can't imagine how much it changes. I remember when I was in middle school, I worked a few months in a small factory. When I heard Chairman Mao was dead, I felt very sad, like everybody else in China. At least 90 per cent of people felt sad. We can't imagine what we will do without Chairman Mao, what our life will become. It seems we can't do anything without him . . . we had such ideas about one man. But nowadays after only ten years I think most people will not think like that. Some of them forget Chairman Mao because we realise that he cannot decide their lives. Some of them think they should protect themselves by themselves. Ideas have changed a lot especially in the young generation.

It can be argued that the revised evaluation of Mao represents a strand of compliance with official policies. Qiu, Gao and Zhang had respected Mao when they had been taught to do so; later they ceased to do this at the behest of the new regime. They can be seen as accepting the propaganda even though Qiu was quite adamant that they would not be 'cheated' again. In one sense this was true but there remained a tendency to believe aspects of the official ideology. This can be seen in the lack of references to Lin Biao and Liu Shaoqi, two former high ranking Party officials who had been discredited by the CCP. There had been an anti-Lin Biao campaign after his somewhat mysterious death in 1971. His status in the reform decade was still uncertain and there were few official mentions of him.

Liu Shaoqi, who had been classified as a moderniser at a time when the leadership were stressing class struggle, had more in common with the contemporary leadership but by 1988 had not been totally rehabilitated. The absence of these figures from the students' replies implies some success for the official propaganda. If respondents had been less conformist they may have cited Lin Biao as the one person who tried to oppose Mao, or Liu Shaoqi, who died in 1969, as a forward-thinking reformist who was ahead of his time. Neither of these judgements were verbalised. Respondents may have been ambivalent about the two personalities and avoided mentioning them. This could also have accounted for the relative absence of Mao in the replies. Avoiding the issue may have been easier and less risky for those concerned about the effect of these conversations with a foreign researcher.

Respondents felt more confident about citing Zhou Enlai as the person they most respected when they were younger and his name was mentioned more than any other. This past popularity and respect for Zhou Enlai was also in line with the contemporary official doctrine. He was not only a revolutionary hero and important political leader but also a moderniser. No other former leaders were mentioned, such as Hua Guofeng who had succeeded temporarily to the leadership after Mao's death. He seemed to have made little impression on the respondents in the light of subsequent leadership changes and policy shifts.

Zhou's predominance can be partly accounted for by successful ideological work carried out by the Party to make him the hero of the 1980s generation. His image was also subject to the process of reworking mentioned above and was more easily associated with people's everyday experiences of politics, particularly during the 1960s when his influence had curbed some of the Red Guard excesses. 'When he was alive, we were still very young. That was during the Cultural Revolution and we loved him very much', commented Wen. 'He always offered help to those who had difficulties'. Chen also perceived him as doing things 'totally for the benefit of the people' in contrast to politicians who cared only for themselves. This comparison with other leaders who were seen to create difficulties for intellectuals, as Mao had done, was not untypical.

'Premier Zhou did a lot under difficult conditions. At that time the situation was unfavourable for him but he still tried to help others', remarked Lili enthusiastically although she was quite young when he died, as were a number of his other supporters. They held vivid images of him, probably from educational and propaganda materials. 'He was a strong and good man', said Lu. Zhou Enlai was mentioned by both younger and older members of the sample as the intellectuals' hero who attempted to improve the educational situation of China. He was also seen to possess diplomatic capability. 'His ways of dealing with people were worthy of admiration', remarked Wen. 'When he met people for the first time, he always managed to remember their names and their specific conditions', she continued.

Zhou received none of the criticisms which were levelled at Mao. Respondents' admiration appeared as sincere rather than the result of propaganda campaigns, but the latter had clearly had had an effect. They were judging him by his actions rather than his words. At the end of the Cultural Revolution, when both he and Mao were terminally ill, it was Zhou who was destined to become the 'people's leader', according to respondents' comments. He may have benefited in terms of respect by not holding the post of supreme leader of the Chinese state as Mao had done. It was Mao who was subsequently blamed for the problems.

This sort of process of association may have been the reason why Deng Xiaoping was also rarely cited. Only two gave his name as someone they respected when they were at middle school yet overseas Deng had been 'Man of the Year' twice, in 1978 and 1985 (ZGQN, 1988:6). Hua referred to Deng elsewhere in the interview, along with Zhou Enlai. 'I personally admire two Chinese leaders, Deng Xiaoping and Zhou Enlai', he stated. As the main figure of authority in the government for ten years, Deng received both praise and criticism from young intellectuals. His relatively low profile could be due to the fact that unlike Zhou Enlai, Deng was politically impotent during most of the Cultural Revolution, having been labelled a 'capitalist roader' and exiled to the countryside. He had few opportunities to endear himself to the people because he was not in the public arena.

He was also still alive whereas Zhou was dead. It is more of a risky venture to evaluate the contribution and significance of a living leadership figure in China. The political scene has been subject to a number of shifts with manoeuvring by both Party personnel and citizens. The example of what could happen to people who criticised Deng Xiaoping occurring at the outset of the reform period probably still influenced young people ten years on. Respondents seemed reluctant to mention him possibly because they were anxious about having their views recorded by a foreigner. Also, discussing people considered worthy of respect implicitly involves an expression of opinion about China's political arrangements. By presenting positive and negative evaluations of former leaders, respondents were offering the qualities which they respected in politicians and those they found unacceptable. There were indirect criticisms of contemporary politicians in their comments. Too few, by implication, possessed the qualities of Zhou Enlai. Respondents had little to say about Mao and Deng yet their aspirations for the future were closely associated with these '*yinghao ren*'.

Another shift away from earlier patterns of respect is the case of teachers, heavily criticised during the 1960s, along with other academics, because of Maoist policies and their inherent attack on intellectuals. Teachers were mentioned almost as frequently as Zhou Enlai, either as part of a social group or as individuals whose assistance and hard work had earned the respect of their charges. Respecting teachers is also in line with the high value placed on education by those actively involved in it, that is students and young teachers who formed most of this sample. Teachers were also closer to the respondents, actively helping them in their education. Feelings of gratitude coexisted with sentiments of respect in some statements. 'I respect teachers because from entering school, they told me how to face society, how to do things and how to think. I think teachers are the most hardworking people in China', said Chen. 'An English teacher' cited Hua who had himself entered this profession. 'He liked me and encouraged me for which I am grateful'.

Other people cited were parents, mentioned by two respondents. Karl Marx only managed two references, implying that the 'father of socialism' was not a modern model of admiration. Zhou, Xiu and Yu claimed not to have respected anyone in particular in the past. Xiu said this was because she was a 'romantic' and not easily influenced by others. Yu said that he could not find a person in reality to respect but 'could just imagine one. My ideal is a fair person, he could help others and he must also care about our society and our country. Mustn't be private, selfish and he must be a learned man'. This ideal is an expression of hope, perhaps also of unfulfilled expectations. Education is an important quality which reflects the background of the respondent, and the strong link between patriotic ideals and educated youth has already been described. The fact that Yu felt the need to invent a hero indicates the rejection of officially sanctioned ones.

Contemporary Models

By the late 1980s, the 'no more heroes' phenomenon had become a more serious issue related to a high level of political alienation. A majority of respondents, 14 of them, claimed to respect 'no-one in particular' at the time of questioning. 'Now we cannot do as we did in the past. People just stress themselves, they are just self-centred', claimed Lili, linking this to the reform decade's social context of competition and materialism. Wen said that 'Nowadays, the worship of others is insignificant'. This view was echoed by Hua who said simply 'Nobody now. I'm too preoccupied with my work. I get so tired that the only thing I respect is sleep'.

Deng Xiaoping was mentioned only twice in the contemporary period. The relatively conformist Lu referred to his record of achievement. 'Although he is very old he still gets some good ideas such as economic reforms for people in the country. He changed a lot of ideas, a lot of things so is most respected', he said. On the verge of going abroad to study, Lu did not say anything which could have been considered as radical. Qiu felt that Deng Xiaoping, Zhao Ziyang and Hu Yaobang were all 'great men because China is very hard to manage. I think they are honest to the construction of China, to the future. I respect them'. Qiu's positive evaluation may have been linked to the fact that without them, he may not have had the opportunity to go to university. On the whole, however, it seemed that Deng's standing had not changed much since the earlier period. In spite of being behind *gaige kaifang* policies, young intellectuals were reserving judgement possibly because he was linked to the perceived social decline of intellectuals and the problems of reforms.

Deng's proteges, Hu Yaobang and Zhao Ziyang, were only mentioned by Qiu whereas Fang Lizhi was cited twice, the same as Deng Xiaoping, as a contemporary figure of respect. Zhang held him up as a possible role model for young people. 'His spirit is worth the youth generation to study. He dares to speak out. I think this is good for the country but most of the people lack this spirit'. This unofficial role model was a cause of concern for the government because of his obvious influence upon young intellectuals. Gao expressed some support for Fang and other leading intellectuals. He felt that they understood educated youth and should be respected to some extent but with reservations. 'We don't respect them very much, we don't know them but agree with their ideas'. Perhaps the levels of respect awarded to people in the past were not possible in the changed circumstances and young intellectuals were careful about who they admired and trusted.

Guo discussed the changing fortunes of scientists in general over the years, reminiscing upon the stress placed upon technology in 1978. 'Scientists were respected a lot. Students wanted to be scientists'. The situation had changed for the worse because 'scientists are not respected in recent years. They get little money and live in poverty but some *getihu* and businessmen are rich'. This was a common theme of earlier discussions and links patterns of respect to the changing social circumstances of a particular group of intellectuals. In spite of an emphasis upon the four modernisations, scientists were not the most respected group and the words of politicians had to be treated carefully.

Sports and singing stars were referred to by two respondents as people they respected which indicates another aspect of change. There were few mentions of model heroes such as Lei Feng, although all the respondents had been subject to emulation campaigns at various points in their lives. The official models presented to young people thoughout their primary political socialisation had not gone unquestioned and there appeared to be a process of reworking the official messages to match actual experiences. Sample data supported Hooper's observation that young people were not easily impressed with the models which were more likely to provoke cynicism than admiration or respect.

Only Zhao cited the official model of Lei Feng. As one of the youngest in the sample, he was not even born at the time of the first 'Study from Lei Feng' campaign. He claimed to admire 'those people praised by the government such as Lei Feng and Zhang Haidi and also the leaders of the country'. His apparent acceptance of the models shows that mass campaigns among youth were not complete failures but his compliance was in line with a relatively conservative stance on other issues. Coming from the outlying Gansu province, he did not share the cynicism of his more urban counterparts. He criticised young intellectuals who 'separate themselves from society, forming a kind of ideal kingdom (*lixiang guojia*)'. Zhao is not typical in this respect as no-one else referred to any of these socialist heroes as role models.

From these responses, it seemed that Deng's generation had a tendency to respect only one former political leader, that is Zhou Enlai. There was also a degree of mistrust of political leaders in power. The trend of not respecting anyone reflected the high levels of political alienation commented upon elsewhere. Several people noted that in a changing society the patterns of respect would alter. The unwillingness to respect anyone, especially the official models, suggested that Deng's generation were looking elsewhere for role models and that their behaviour could be influenced by people not officially sanctioned by the Party, such as Fang Lizhi and people within their own spheres of social interaction, such as friends.

To conclude this chapter, it can be seen that Deng's generation were involved in a diverse range of activities, from making money to watching films, with explorations within the ideological as well as leisure spheres. To some observers, such as veterans of previous political campaigns, this generation of students was 'immature' and not at all concerned with politics. 'Their interests focused on playing mahjong and winning a place at a US university' (Macartney, 1990:3). Few of them attended the 'salons' for discussions on democracy or showed much interest in these matters. On the other hand 'drinking parties were common' (*op. cit*:4).

The disappointed older activists looked anxiously to the younger generation to continue previous struggles. This may have been a misunderstanding of the strategies which were attempts to change things or at least offer some diversions in a situation where it was felt not much could be done. The subculture of young intellectuals may have appeared as largely conformist or 'official' but there were unofficial elements with many of them doing what they wanted to do, rather than what they were told to do, whether it was in their personal relationships or what they were reading. The enthusiasm for western things, including philosophical ideas as well as music and fashion, often went beyond what was considered acceptable by the government who had, ironically, made such interests possible by opening up China to the outside world.

By the spring of 1989, students and other young intellectuals showed themselves ready to abandon some of these activities and take up a more overtly political cause. The diversions of previous years were put to one side as they expressed their pent up grievances after the death of Hu Yaobang in April 1989. It should also be remembered that going on protest marches and holding meetings could be viewed as a form of enjoyment but ultimately the demonstrations were serious, as, indeed, was the outcome. Trends within the political sphere will be examined next.

5 A Democratic Generation? Conformity and Activism

Deng's generation appears to be one that rejected official political arrangements and, in seeking to instigate change, became associated with pro-democracy movements. The reform decade began and ended with two such movements and political alienation and apathy were rife amongst young intellectuals at the outset of the decade. The younger ones were, at first, more optimistic but they came to share the frustrations of their seniors. By the late 1980s organisations such as the CYL were viewed as little more than useful for arranging parties. Apathy did not always translate itself into political dissidence and it will be shown how a pragmatic approach was more likely with some forms of activism acceptable to the young intellectuals at certain points in time. The notable outbreaks of protests in 1980, 1985 and the winter of 1986–87 have already been referred to and views about these protests will be discussed as well as their implications.

Whilst there was a degree of disillusionment, there was also conformity. This will be explored further in the attempt to explain why Deng's generation ultimately became associated with mass political activism in early 1989. They did not passively accept the political ideology presented to them but reworked it for their own purposes. Attention will be paid to the level of attachment to conformity and activism, and the possible reasons why they were adopted or abandoned at any particular point. Deng's generation can be summed up as one which had learnt to cautiously take calculated risks in the political sphere.

Replies to a number of politically oriented questions will be discussed along with other data to elucidate their political characteristics. Such issues were approached indirectly because even in the relatively open year of 1988, punishments were still likely for anyone overtly critical of the state, especially in front of foreigners. The outbreak of a poster campaign at the time of the first interviews heightened this sensitivity. Several interviewees

159

were quite outspoken and some expressed views not only about student movements but also the government's handling of them. Additional comments were made in confidence with anxiety expressed about the repercussions if they were discovered by the authorities (see the Appendix).

Political Activism and Conformity

Activism is neither inherently conformist nor oppositional and the divide is not always obvious. Conformist activism was found to be not so clear-cut in, for example, Chan's work on the Red Guard generation (1985). The aim here is to discern the radical from the conformist in the political thought and actions of Deng's generation. Activism could include putting up *dazibao*, holding political forums or 'salons' and participating in demonstrations and other protests. These proscribed activities were observed during student movements throughout the 1980s and whilst not all those who took part can be thought of as radicals, this behaviour can be viewed as a form of dissidence. Zhen, an activist supporter, was quick to point out that '*Dazibao* are illegal and demonstrations. You will have to get the permission from the government'.

Lying somewhere in the middle is nonconformity which implies a rejection or suspension of the acceptance of the dominant political orthodoxy but does not necessarily entail conscious activism. It will be argued that this is where many of Deng's generation could be located, being ambivalent or alienated conformists weakly attached to this strategy but unlikely to be won over to activism unless some significant event occurred, as happened in 1989. Conformity and activism are also linked to social closure processes because they may be related to the demaraction of young intellectuals from other groups. This, again, was the case in 1989, when young intellectuals tried to show their historic role as critics of the government by the adoption of activism. The support of other social groups was welcome but they were the ones who had to occupy, for example, Tiananmen Square and physically exclude other groups in a literal expression of social closure.

Respondents showed conformist traits whilst simultaneously being dismissive of official propaganda. It is unwise to slot people firmly into one camp or the other because both were contingent upon several factors, being tentative, changeable and liable to be abruptly abandoned. Interviewees also tended to oscillate between the two stances, with both acceptance and rejection of official ideas in their views, indicating that they were in a state of flux. This was because they were maturing at the same time as China was undergoing rapid transformations. Few respondents admitted to participation in protest campaigns but that does not indicate they were all conformists. Several indicated tendencies more on one side than the other, such as Lu, a relative conformist along with Xiu. There were no obvious political activists except for Wang who referred to his involvement in earlier protests. Gao mentioned some college disturbances in the late 1970s in which he had been involved.

Inter-generational Comparisons

There appeared to be a prevailing attitude of 'we won't get fooled again' which implied a number of comparisons with the past. Deng's generation saw themselves as more politically sophisticated than their predecessors who were judged as naive and misled. They emphasised their own maturity achieved partly as a result of the *gaige kaifang* policies. This generation were more aware of what was happening in the world and their higher education added to this feeling of confidence.

Interviewees' comments confirmed their belief in their own generational distinctiveness as being more sophisticated. Other sources of information also pointed to this conclusion. Deng's generation wished to be more active and influential, which contrasted to prevailing perceptions of their predecessors within the communist era, especially the 1950s generation, described by Qiu as 'tame'. He said 'In the past, people, especially the intellectuals, were as tame as sheep. They daren't do anything the leaders didn't allow. Now very few people mind what the leaders say. They are not willing to starve. They are not tame anymore.'

Similarly, Liu believed that 1950s youth ' . . . did what the Party told them to'. Chen said that this generation had ' . . . just devoted themselves to society', putting collective interests first as intructed by the Party. This attitude was raised elsewhere. The consensus view was that 1950s young intellectuals were politically compliant. Zhen felt that many youth in the 1950s and 1960s obeyed the slogan of 'do what the Party wants you to do'. She also felt that her generation sometimes rebelled and had changed their ideas. The passivity of the 1950s generation was contrasted to the activist tendencies of the 1980s generation. 'Now they dare to think about what they should do but in the past only did what was demanded by the state.'

The 1960s generation were criticised for being negatively active in politics. Liu described them as 'really crazy' compared to the 1980s when things changed. 'We began to doubt many things, no longer take it for granted. Their thoughts are more active.' Wen claimed, similarly, that 'Now they dare to think about what they should do but in the past only did what was demanded by the state.' It was thought that Deng's generation were more likely to consider their actions, be more independent than their 1950s and 1960s counterparts and less prepared to unquestioningly follow the leadership. That they were unwilling to be held back was suggested by Xiu who characterised them as 'more active in thought than ever' and used a Chinese proverb to describe this. 'New born calves aren't afraid of tigers.' One informant pointed out that amongst older intellectuals there were ' . . . a lot of teachers, lecturers and professors who support the students. The students say a lot of things the adults want to say.' They may have done so in previous campaigns and been punished. This inter-generational comparison was also noted by Rice (1992) who described older intellectuals standing by and watching the students in 1989.

Qiu described how 'Most people had to think what the Party thought. They couldn't say anything different. As for doing, if you did something different from the Party, it was dangerous for you. You might be sentenced as anti-revolutionary. But after the Cultural Revolution there is a long course. At first people can think freely, then speak freely. Now, do freely. There is little danger to do or say. But still not absolutely free.' In comparison with those earlier periods, the late 1980s were relatively open and this perception was promoted by the authorities. In a similar vein was Yu's belief that the 'most important change is people's ideas. Nowadays people have their own brains to think. They don't believe what the government and leaders say. They don't believe it easily.' Restrictions did remain though on thinking, speaking and doing, and there were causing concern to young intellectuals.

It is noticeable, that these evaluations of previous generations as well as of their own were not unlike official ones. The Red Guard generation was frequently referred to by the authorities as one likely to go to political excess with their violent, anti-social behaviour and unquestioning acceptance of Maoism. It became, in fact, standard official practice to label any outbreak of protest action in the 1980s as unacceptable behaviour too reminiscent of the Red Guards and the *da luan* (chaos) they created. The authorities used that as some sort of guideline and always warned of a dangerous slippery slope back to the 'bad old days' if young people persisted with protests. An informant made this point, claiming that 'Old people always have the psychology of fearing that young people will do wrong. Many of them often show up the young people, how dangerous they were in the Cultural revolution.' One of the articles that angered the students and further inflamed feelings during Spring 1989, for example, was a key editorial comparing them to Red Guards (RMRB, 26 April 1989).

The students did not accept that their actions were in any way like those of the Red Guards but there was a tendency to perceive earlier generations of young intellectuals in the official terms. This indicates a degree of conformity to, rather than total rejection of, what had been preordained for them, at least at the level of ideology, by the 'old men' still in power. This extends to their own designated role as 'modernisation successors', or 'reformist youth', phrases used to describe the official model of Deng's generation.

This then calls into question their claims to be more open in their political thought. According to Zhao, they could compare 'the oriental culture with the western culture and form their own ideas and opinions', echoing the message of the *He Shang* series. Reformers had encouraged young people to 'open their minds' and 'seek truth from facts' but within the limits set by the CCP. The socio-economic context had changed but the Party had retained a paternalistic attitude, trying to control the political development of young intellectuals by ideological work (*sixiang gongzuo*) and propaganda. Official pronouncements warned that 'Some mistaken concepts have appeared such as "China lacks capitalism." Also, the mistaken idea of checks and balances, also democracy and freedom . . . the younger generation bear the mark of their time . . . they need to be guided in the concept of reform' (*Gaojiao yu Rencai*, 1988.3:1). According to the predominant views, however, they did not relish being subjected to this official guidance.

Complaints about the existing political arrangements often referred to the lack of democratisation, insufficient independence for intellectuals as well as lack of free media. Zhang was convinced that 'Young intellectuals realise our country should take democracy. It is hopeless without democracy. If a country is held by one person, the country is hopeless. This is true in the history of our country and other countries'. Gao expressed his belief that 'checks and balances' were needed in China and was critical of the one-party system which gave rise to student protests. Guo felt that young intellectuals should have ' . . . more power and higher position especially in leadership because the government officials are always quite old. They don't know many things that are happening in the outside world. They manage China like an army.' Some wished to continue the political debates of previous years and their hopes were related to these. It is probably likely that the tendencies towards activism were related to factions within the Party and their relative predomin-ance at any one point in time.

Whilst there was a degree of convergence between the official expectations and their emerging political characteristics, there were also indications that clashes of opinion were quite likely about acceptable forms of political behaviour. Inter-generational clashes can be the motor for social and political change and the 1980s young intellectuals were well aware of this but their attempts were usually thwarted by the continuing power of their seniors. Members of Deng's generation probably began to de-velop an antagonistic 'generational style' from around the mid-1980s, which was 'separate from and perhaps opposed to, the dominant style of the adult generation' (Murdock and McCron, 1976:196).

Early in the decade there had been clashes with the authorities as students attempted to hold western-style campaigning on campuses during the 1980 elections. Coming with the rise of the new regime, their enthusiasm for such campaigning was deemed unsuitable for China and the student activities were squashed. Without legitimate avenues for exercising their initiative, the confident younger members of the generation could also have been tempted to adopt unacceptable political tactics and the transformation of protests into something more radical and in conflict with the authorities. During the pro-democracy move-ment, this appeared to have happened.

The apparent trend of diminishing acquiescence in the political sphere amongst young intellectuals was expected to continue. There were implications that the 1980s generation had not been able to go far enough along the road of political independence. Liu, for example, felt that future young intellectuals would be 'more active in politics'. They would be less easily restrained than Deng's generation which still had some shortcomings because of the previous political movements and events of the 1980s. Gao saw a difference between his generational unit, that is older youth, and the younger ones in this respect. His response contains the predominant views of the sample about not only an emerging generation gap but also about unfulfilled expectations being passed on.

> I feel the generation below us are much more different to us. A gap has been formed between us ... I find this new generation of intellectual youth more brave than us. Maybe it's China's hope. In our generation, intellectual youth like us, dare not take advantage, or adventure. Maybe because of the experience of the Cultural Revolution we are law-abiding – *anfensi*. If they can live by their salary, they never think of taking some risk to make money, to make life better. But this new generation, many of them dare to take some risk, do something ... 1985 or 1984, maybe it's a line of demarcation for the 1980s generation.

Similarly, Zhang felt that 'The new generation is better than the old one. The next will be better than ours. I graduated in 1984 but nowadays students are more sensitive and more bold. The older generation is more obliged because of their experience. Most of them have no idea about political affairs. They were depressed too much during the Cultural Revolution and the anti-rightist movement.' He further explained how their predecessors in the 1950s were 'punished for speaking out' and this dampened their enthusiasm. 'They should take part in political affairs but nowadays most of them can't do it. They have misgivings – *gulu* – and are afraid of being punished by the leaders.'

Older educated youth were viewed, and viewed themselves, as deterred from political activity by adverse experiences. Zhen felt that 'The early 1980s youth still have some characteristics of the older generation. But later 80s youth, they do not . . . the big difference is that generally we are not as disciplined as the older generation.' Similarly, Xiu saw them as 'more active in thought than ever'. The line of demarcation for a possible generational divide was given as the mid-point in the decade. There were outbreaks of student protests at this time and it was possible that differences between the younger and older members of the reform generation were already setting the basis for a 'post-reform' generation.

Protesters during the movement at the end of 1986 were keen to express their support for reforms but wanted more opportunities as well as more rights and freedoms. Nathan (1990) reminds us that great hopes were raised and encouraged by Deng Xiaoping but the subsequent campaign against 'bourgeois liberalisation' in 1987 was a deep disappointment. The students did not necessarily wish to overturn government policies but different generational issues and priorities existed which were inadequately resolved through the usual CCP organisational channels. Deng's generation wished to see reforms continued but with ensured development of their own role as intellectuals with adequate recognition and rewards.

Any overlap of values between younger and older intellectuals did not mean there was agreement about the ways of expressing them. Hua felt that they were not expected to be so 'aggressive'. Unofficial movements fell outside the boundaries of acceptability even in the 1980s and represented a clash of opinions between young people and the authorities about the correct expression of patriotic values. According to Hua, student demonstrations in previous decades had been officially orchestrated ' . . . to serve the government's goals or foreign policies. Chairman Mao often led this kind of movement such as against the US invasion in Vietnam and Korea. There were no demonstrations organised by the students themselves.' This reiterates the view of these generations as politically compliant. Wang also pointed out that until the 1980s, there were few unofficial student demonstrations but after this time, they occured almost annually, even if usually centred on Beijing University. This form of activism distinguished Deng's generation from its predecessor but whether it was the behaviour of a vocal minority rather than being a more widespread characteristic can be considered.

The limits imposed by the older generation were not universally accepted. Intensifying ideological work amongst young people with increased doses of Marxism–Leninism–Mao Zedong thought was increasingly ineffective. ' . . . few bothered to pretend an interest in Marxism; many openly treated it as a joke' (Nathan, 1988:112). Rosen (1993) uncovered similar cynicism whilst Kelly (1990) noted how the CCP no longer seemed to have the ideological authority or the political will to induce intellectual conformity. As designated 'modernisation successors', young intellectuals viewed their seniors as offering outdated solutions to contemporary problems. Their words and advice often fell on deaf ears and this exacerbated the potential for inter-generational conflict. Their ambivalent conformity could be turned into activism given the existence of other key variables located within the social context and their own position.

FACTORS AFFECTING ACTIVISM AND CONFORMISM

Historical Antecedents

One important continuity was the self-perception of being a vanguard with a historic role to play. Patriotic values formed part of the official discourse and the links between notions of national salvation and young intellectuals remained strong. For Chen 'The most important thing university students have to have is responsibility for this country'. Hua similarly felt that 'Loving the motherland is their duty', a central value of Chinese communism present in much of the propaganda. Other respondents accepted this traditional activist role. According to Qiu 'If the students didn't hold demonstrations who in China can put pressure on the government? Only students have the right to speak the people's thoughts. Other people, except the students, dare not do this', reiterating the idea of their special role. This statement also implies a degree of immunity which other social groups did not possess. He gave the example of Shanghai where some 'workers' were arrested for taking part in the 1986 demonstrations but no students. The perception of protection could be a key factor. When this is strong, involvement in some form of activism might be more likely than when it is perceived as weak.

If speaking out was their historic duty, then it becomes a type of conformism although having the appearance of rebellion. The data indicated that a major source of motivation for activism was compliance with patriotic duty. Protesters wanted to draw attention not just to their own unsatisfactory situation but to the nation's problems. One informant expressed it in this way. 'It's very difficult for us to talk with the senior leaders so there is no other way. Demonstrations remind the government of some problems that exist in the society. The students just think about the fate of our country and want to change the bad things at present.' They shared a habitus predisposing them towards certain actions which also gave rise to this evaluation of activism in terms of fulfilling the role allocated to them as establishment intellectuals.

Other interviewees referred to something similar to Gao's notion of students having a 'sense of social responsibility' and concern with political affairs by holding demonstrations and writing posters. Others mentioned 'putting pressure' on the government and 'advising the state'. Guo said that 'They want to do something about China, want to take part in the reforms, to give their opinions and ideas openly, to tell people what they think about China.' This view was shared by Qiu who said that students did not want to 'overthrow the government, just only to show their feelings or ideas about the problems in society'. Such a reply distanced the respondent from open rebellion but participation in demonstrations could lead to the dissident label, depending on who was in power. Writing *dazibao* during the June poster campaign was viewed as in line with this tradition.

The historic importance of Beijing University was noted by many respondents. They expected this university to act as 'spokesman' for all the others. 'We should preserve this tradition because *Beida* is famous for its democratic and scientific attitude and if we do not do anything, there will be no-one to do it. *Beida* students are very sensitive to political change, they are quick minded', Chen said proudly. It could also be the case that they were an untypically active minority with a reputation to live up to but generally their actions were viewed as important. There was support for Chu's view that knowing and understanding *Beida* students leads to the understanding of all Chinese students.

According to Guo 'There is still some custom (*chuan tong*) or tradition at *Beida*, they're always very active in politics. During May Fourth and the Cultural Revolution, they were the first ones to say what we should do.' Sun also mentioned that *Beida* students 'have a kind of tradition, to be very radical', whilst Yang considered this as a 'characteristic' of this university. Students there may be expected to speak out and instigate political activity in certain situations. Activism may be partly institutional, like conformity, with some places more likely to start student movements than others. Students and staff might have such an ethos as part of their shared identity although this should not be over-emphasised. There is, however, some historical background for this view with campus culture contributing to predominant trends of behaviour.

Although university authorities may not take an openly confrontational line with the government they can promote a particular image of themselves which may then be taken up both by staff and students. In the mid-1980s, the Science and Technology University in Hefei also became known as a radical place and students there were seen to be influenced by the outspoken professor of astrophysics, Fang Lizhi, who taught there at that time. Fang was a respected academic of international renown but made no secret of his pro-democratic views and his speeches were enthusiastically greeted by younger intellectuals. He was something of a role model and his high profile gave him, to some extent, a degree of immunity especially when the reformists were predominant in the Party. The university saw the first actions in what transpired to be a nationwide student movement in late 1986.

Other Beijing campuses such as the Teachers' (Normal) University (*Beishida*), could be described as potential 'hotbeds' of activism. Not all the causes of activism and conformity, however, were related to the notion of historic duty or institutional identity. It was customary for young intellectuals to employ the rhetoric of the official discourse when expressing their personal interests.

Personal Interests: Rewards and Punishments

The tension between personal concerns and national ones was never far from the surface during the 1980s. At one level, student protesters may have been expressing disgust with the phenomenon of corruption amongst Party leaders, for example, but it was also prevalent in everyday life and may have been interfering with their own personal progress. Yu talked of students unable to put up with 'unfair things, degeneration, corruption, embezzlement, bureaucracy'.

There were also daily concerns and frustrations which may have motivated some people to write posters. Lili stated that '*dazibao* reflect many detailed problems in the universities', with 'terrible food in the canteens and drawbacks in the university administration' mentioned. She considered these to be important when discussing why some young people chose activism but pointed out that 'We can't compare the students to those revolutionaries before Liberation'. Contemporary activists in her view adopted this tactic to complain about their own problems rather than those of the nation. Although they may have felt that their posters were written in the 'May Fourth' spirit, in her view there was a good deal of difference.

Liu similarly claimed that few participants of the June 1988 campaign were really concerned with the death of postgraduate student Chai Qing Feng. 'Some students just wanted to use this activity, to take this opportunity for their own purpose', she said without stating what the ulterior motive might be. It was implied that 'causing trouble' may have been their aim but this was not specified. This view was not widely shared, however, with most respondents stressing that it was the general concerns about Chinese society which were uppermost in protesters' minds rather than the quality of canteen food. These issues were described as being symptomatic of a wider malaise brought about by the reform policies, as already shown.

Li and Zhen described the strategy of activism as 'risky' but 'brave'. On the other hand, there were possible rewards for those who conformed. Favourable life chances in terms of state jobs, secure incomes, promotion and possible perks, such as going abroad, were the main rewards expected in the late-1980s. Being noticed as a faithful Party follower could bring about tangible benefits and people with 'clean' political records, that is no history of misdemeanours, would be more likely to benefit. The latter point is important given the nature of this particular sample, many of whom were preparing or planning to go abroad. Lu, for example, seemed willing to conform because he was going to study in the West but he recognised that problems existed in China.

Others were conscious that their employment prospects could be detrimentally affected by activism. Guo claimed that 'After last year's demonstrations (1986–7) the government didn't want any students in work. So those students had to go into lower levels of work. The government punished the students because of the demonstration.' This view can be illustrated by the case of a young man, not a sample member, who had participated in these protests. His previously assigned 'iron rice bowl' was subsequently downgraded and his job failed to use his specialist skills; he suffered with poor conditions and few prospects. Although disappointed, he wished to stress that his reasons for demonstrating were patriotically inspired, wanting to contribute to his country's development. His sentiments had not been expressed in an acceptable manner, hence the punishment rather than reward.

Caution may have been a byword for the respondents when considering political matters given the fact that the authorities could deal very strictly with activists and their degree of immunity could not be guaranteed. Accepting the Party's own definitions, even if vague, can be viewed as one tactic for improving social position. Some other 'official liners' were possibly reiterating government slogans so as to appear as loyal subjects due to personal concerns or because they did want to be classified as political deviants.

Hua considered the personal files kept by the *danwei* as effective deterrents against activism. 'Every work unit pays attention to this file. If you participate in a demonstration or put up *dazibao*, this will be put as something bad in the file. It will directly affect the work arrangement after graduation.' He believed, wrongly as it turned out, that protests such as those of 1986 would not reoccur. In his own calculations, the risks were too great to offset the justifications which might have existed for adopting activism. The authorities were able to exercise control over students, behaviour which curbed their actions and maximised conformity.

The process of calculation is important because this is exactly what many young intellectuals were doing, either consciously or unconsciously, when selecting political tactics. They were working out the relative chances of conformism and activism paying off in terms of improving their life chances, status and so on. Given the system of rewards and punishments, it is not surprising that activism was considered as risky but it is suggested here that at some point, they may have calculated that it would succeed and, in fact, be seen as the ultimate form of conformism. This was the case in 1989 when the mass adoption of activism contrasted to one year earlier and those involved believed they were the 'true patriots'. They had also calculated that other political tactics and, indeed, other strategies, would not bring about the rewards they desired.

Punishments certainly acted as deterrents but there was another part to the calculation and that was the relative possibility of the punishments actually being meted out. Perceptions of immunity and safety become relevant here. It is suggested that in 1988 there was a sense that it was not very safe to demonstrate or continue the poster campaign with a high likelihood of punishment for the activists. During an informal discussion at the time of the June poster campaign, a young state employee expressed the opinion that if the situation had grown more serious, the government would have resorted to force, threatening imprisonment for student leaders and not just poor job assignments.

By 1989 this had changed to some extent, with a common perception, perhaps with the benefit of hindsight we could now say common self-deception, that a level of protection existed which would reduce the possibility of official reprisals. That is to say, the threat of punishments which the 1988 sample were so conscious of was suspended by those taking calculated risks in the Spring of 1989 and there was also an element of the peer group influence. The length of the 1989 movement and the way it spread to include millions of people would also add to this feeling of relative safety and protection from those punishments which young intellectuals were so keenly aware of. The importance of the peer group will be considered next.

Peer Group Influences

Parents and teachers were earlier shown as influential in shaping ambitions and expectations but whilst these social actors remain important, it emerged that the peer group became predominant within the higher education setting. Although there may have been differences between the activists and the bystanders, their shared social position gave rise to the predominant trends of thought and dissatisfactions identified elsewhere in this work.

Chinese students usually live very closely together in crowded dormitories. Communal living, studying and socialising have clear implications for the development of peer group identity, especially with those in the same grade or year. These interactional aspects are important both as a source of influence and pressure. When there is a consensus towards conformity, then nonconformists will stand out whereas when nonconformity becomes the norm everyone is expected to behave in a similar fashion. Peer pressure could override the influence of parents and lecturers, even of the CCP authorities, and peer group conformity can be in conflict with the official model of conformist youth.

It is also safer when nonconformity is a group-based strategy rather than an individual one because lone activists are more easily apprehended and punished. There is a sense of 'safety in numbers' which Yu alluded to with his reference to a classical Chinese saying. 'Laws cannot punish the masses. If one of them breaks the law, he will be punished but if so many people break the laws, the laws couldn't punish all of them.' This is a significant point because it seems to be the case that once a group of activists have taken the initial risk then it becomes easier and perceived as less dangerous for others to join in. Someone had to be brave enough to go first.

Referring to June 1988, it was felt that some poster writers copied others after the initial outbreak had gone unpunished and went along with everyone else. Chen referred to those participants who merely 'follow the wave', that is to say they become overwhelmed by peer group actions. Qiu talked of those who just follow like 'sheep' and did not have their own theories clearly thought out. In his view this was a negative point of the campaign and should have been avoided by better organisation and making clearer objectives. Guo believed there was an element of seeking 'fun' or excitement. 'Other students go on a demonstration and follow others, making a disturbance.' Whether participation was more to do with entertainment than politics is an interesting issue but the influence of the peer group is a key point. It appeared to be insufficiently strong in 1988 to cause more than a short, localised outburst of political activism. One year later, this had changed and the influence was sufficiently strong and exercised under conditions which were more 'ripe' (*chengshu*) for the widespread adoption of the activist strategy.

Government and Party organisations discourage any predilections for radicalism but it must be remembered that the government was not a united body. The existence of factions has already been pointed out as well as power struggles within the leadership. Although there may have been an official line about the types of acceptable behaviour and opinions which young intellectuals were to follow, there may have been different messages emanating from the factions.

To conclude this section, it can be seen that various factors influenced the selection of political tactics which interacted with each other, being affected by the context of the decision-making process in terms of prevailing social and economic trends. Even though conformity remained a recommended strategy given the existing political and legal systems in China there were trends encouraging nonconformity. One conformist tactic for young intellectuals was to join the CYL and the apathy felt towards this organisation will be discussed now in further detail.

THE CYL: A REVOLUTIONARY VANGUARD OR SOCIAL CLUB?

Joining the CYL can be viewed as a tactic inspired not so much by political fervour than of self-interest, with potential benefits to be gained in terms of economic and social position. A number of respondents described their sense of alienation yet remained attached to it for instrumental reasons, with middle school recruits tending to retain their membership throughout university. Most of them saw membership as the usual course of action for those pupils destined for higher education. There were also indications of it being a leisure and entertainment strategy.

According to Wen 'We joined in junior high school because at that time we were curious about the Youth League. As we became older, we paid less and less attention to it.' Lili described how ideological education typically began in primary school and it was normal procedure to apply for membership. If they did not apply, other pupils would think that they 'had some trouble', since 'all good middle school students become members', according to Liu. The entry requirements enhanced its elite status, adding to the social closure processes of young intellectuals, and membership was a means of attaining a certain social position. Those who joined were 'good youth', being 'honest and hard working', according to official writings. Xiu paraphrased official Party slogans about the CYL, saying that 'In China, there prevails such an idea, all those honest young people take part in the activities organised by the League'.

This was related to the fact that the organisation only selected those with 'good moral qualities and sound working attitude' for membership. Being a passive member was judged to be sufficient. In Xiu's case, it appeared that this method of working within the system in order to gain personal benefits had been successful. Other respondents held similar ambitions which may have been helped by a good CYL record. Membership was not an expression of youthful political commitment nor necessarily conformity but was a tried and tested tactic which parents and teachers expected the young people to adopt.

Yang pointed out that membership was not just a formality but had been 'socially and politically important' as it assisted subsequent application for the CCP. He had applied for membership but had been turned down. He saw himself as disadvantaged both socially and professionally because of this so his view was more negative. 'Not everyone who wants to take part is accepted, it's difficult to be accepted.' He contrasted membership procedures to those in the West where, he believed, it is relatively easy to join a political party. This idea of it being a formality is important when considering views not only about the League but other political organisations.

CYL membership suggested not expressive but compliant behaviour dominated by instrumental motivations which were partly conveyed to young people by the older generation of intellectuals. These pragmatic members were different from the ideologically inspired and unselfish youth portrayed in the Party literature and their attitudes were indicative of disparities between the official discourse and actual social realities. The gap between initial expectations and subsequent experience may not, however, have been very great as there were indications that respondents had started off with a realistic rather than idealistic view of the CYL. Political activity was not part of this. 'We just hand in our League fee each month', said Li.

Yet the CYL was supposed to be 'the Chinese Communist Party's leading mass organisation of advanced youth, the school for carrying out the study of communism for the broad masses of youth and the CCP's assistant and reserve army' (CYL Constitution, 1983:1). Zhang countered this official description by saying that 'The CYL should be the assistant of the Party but nowadays in China most League groups can't do that'. Jiang also expressed doubts about its political role saying that he did not believe it promoted socialism. 'It's not a school, just a name.'

The CYL was also meant to 'arm' young people with the correct ideology and political doctrines. Zhang again contradicted the propaganda, stating that 'In the old days, the League organised young people to study Marxism–Leninism–Mao Zedong thought but now nobody believes it so nobody studies it'. This statement supported the notion of Deng's generation being less likely to follow official ideology without questioning it. Not all statements were so critical but most were dismissive of the League's political role. A large gulf was evident between official views and those of this sample. Respondents had earlier described how they should take the 'leading role' in Chinese society and official descriptions of the CYL also emphasised this but there was some confusion about what this actually meant.

Organising political study sessions was referred to by seven interviewees either because their local League branch held weekly, in one case monthly, meetings, or were supposed to do but rarely did. 'Theoretically they should organise political meetings. We have for each unit a set afternoon for political meetings. But I don't know. They seldom discuss anything political, just complain about small things or just gossip.' That was the view of Sun who was antagonistic towards these meetings. 'I hate it. I never want to attend any kind of meetings. Once my leader said if I didn't go then they will take off some of my bonus. I said I didn't care.' She took a stance against these meetings but her view that they were a waste of time was common.

Gao had a similar attitude. Party cadres in his institution planned two afternoons of political study each week. 'We can certainly promise them we do that, but don't do that actually. Maybe we can sit there, have a discussion about our research, about teaching.' He could remember his own college days during the early 1980s when political study had been more rigorously carried out. This comparison with the past is important because it implies that the CYL had been more active earlier on. A decline was apparent but there was still the process of going through the motions, showing up for political study meetings for example, but not actually doing much.

Even the task of keeping up political appearance was proving difficult in some units. 'For the activities I join in, not too much political. Just like a social thing', replied Lu who referred to the picnics and events for members such as on 4 May. He enjoyed these and other social events such as dance parties. Zhou thought young people should take part in the League because it was a socialist organisation but did not elaborate on this claim.

League membership was viewed in passive rather than active terms, being too compliant for the 1980s generation. The CYL had become an anachronism with its messages out of date and the activities 'dull' according to Gao. Li declared that it was useless. Her view was not untypical and it did not seem to matter whether these young people were active in anything other than picnics or dance meetings. Four respondents' views could be classified as neutral with their relatively short responses containing no clear views. These were Chen, Zhao, Hua and Deng who all tended towards conformism.

Chen was no longer a member and 'stood by' rather than participated in anything. Zhao was a member but 'seldom' participated in such things as dance parties. Their attitudes emphasise the weak attachment to the CYL whose local branches were viewed as inefficient in organising social activities for members, another aspect of its designated work. A number of 'healthy' pastimes for young people were supposed to be available which would develop their collective consciousness as well as provide officially sanctioned entertainment. Visits to scenic and historical sites, picnics on national holidays and, more recently, dances were the major activities cited. There were also the more socially inspired activities of tree planting and sweeping out tombs at *Qing Ming*.[1] The organisation may be more of a forum for social meetings than part of a politically conformist tactic. Dance parties provided chances for young people to mix more freely than in everyday life and in this sense the CYL may be viewed as a socialist 'dating agency' or social club.

Most respondents believed that there were fewer recreational pursuits arranged by local branches than before. Lili said that 'Nowadays the activities are becoming fewer. They're limited to tree-planting.' Her friend Wen supported this by saying that instead it was the students themselves who organised activities. There was an indication of some regret about the decline. 'They seldom do things like we did in middle school.' A few respondents looked back with some nostalgia but basically had always been pragmatic rather than idealistic in their evaluation of this organisation.

There remained, however, an emphasis on political ideology even though instrumentalism and materialism were on the rise.

The lack of fit between the official discourse and social realities further tarnished the League's image. According to Gao 'The organisation of the League has actually disappeared, only the name exists. It has no effect on young people, no power in political life.' As a senior sample member, he was able to take a more retrospective view but it was not dissimilar to those of 20 year old Li. For the older, employed members, it was less relevant. Hua pointed out that 'When people start work, their activities are mainly organised by the Communist Party, not the League'. Age did not seem to correlate with negative or positive opinions amongst the sample because most felt it had little to do with communism. Its major function as an officially appointed agent in the process of political socialisation of young people in China was in doubt.

It appeared that, as with other social institutions, the CYL was changing because of reforms but this was often viewed negatively. 'Many young people are not interested in politics now', claimed Liu. Zhang also thought this was true and mentioned the difficult task that CYL workers faced in promoting their cause whilst young people had other interests. The responses implied that within the reform context mass campaigns were more difficult to mobilise effectively. 'If there are some problems, they can't explain or persuade people: they do *sixiang gongzuo* – ideological work – to solve the people's thought problems but the Party and League can't solve the mind problems [*sic*] very well', said Zhang.

The theme of the lack of interest in politics raises again the question of the definition of the term. A sustained and active interest in unofficial political issues had been visible throughout the decade with a succession of student protests. Increasing dissatisfaction with official political organisations and their activities partly distinguished this generation from previous ones and negative evaluations of the CYL indicated a continuing of alienation. They were unwilling to unquestioningly follow Party orthodoxy but remained muted in their criticisms.

The case of Wang illustrates this. He had been a CYL secretary at university but was 'driven out', as he put it, after participating in the student demonstrations in 1986–7. He identified a conflict between the CYL and those students who wanted to freely discuss their own views, as he had tried to. 'I think it's natural and necessary for students to express their own ideas or demands in a way like student demonstrations.' The League, however, could not allow this. He lost his position and was replaced by someone more conformist. Other student activists may have encountered more serious problems.

There appeared to be little room for independent aspirations, but without major changes in political arrangements this was the system young intellectuals had to work within. There was no alternative organisation and most respondents, therefore, re tained their membership for what it could do for them rather than what they could do as a result of active participation. It is suggested here that as they did not feel strongly attached to the official youth organisation, they could easily dispense with it should the opportunity arise and the possibility existed for the creation and development of their own version.

Similar feelings existed about the League's controlling body, the CCP. Amongst the respondents of the 'Roots' survey, only 17 per cent wanted to join because they had faith in communism but a larger proportion, 35.2 per cent thought it would enable them to 'adapt to society' and make life a little easier. Many of the respondents, 37.4 per cent had no intention of applying for Party membership at all. This theme of political alienation and weak attachment to conformity was also prevalent in the replies about one of the major political slogans of the period, to be discussed next.

'SOCIALISM WITH CHINESE CHARACTERISTICS'

There were a number of officially promoted phrases frequently used in the late 1980s which appeared as slogans (*kouhao*), or what Li described as 'fashionable definitions'. They contained refer- ences to both official ideology and policy. Frequently, one phrase was explained by reference to others. The one presented to interviewees as a vehicle for assessing their acceptance of official political ideology was *Zhongguo tese de shehui zhuyi* because it appeared to embody the major aspects and objectives of the reform programme. This phrase offered a way of exploring the degree of correlation or divergence between official political statements and the opinions of young intellectuals, with the latter being seen as further evidence of political alienation.

Lying somewhere between political ideology and economic policy, 'Chinese style socialism' was what China was supposedly heading towards. Building socialism had always been the stated aim of the CCP but the nature of the socialist endeavour was changing. Pronouncements were becoming less rigid and the 'correct' path was open to structured discussion and debate. Some long-standing dogmas from previous eras were rejected in the process of what was termed 'seeking truth from facts', another important political phrase related to the Deng Xiaoping era. The necessity of a form of socialism which suited actual Chinese conditions was emphasised. *Zhongguo tese* allowed for and justified social and economic change, along with emerging inequalities, including those that indicated China was 'turning capitalist' because of the introduction of elements of the market economy.

Most replies contained references to official statements in this area. Four major themes were recognised. These were: the revision of Marxist/Leninist theory to make it more suitable for contemporary China; learning from other countries, especially western capitalist ones; following Deng Xiaoping's recommendations; and finally, revising judgements about Mao and his policies. Ten respondents could be placed on the official side in their explanations of the phrase because they referred to one or more of these categories. Some of the more unofficial replies, nine in all, also included several of these ideas in their discussions but can be distinguished by other considerations which veered away from the Party line.

Although the 'official liners' tended to stay within the boundaries of political conformity, not all of them expressed equal acceptance of 'Chinese style socialism' either as a part of an overall ideology or actual policy. At one end of the continuum was Lu who felt that *Zhongguo tese* was a 'good phrase to express our ideas of our system what kind of things they do. It's our goal.' Xiu also indicated that she accepted the official version rather than genuinely believing it was a good policy. She prioritised personal interests whilst acknowledging Party ideology and it is worth quoting some of her comments.

She began as many others did by stating that she could not give a clear definition of the term because '. . . this concept sounds vague to ordinary citizens'. She then proceeded to suggest that it was best to conform even without a clear understanding of the policy. 'Everyone has his own experiences but on political issues I think it's better for us to follow what our leaders have said. If the policy doesn't arouse our personal disgust we'd better support it.' Her message was simply that it was best to go along with the government as dissent could lead to personal problems. It was not necessary to believe in everything. In her case, conformity had been rewarded and she was not exactly an ordinary person because she was part of an educated elite and preparing to go abroad. Xiu can be seen as representative of other conformists who sought to gain personal benefits by accepting the propaganda.

Generally speaking, revising Marxism and moving away from previous policies were supported. This reinforced an earlier conclusion that the post-Mao government had in some ways been successful in terms of political resocialisation. The dominant leadership faction had been seen to transform Marxism to suit their needs and young intellectuals had largely done the same. There were no expressions of a desire to return to past policies and in this one important respect, all the respondents can be seen to be conformist. Although a high degree of alienation and ambivalence was noted, this was probably considered less problematic for the authorities than the retention of 'leftist' policies from the previous era. Another point is that the respondents' misgivings indicated again the state of flux in their thinking and their views could change, becoming more positive or negative according to how events unfolded.

Some respondents indicated that they hoped the situation would become clearer in time so a 'wait and see' attitude was adopted which affected their overall view. Their ambivalent, even contradictory views can be explained in terms of their being both supporters of the present regime and its main critics. These responses also show that if the situation of young intellectuals deteriorated further then ambivalent conformity could change into activism. Even conformist replies contained elements of dissatisfaction with existing political arrangements.

In spite of the uncertainty about the meaning of the slogan, respondents attempted to make links between official policies and everyday life. The majority of them began with negative comments such as 'it's meaningless, just a phrase', or 'I don't know, nobody knows', or 'I can't give a clear definition of this'. They had to make some sense of it in order to envisage their own as well as the country's future development. As educated people, they reflected on its philosophical, historical, political and economic strands. Vagueness was evident with implications that the government were using it to justify a lack of political reforms to parallel economic ones. Respondents generally noted this and pointed to the inherent contradictions of trying to maintain a socialist system whilst introducing elements of capitalist economics. 'Sometimes the reform and modernisation policies are contradictory with socialism. They conflict. So our top leaders have to use this term, *Zhongguo tese*', remarked Gao who viewed the phrase as an attempt to resolve this ideological conflict.

Others expressed doubt that this ideological clash could be resolved. Zhen thought that by combining the two 'you get something worse'. This contrasted to the official view that China could take the best from both systems to produce a better way. Zhou echoed the view that the phrase implied knowing China's own strong points and combining them with those of other countries. The idea of combining the best from the East and West, expressed in different ways, was put forward by five respondents and is reminiscent of the *ti yong* policy of a hundred years before. In the contemporary context the *ti* is Marxism–Leninism rather than Confucianism (Goldman, 1992:197). 'We must find a road between the two extremes', suggested Lili referring to capitalist and socialist systems. It was important for them that a balance was found because when considering the recent past they saw serious political mistakes emanating from extreme views. Having been brought up within a socialist system, however, they also had an interest in the maintaining the status quo.

Those who were more sceptical saw it as a licence to do 'anything you want'. It allowed the Party to implement previously unacceptable economic policies. 'It's a good excuse to do something that formerly we thought was wrong', said Guo. As well as offering explanations for shifts away from socialism, the phrase permitted a rewriting of history. There was an associated reconstruction of past policies, particularly those of the Cultural Revolution. There were six references to correcting past mistakes and five respondents mentioned the revision of the ideas of Marx, Engels and Lenin. According to Zhang 'Socialism is not the style, the model written by Marx. It should be created by people themselves.' Chen expressed a similiar view, stating that 'Marx defined the word but we should consider it very practically. You see the society is not just like the society 200 years ago. This is China and not Germany.'

The desire to redefine socialist principles and adopt selected capitalist practices was in evidence with eight respondents talking of learning from other countries in order to improve the Chinese situation. Several of these stressed that it should not just be imitation. Liu, for example, felt that her country should not 'simply copy from the West'. The notion of selective modernity reemerges in this discussion with certain items being accepted, others rejected.

Others respondents saw the error of the earlier policy of following the Soviet Union. Only two mentioned Deng Xiaoping's speeches directly but several rephrased some of his well-publicised views. These can be seen as variations of the 'seeking truth from facts' maxim and respondents explained that whatever economic reforms were implemented they had to be based on the concrete Chinese situation rather than pure ideology or imitation of other countries. Again, this had been stressed by CCP leaders, especially Deng, with these sorts of views appearing in official discussions of *Zhongguo tese* and other slogans.

The sort of practical steps identified as necessary for the realisation of Chinese style socialism included 'absorbing Western knowledge and technology', 'improving management and efficiency', 'developing the coastal areas of China first', and 'knowing and developing our own strong points'. Lili mentioned the setting up of Special Economic Zones such as Shenzhen which would lead the way for other areas. Wen supported this view, saying that 'China should develop the economy from this coastal area inwards to the inland places. A gradual development starting from the coastal places will prepare the way for the four modernisations.' This idea of certain areas being developed first was official policy and justified unequal economic development. It was stated as a necessary process for overall increases in standards of living. Lili accepted this policy but she did point out the need for special attention to be paid to the more backward areas of China. 'If you go to Xinjiang, you'll be shocked by the backwardness there. So the disparity between different places in China is astonishingly great', she said.

Qiu believed that as China developed, more capitalism would be introduced. Socialism, he implied, was only suitable for poor and backward countries, as China had been earlier in the century. 'If something is of benefit to the people, we can do that regardless of it being capitalist or socialist.' This view is similar to the justification for introducing elements of free market economy in order to raise the general living standards of Chinese people, the 'cat and mouse' argument referred to earlier.

Gao suggested that ideology should be forgotten in order to make progress. Although he began with dismissive comments about the phrase, saying that it was 'not very clear, just propaganda', he went on to offer a more conformist view. It reflected the leadership's own ideological arguments for introducing elements of the free market to boost the nation's economy and bring about greater prosperity. Gao claimed that ideology used to be ' . . . very strong. That influenced our policy so we didn't do business with other capitalist countries at that time. I think if China wants to become modernised we must at some point forget ideology. Socialist or capitalist, it doesn't matter. If the country can develop, I think that is important.' This is another example of the 'cat and mouse' doctrine which was very common amongst the sample.

Lu also explained how private ownership was formerly prohibited with the interest of the state best served by the collective but conditions had changed. 'Our new situation has never occured in other countries nor has been explained by Marx or Engels. We still aim at socialism but we take methods which are different to those of the past.' There were doubts expressed, however, about whether the combination of socialism and capitalism could be carried out. 'I think it can be said easily but cannot be done so easily', said Hua who believed that there would be changes but not the political order. This he considered as part of the 'tradition'. Zhou advocated political reform which, although not copying from the West, ought to include the 'three main points of equality, freedom and reasonable thought'.

Zhen thought that it was probably just a political phrase which meant nothing. She said the government wanted to retain socialism but were in a dilemma because 'After thirty years they found out that it didn't work so well and then they want capitalism as well but since they are socialist they cannot give this up'. This view was shared by Qiu who, as the oldest interviewee, had given such shifts a good deal of consideration. He described the problems facing the Party who had to remain committed to socialism even though they realised that some of theory was wrong and that the situation had changed. 'They can't negate Marxism, it's the fundamental theory of the Communist Party. If they negate socialism, they have to change their name. It's complicated. It will meet a lot of trouble. It will bring the risk of being overthrown. It will make people confused about the difference between the Communist Party and Guomindang. So they have to persist.'

Qiu believed that socialism had earlier saved China but something different was needed to reverse the ongoing decline. 'After the revolution, China was very, very poor. The government can't carry out capitalism. If it does so in this poor background, there are a lot of people who will die of hunger. One of the aims of the Communist Party was to eliminate starvation, to give everybody food to eat, clothes to wear. So, at that time, I think socialism, is actually the social averaging. Maybe it's not true socialism. I think the Communist Party did a lot of good things for the Chinese people.' This implied that although socialism had previously worked to some extent it no longer did, yet this could not be openly admitted. 'We do not have the successful experience in building a socialist country', claimed Jiang. Others expressed their doubts. 'I can't be sure whether our system is socialist or not', said Li. The attempt to make socialism work in the changed environment was not assured of success.

Yu linked the phrase to the drive for modernisation, which was different from the situation of capitalist countries, 'so we call it Chinese specialised socialism'. He queried how the 'modernisation of people' would occur because changing the structures was not enough in his view if people's ideas remained traditional. He implied that reform policies would fail if people did not change as well. Jiang was hesitant about accepting the government's explanation loosely brought together under the term *Zhongguo tese*.

Several people saw economic reforms as benefiting the nation. This was directly linked to the government's intentions of prioritising development. Jiang felt that the most important thing was 'to develop the Chinese economy fast' with the leaders subsequently having new theories to explain what they are doing. The negative aspects of previous socialist policies were criticised as in need of revision and a controlled form of capitalism necessary for China's modernisation. Zhang declared that it did not matter whether the way ahead lay was capitalist, as long as it benefited the country which was yet another version of the 'cat and mouse' argument.

The emphasis placed by conformists and indeed some noncon-
formists on economic development was a major part of their
views. The continuing sense of nationalistic fervour passed down
from earlier generations survived into the reform decade, albeit
with some modifications. Qiu expressed the need for socialism to
be transformed, although he was sceptical of *Zhongguo tese*. He was
patriotic in believing that socialism should not be for socialism's
sake but for the country's benefit. Zhao simply said that it was
'according to China's real situation. When China is going ahead
it should do everything based on its reality and that's enough.'

There were some short and negative answers, such as Gu's who
said 'I don't know. I think no-one knows. The reform is going
very fast and I think this is one of the features.' For Sun, it was
'always confusing. There are many of these kind of phrases in
China but I never really take it so seriously.' Her reply reinforced
a lack of interest in politics and her desire to concentrate on her
career. This could viewed as a tactic, trying to avoid any
outspoken opinions. 'My family sometimes argues about these
kinds of things and when friends of theirs come they also argue
about it.' She herself did not participate in these arguments.

From this analysis of views on *Zhongguo tese*, the previously
noted political ambivalence was evident. Whilst accepting the
need for political changes to accompany those occurring within
the economic sphere, interviewees were unwilling to totally reject
the official line. They reworked it instead and their replies
contained many of the original themes, indicating a degree of
success in the political socialisation of Deng's generation. Their
views ranged from close alignment with official statements to
outright rejection with some people oscillating between the two
extremes. Overall there was a large degree of convergence and
Hua summarised the slogan as being a policy which is able to
adapt capitalist economic practices but 'as for our political order,
we will stick to our tradition'.

The acceptability of maintaining this tradition was questioned,
however, during the June poster campaign. Ambivalent support
for the existing political arrangements was temporarily withdrawn
by the activists who conformed instead to the tradition of protest,
thus raising tension between young intellectuals and their elders.
This campaign was the unanticipated context of the first few
interviews and respondents were asked what they thought about
posters and demonstrations. The main sources of motivation were

investigated as well as reasons for subsequently retaining or abandoning this tactic. The official limits were tested to some extent at this time and then exceeded in 1989. The following analysis provides support for viewing alienated conformity as potential activism which occured on a small scale in June 1988.

ADOPTING, RETAINING AND ABANDONING ACTIVIST TACTICS

The recourse to activism was explained in terms of the desire to express feelings, ideas, opinions and also complaints about the lack of other, more effective means of making themselves heard. A central theme was freedom of speech and of the media (*yanlun ziyou*) because the reform decade had not brought the openness demanded during 'Democracy Wall' ten years earlier.

'*Dazibao* are an important means for students to express their ideas. If they just sit in their dormitory and complain about things, the upper class will not pay attention to us. If we go to Tiananmen Square, through the media broadcast people will know what we think', stated Liu. This view reflected the reality for students who spent time holding 'bedroom conferences' in their dormitories about important social and economic issues. The interactive aspects of the peer group, as previously mentioned, were important in these informal forums. Liu realised that keeping complaints to themselves achieved nothing because no-one took any notice and feelings of alienation could intensify if grievances were not aired. 'There is no other way. People always complain but just privately, they cannot say something because the press is not free', said one informant.

These frustrations came up during discussions with some people saying they could only 'keep quiet'. More independent channels of communication would enable them to carry out some of the activities mentioned earlier in relation to their social role, such as inspiring and educating the people. The respondent Deng linked newspaper freedom to democracy which he hoped would be established in the future. 'More people will dominate the country and all people can have the expression of their opinions.' He implied that this progression would be a natural one, without resorting to activism.

Writing letters to official publications was a legitimate channel for airing grievances but respondents generally did not cite the pages of ZGQN, for example, as a suitable forum. Jiang, in fact, described its uselessness. 'If we write some letters to the authorities at the college and university, they do not care, maybe it is not effective.' He viewed more radical actions as natural because, 'it's a way for students to express their feelings'. Others pointed to the deficiencies in existing channels of communication. 'You can't discuss it in newspapers so during those times they have to put those ideas in posters', said Guo. Frustration at not being able to say openly what they felt was sometimes uncontainable and spilled over into protest activities. Freedom of speech remained a key issue for the more outspoken and nonconformist respondents. Wen, on the other hand, disliked posters and suggested that writing letters to the leaders was preferable, along with 'making propaganda among the peasants and workers so that they can understand the students'.

One question in the 'Roots' survey investigated suitable ways of expressing dissatisfaction about social problems. Seven possible options included writing *dazibao*, getting in touch with higher authorities in the student organisation and other official organisations, joining protest movements and talking privately with friends. The most popular response was discussing it privately or personally with classmates and friends, which scored 53.7 per cent. The next most popular selection was to 'keep it to themselves', at 35.3 per cent. Over 24 per cent selected the option of delivering a letter to a news organisation. Protest activity and public forums did not seem to be a suitable way of expressing dissatisfaction, at only 13.9 per cent. Another question pursued this theme and asked whether there were any other effective channels for expressing aspirations and opinions apart from demonstrating. Those who said 'none' outnumbered those who said 'yes', by 52.4 per cent to 47.6 per cent. What these channels might have been were not indicated.

'*Dixia kanwu*' or underground journals were a possibility and the informant Chu had access to several of these. They were not particularly radical in content, unlike the 'Democracy Wall' journals but were significant nonetheless, being independently produced by students and other young intellectuals who had access to printing presses. By using social connections, they had supplies of paper and reprographic facilities, both of which were scarce resources. They also used their own money to fund the process.

One of these journals, *Yanyuan Xinwen She* (Yanyuan News Agency), printed in 1987, discussed the implications of decisions and policies made at the Thirteenth Party Congress in late 1987. Another one was about *Beida* being a political 'thermometer' of Chinese students. It warned that although the university appeared 'quiet', this was not really the case and that the students' acquiescence and conformity could be withdrawn at any point. Producing these journals was illegal and incurred risks for those involved. Guo referred to them a short time after I was alerted to their existence. He said that 'Some journals edited by students have been closed by the university because they say they are too active. There's a magazine that has a paper about Fang Lizhi. It said our country needs such kinds of scholars and at the end had made some trouble, and the magazine had been stopped.' The link with Fang is significant because he had called for greater freedom of speech in the promotion of democracy.

Young intellectuals realised, however, the problems of being highly visible in expressing grievances. Possible motivations for participation, then, lay in their frustration at the lack of free expression. The initial decision to write posters or demonstrate and subsequent commitment to following such a course of action indicates two main characteristic features of the activist young intellectual. These are the desire to air grievances and opinions and the dissatisfaction with more legitimate channels of communication.

The consensus view was that posters and demonstrations were basically correct and students who resorted to these were in, the main, judged as justified. The majority of interviewees, 13 out of the 19 questioned in this area, expressed a degree of support for student activists. This ranged from very strong, for example, 'I agree with their ideas and I support their behaviour' from Gao or 'their enthusiasm should be encouraged' as expressed by Chen, to fairly weak but not oppositional such as 'I don't oppose it' from Li. During informal discussions there were statements such as 'I don't think the government should inhibit it'.

Zhao expressed little more than sympathy with them. 'It's a new way to push reform.' Amongst the supporters, there were at least five who expressed concern that students sometimes went too far. Lu, for example, remarked that 'the main force of their ideas is good, though some of their opinions are too radical'. At university, he used to be president of the Student Union and in this position he felt he could not become involved in any radical activity. Problems amongst students were reported to him and he could channel them to the university authorities. Lu's position gave him a direct line of communication with the administration which was denied to others. As a result, he was less inclined to support such actions as writing posters although in agreement with some of the contents and motivations.

Li also also expressed the idea that activism was 'out of bounds' (*chugui*). A distinction can be made between support for views expressed during student movements and the way of expressing them. Although most agreed with both the message and the initial recourse to activism, there were concerns about the possible repercussions. Li said that 'It will possibly lead to chaos, make trouble . . . that will only sharpen the contradictions'. Wen, somewhat a conformist in this respect, said that 'I don't think their thoughts are wrong but the way they do things is not reasonable. The demonstrations in Shanghai (1986) seriously blocked transportation and as a result hundreds of workers couldn't get to work. This caused chaos.' This sounds quite similar to the official pronouncements.

A minority disagreed with activism but offered some support for the motivations. 'I don't like this sort of behaviour. Some problems can be solved in a more peaceful way as we cannot have a good solution if we go about solving these problems by sharpening the contradictions', said Xiu. Deng was concerned about the success of reforms and the negative impact of demonstrations on society. 'I am opposed to processions as it will arouse social repercussions without achieving its own aim.'

The repercussions, then, could be a major reason for abandoning support for activism. Many supporters of activism indicated under what circumstances it might be withdrawn. The majority, ten, qualified their statements by discussing specific cases of protests. The most frequently selected example was of Beijing University with the timing and location of the fieldwork largely accounting for this, but its reputation has also been taken into consideration. This university might have gained a prominent position in replies even if the interviews had been conducted outside the capital and not in the wake of a *Beida* poster campaign.

One person expressed some reservations about students there, viewed as 'ridiculous' because of their attitude towards the dead student in 1988. In wanting to promote him as a 'servant who died for his country', Liu thought the students were going too far. 'Because he is a *Beida* student, people pay more attention but if he is a stranger, he would have died silently.' The self-perception of *Beida* students as important citizens in China is questioned in her response. 'People are equal in the face of the law', she stated. This view was not common, however, as it was suggested that the special social position of students offered a degree of immunity. Liu did consider the main complaints in the posters as legitimate.

Three respondents made references to *Beida* as well as to the demonstrations in Shanghai and other cities in 1986–7. They also referred to evaluations of such activities made by the rest of society, notably the government and other official bodies. Whilst the sample mostly supported activism, a feeling of impotence predominated since ultimately the students had no power. Li said 'I think they are very brave. But it's useless.' She may have been considering the lack of concrete achievements after previous protest movements and the authorities' power to punish participants.

The youngest respondents in the sample would have been at middle school and too young to participate in either the 1985 or winter 1986–7 demonstrations. The June 1988 poster campaign was a contemporaneous event and many had the opportunity to participate by writing or reading *dazibao* as well as attending the open political 'forums'. Li stated quite clearly that she would not personally participate in such activities although it was acceptable for others. 'Everyone has his own right and freedom to express himself, and should not be deprived of such right and freedom. Of course I don't want to take part in such activities.' Sun said she really had no interest in politics and would not join in but felt it to be a good thing. One informant described one of his friends as a 'student leader' who had taken part in demonstrations and used this contact to put forward his own generally positive views about student activism.

Other evaluations of the poster campaign included terms like 'progressive', 'frank and reasonable', and 'the right thinking'. Liu and Lu felt that the participant students went 'too far'. 'I don't think demonstrations will really solve the problem. It can only give the government a stir', said Hua. Deng's generation perceived themselves as more likely to act in unofficial ways but they showed a high degree of conformity by accepting this view of themselves.

Gao also referred to political campaigns in communist China but reached a different conclusion. 'We need something because you know since Liberation, about 30 years in China, we have no demonstrations. We have no strikes, no workers strike. The students just study, do what their teachers say. We should have our own ideas, should express our power if we have such ideas.' He viewed the demonstrations and other protests that had occurred as exceptions and suggested that China's students should make 'some noise' about the problems they were experiencing and those of society. Gao may be considered as a typical conformist/passive activist because he stressed the nationalistic motivations for adopting and retaining activist tactics. In Jiang's view people were less fearful of demonstrating than before because their ideas and minds had changed. 'Ten years ago people were afraid. They feared to demonstrate their own views but now they dare.' Their bravery, however, was still understandably limited.

Liu felt that 'political reform will work more efficiently but we do not hope much. It's not easy for the political reform to be carried out. Many old cadres have conservative ideas about things.' These hopes were shared by Qiu and Chen, as well as Zhang. Chen warned that if the political situation did not change then there could be a massive outbreak of activism. 'The understanding between the government and the people should be emphasised. The policies must be understood by the people because if not they will not support them. They will complain about society or may be they will rise up, just to tell the government they don't want to support them. Maybe this can happen.' One year later it did, with the students making the initial moves before hundreds of thousands of citizens joined in, but in 1988 the support for activism remained largely passive.

Some younger respondents believed activism could be partly attributed to a lack of social experience. Liu, who had described some students as 'ridiculous' also claimed that many are not 'realistic', having gone straight from school to university. 'We have no experience in society', a view which is in line with more official evaulations of student protest. She was conformist in this sense but her disappointment led to some sympathy with the demonstrators. 'We hoped, and expected things would be different. The situation is not what we expect.'

According to Wen 'The leaders don't usually understand the students' thinking. They also misunderstand that their original aim is to do something good for the country by showing their deep concern about this state. The leaders tend to regard the students as a destructive force.' She was against activism, believing there to be better ways to express grievances which would not give the wrong impression about students. Lili, as usual, agreed with her friend. 'People also tend to misunderstand the students. They think that the students are simply too idle in the universities so they will write *dazibao* and hold demonstrations to kill time.'

Zhen disagreed with the criticisms of her generation as 'too radical, too irritated, not experienced, not old hand'. These views were evidence of the generation gap, noted earlier, with young intellectuals castigated by their senior counterparts for their impatience. Demonstrations and posters received some criticism but overall were accepted as ways of gaining the attention of key people in the society, to remonstrate about the problems facing China, and those facing young intellectuals. Most respondents were aware of the potential problems for activists in a political system which does not allow for spontaneous protests and they incorporated these concerns into their replies.

Considering these evaluations, activism emerged as a strategy supported by many but adopted only by the 'brave' few. It involved the 'venting' of opinions and grievances and was possibly psychologically valuable but it was not generally considered as a useful way of improving the position of young intellectuals in China. There were too many risks which could lead to further deterioration of their situation as well as causing social unrest. It was, however, closely related to the historical tradition of remonstrance and not necessarily viewed as nonconformism. On the contrary, young intellectuals were expected to speak out in whatever ways they could in line with their inherited tradition, especially those at Beijing University which appeared to occupy a unique postion.

Similar evaluations of political activism strategy emerged from the the 'Roots' survey. On the issue of student movements, questions were asked about the September 1985 and 1986–7 protests. With regard to 1985, a small majority, 53.5 per cent, said they had participated whilst just under 40 per cent stated that they had not. It was not clear whether only those who were in Beijing in 1985, that is the more senior students, were instructed to answer this part of the question. A considerable number, nearly 35 per cent of first and second years plus some graduates, were not at *Beida* at that time. It could be presumed that some of those who responded negatively did so simply because they were not at university or in the capital in 1985.

One question referred specifically to the reasons for the protests. Respondents could select two items and the largest response was 'to arouse the whole people to be conscious of the suffering of the nation', with 58.1 per cent. This follows the theme of patriotism and their historical role as remonstrators. The next most popular response about the stated purpose of the 1985 demonstrations, with 33 per cent, was to bring attention to Japanese economic policies in China. This item also included the view that the government should strengthen its stance towards their neighbour instead of allowing an economic 'invasion' of China.

Twenty-one point five per cent of respondents felt that the protests were 'to show the role and power of the students in the middle of the process of drastic social change'. The other items included 'expressing a lack of faith in the government', with 20.8 per cent. A more negative response was that 'a few people have a reason enough to make decisions but most only have the sense to follow them and make trouble'. The view that many people are influenced by a small group of activists is discussed elsewhere in this work and this seems to further emphasise this factor. Just over 11 per cent selected this response.

Eighteen point two per cent selected the reason that 'student life is dull and depressing, so they want to vent their feelings' for the 1985 demonstrations, but for the 1986–7 student movement, the lower figure of 11.5 per cent was recorded. These were clearly considered as significant factors but not the main reasons behind these two previous outbreaks of protest. The state of the nation might be important but this brought the issue closer to the personal situation of students. The final reason, which received little attention (1.1 per cent) was that the reforms at that time (1985) had some contradictions which needed to be pointed out.

When asked about the 1986 demonstrations, respondents were presented with some different possible reasons probably because of the changed context and the national rather than local nature of these protests. The most common response was that 'students' consciousness of and participation in democracy and politics is growing stronger day by day', with 62.4 per cent. This indicates a desire for democracy and also a willingness to speak their minds not only in patriotic terms. The second most popular item was 'In society there are some people who don't understand students and whose adoption of unsuitable countermeasures mean the greater the changes, the bigger the problems.' This received just over 36 per cent.

The other items all received less than 20 per cent. The most favoured of these was 'reform of the political system is slow in manifesting itself', with 18.5 per cent. Reforms of the economic system were also considered too 'sluggish' (*jing ji tizhi gaige jinzhan chihuan*) at 11.1 per cent. Just over 13 per cent expressed criticism by selecting the item stating that the students who joined the protests lacked thorough knowledge of society and their simple ideas led them into radical actions. Also in this questionnaire the main goals of any possible demonstrations during the June poster campaign were hypothesised. The highest score, 76.4 per cent, was for the item 'removing newspaper restrictions'. This reiterates the previously discussed desire for mass media freedom and the fact that there may have been no effective way of expressing opinions or changing anything through official channels.

Another question explored the roles they would have selected if they had participated in a student movement: organiser, participant or onlooker. Not surprisingly, the lowest figure was for that of 'organiser' at ten per cent. This is the most dangerous part to play in any protest because of the possible punishments. 46 per cent opted for 'participant' with over 43 per cent saying they would just be an 'onlooker.' The more or less equal split between onlookers and participants indicates a high level of interest in demonstrations but a concern about the repercussions. Preference for passive involvement and support emerged again here. The traditional sentiments noted earlier were expressed in these replies.

There were deterrents to participation, however, and according to results from another 'Roots' questionnaire, administered after the June *xuechao*, the fear of official retaliation was the major one. Replies to the question enquiring into why student demonstrations failed to materialise paralleled discussions about motivations for student activism in the interview sample. Participation had been abandoned because of the potential negative personal outcomes.

The most commonly selected item at 63.2 per cent was: 'The authorities threatened to take severe action towards the participants'. It appeared that such threats had successfully deterred students from taking their grievances onto the streets, and this was a reminder of the punishments which could follow from participation in protests, as interviewees had described. The outcome of previous campaigns possibly served to weaken the orientation towards activism, and awareness of the experiences of their 'veterans' may have acted as a 'cooling off' factor in so far as protest activity was concerned in 1988. If these deterrents were removed or perceived to be less likely because of mass participation, then demonstrations might occur.

There was also the view that demonstrations did not occur in June 1988 because the aims were unclear with no precise goal. Just over half selected this item as one of three main reasons and this was similar to the 45 per cent response to the 'demonstrations lacked organisation' item. In another question about this, just over 30 per cent selected as one of their three main reasons: 'some classmates, on the basis of experience, believe that demonstrating is useless'. These results suggested, as did the interview data, that demonstrations may have taken place if there had been better planning and clearer aims. More young people may have risked the consequences if the circumstances had been more favourable. It seemed that the timing was not right. Between 1988 and 1989 the context had changed because more young people were prepared to take the risk and openly air their grievances.

The influence of the peer group or 'following the tide' was also included. Eleven per cent selected one reason for the 1985 demonstrations as 'a few people have reason enough to make decisions but most only have the sense to follow them and make trouble'. Respondents were also asked whether they felt society understood the students. On a scale of one to four, ranging from 'very positive understanding' to 'not at all', the results were, 3.3 per cent, 6.7 per cent, 45.7 per cent and 29.8 per cent. These figures indicate that 1980s students felt misunderstood by society at large and that there was a wide gulf between them. Twelve per cent chose the 'don't know' category.

In summary, it can be seen that political activism was viewed as a possible strategy for overcoming the disparities between expectations and experience but one that involved risks. In 1988, passive support of activism was more the norm but the prerequisite conditions were indicated which could transform ambivalent conformism into activism. These appeared to be the removal of the threats or at least the perceived weakening of these threats, peer group activity and pressure, good organisation and goals as well as some initial trigger as with the June campaign which broke out after the violent death of a student during a fight in a snackbar near Beijing University on 2 June.

The June *Xuechao*: a Case Study of Activism

Poster Contents

It was not possible to study every single poster because of the crowds and the tense situation that was developing. The exact number of posters that appeared was also difficult to estimate. Some were short-lived, others remained posted for the duration of the campaign. These limitations stated, however, the account of the posters can be said to be more than an impressionistic view of the events. It is based on several visits to the site and discussions with young intellectuals at *Beida* and other places both before and during the June movement. This information adds to the analysis of poster contents. A conscious effort was made to avoid revising the account of what happened in the light of information that subsequently became available.

The posters could be broadly classified into four main types with respect to their predominant subject matter. These categories are neither rigid nor mutually exclusive, with a degree of overlap in content. Some posters addressed more than one issue and others were more difficult to categorise. These classifications are an attempt to order the content material in line with previous discussions of the major trends of thought and attitudes, as well as to facilitate analysis. Their writers did not intend to do this, however, and would probably have viewed their own messages as individual expressions of opinion rather than as part of recognisable patterns of thought. This said, we can accept that since the participants in this *xuechao* occupied a similar socio-economic position and shared common concerns, previously discussed, the poster contents could be accepted as further indication of the major trends amongst Deng's generation.

The first and most immediate category was of those posters discussing and mourning the dead student. The second includes posters that addressed the 'unhealthy' trends in Chinese society which possibly contributed to the murder, such as increasing crime rates, lack of public security, corruption in the Party at all levels, the devaluation of knowledge and the resulting lowering of intellectuals' social position and other negative aspects of reform. The third category included those posters discussing concepts of democracy and political reform, freedom of speech, of the media and human rights. Finally, there were posters which contained calls for action to be taken by students, teachers, university authorities and the government.

There were both direct and indirect expressions of opinions in the posters and interpretation involved more than simple, literal translation: decoding was necessary to understand some messages and this was done by contextualising the poster material within the contemporary situation as well as elaborating on specific issues where necessary.

Posters containing demands for and discussions of '*renquan*' – human rights, '*minzhu*' – democracy and '*zi you*' – freedom, were present as they had been in previous campaigns because they remained unfulfilled hopes of Deng's generation. Political reforms were deemed essential to ensure the future success of the reforms. There had been some policy shifts but further ones were needed to bring about a more open and civil society as opposed to a state largely controlled from the centre. The discussions in the posters mirrored those that intellectuals had been engaged in during the late 1980s about the desired nature of the state and society in modern China.

One poster addressed three major problems facing China as a developing nation. These were the lack of political participation, the unequal distribution of wealth and so-called 'social clashes'. With regard to political participation, it stated that 'Much progress has been made in 1988 when compared to the previous ten years such as the democratic election at the National People's Congress. But we still don't have enough opportunities to participate in state affairs.' This comparison indicated that insufficient democratisation had taken place with the hope expressed for more communication between the government and the people. 'Social clashes', it implied, like the fight between the *Beida* students and unemployed youth that led to Chai's death would continue to occur under conditions of low political participation and poor communications.

Another poster stated that: 'There can be no success without political reform' which was a recurrent theme in protests throughout the 1980s. Democracy was often described as the 'fifth modernisation'. A lack of democracy was viewed as a cause of the authoritarianism in university life which reduced individual autonomy and freedom. Excessive control over everyday life, for example, had been at the root of earlier protests. Young people wanted to break away from their elders who did not allow them to 'shoulder their own responsibilities'. The responsibility issue can be viewed in two senses: national and personal. The former refers to the young people's social role whilst the latter refers to having greater control over their own lives. This was largely denied them by tight controls both at national and local levels.

The Chinese characters for 'self' (*zi ji*) and 'responsibility' (*zeren*) often appeared, reflecting concern with the personal responsibility issues discussed in the media. In early 1988, a ZGQN article included comments of the growing importance of the 'self' in people's minds with the related increased usage noted of phrases like 'self respect', 'self love' and 'self confidence' (1988:1). Changing the political system, according to the June poster writers, would assist the realisation of the importance of the individual in society with a shift in emphasis away from the subjugation of the self in favour of the masses to acceptance of a greater degree of individuality.

An inherent contradiction was pointed out in the official messages by the poster writers. The authorities talked of 'eliminating old concepts which obstruct reform' (*Gaojiao yu Rencai*:13) yet insisted that young intellectuals should uphold the 'four cardinal principles' and other tenets of traditional communist ideology. It was claimed that between 1985–7, some college students worshipped the 'self' to the extreme and this was partly responsible for the students, movements in this period, especially the nationwide one of the winter of 1986–7. 'Such irresponsible behaviour of the college students only added difficulty to the reform' (*op. cit*:16).

It was recognised that an increase in self-consciousness (*ziwo yishi guannian*) was in part 'a reaction against the previous one-sided emphasis on social demands' (*op. cit*:13) and that society could benefit from this increased self-realisation. A balance between self and society had to be found, however, which according to this article, would only result from following the Party. It seemed that ultimately the authorities were to decide on the 'healthy' direction of individual development for young intellectuals but the June posters disputed such views. Deng's generation wanted to decide for themselves.

The posters suggested that official ideology should be altered to facilitate practical shifts in behaviour for young people, away from dependency on adult-organised agencies. They wanted more personal freedom which was previously described in the discussion of attitudes about the CYL. Calls for the recognition of individualism ran parallel to more general discussions about democracy, freedom of speech and improvements in human rights. They would no longer have to resort to writing posters and taking the risks incurred by the recourse to political activism if these issues were properly addressed.

This disparity between the discussion of human rights in the posters and the treatment of those accused of murder, who were quickly tried, one of them being executed, was pointed out by some students. It reflected an underlying ambiguity in the social situation young intellectuals found themselves in, as well as aspects of their relationship to other youth groups already referred to. The posters did not propose that human rights were the sole privilege of educated people but the emphasis on Chai Qingfeng as a 'victim' rather than the unemployed youths accused of his murder indicated the relative nature of evaluations of different social groups.

This was also evident in the category of posters which demanded action. Intellectuals deserved justice, as poster writers had demanded ten years before, but this begged the question of justice for other groups in a society where few people could speak out. It was made very clear that young intellectuals were the ones with the traditional role to play rather than any other social group, as previously discussed, but this notion is not in itself very democratic because it assumes the elite nature of one particular social stratum. Even if well intentioned and well informed, the idea that intellectuals could speak on behalf on others implied that a political system based on neo-authoritarianism was acceptable for some people. This indeed has been implied in some discussions and writings at this time. There was also a related notion of 'New Confucianism' which called for a return to certain traditions to provide a basis for modern intellectual values. These ideas were part of the ideological and intellectual context for the June *xuechao*.

Overall, as the poster campaign developed it took on an increasingly political slant. The death of the student was seen as almost symbolic of the demise of intellectuals in general but further actions were not taken and it did not extend beyond *Beida*. Just as some informants described the April campaign as well intentioned but misguided, the June posters created a lot of discussion on campuses and, no doubt, CCP officials were concerned about yet another outbreak of localised activism. There were reports of meetings of various bodies to discuss this poster protest and its repercussions.

In conclusion, it can be said that the potential for political activism did exist in 1988 but other factors were working against it. The trajectory was viewed negatively, which is to say that resorting to activism at that time was calculated to incur more costs than rewards and would probably lead to trouble for its participants rather than success. It could also have been the case that an insufficient number of students and young teachers were aroused to take action. Less than one year later, many more were willing to take the risk of the activist strategy, as will be discussed next. This will not be an analysis of the outbreak of this movement, which has been done elsewhere, but an attempt to apply the previously used concepts to the Beijing Spring.

From Passive Bystanders to Active Participants

In early April 1989, another death was the trigger for the nationwide, student-led pro-democracy campaign. It is pertinent to ask the question of how and why students, described by some commentators in 1988 as not at all interested in politics, were transformed into the 1989 activists. It is argued here that it was not so much that they were personally transformed but that the situation had altered sufficiently as to suggest that activist tactics would be more likely to be successful than passive conformity, that activism was, in fact, the way to conform in order to fulfil their historical role. The element of calculated risk had lessened with the mistaken appearance that the government would be less likely to punish the participants of protest movements.

There was certainly the influence of other social actors and agencies, both official and unofficial, to take into consideration. There existed a general feeling of openness in China at that time with several intellectual journals, such as the influential *World Economic Herald* in Shanghai, operating relatively freely and beyond overt state control. The government appeared to tolerate a

greater degree of criticism as the reform programme continued
to exhibit failures as well as successes.

Early in 1989, a group of leading intellectuals started a petition
calling for the release of 'Democracy Wall' activist, Wei Jingsheng. This action may have signalled to younger people that it
was feasible to make demands on the authorities should the
occasion arise. The prominent intellectual Fang Lizhi was involved and his stature amongst young intellectuals has already
been discussed. His continued involvement with pro-democratic
organisations and behaviour verging on the dissident probably
inspired some sections of the young intelligentsia.

In terms of the social, economic and political contexts, there
were positive and negative factors operating simultaneously.
Young intellectuals desiring more freedom of speech were probably encouraged by what seemed to be an air of liberalisation
which was also fostered earlier by the *He Shang* phenomenon. The
prominence of pro-reformer, Zhao Ziyang, was another favourable feature and he was viewed more positively than Li Peng.
Overall, however, there was a 'crisis of confidence' in the leaders
and even in themselves as a nation. 'This social and intellectual
crisis is a major political irony of the reforms' (Nathan, 1990:108).
Views about political leaders were discussed previously and
no-one emerged as particularly impressive.

There were increasing personal attacks on political leaders and
their families as part of the general intellectual mood of 'profound
questioning' of the political system and even of the national
culture and character (*op. cit.* 1990:113). I was alerted to one
poster which was in cartoon form, with caricatures of Deng
Xiaoping, Li Peng and Zhao Ziyang all in a boat with Deng at
the helm. When the other two ask 'where are we heading?' Deng
replies, 'I don't know. Anywhere is fine.' This rather cynical
cartoon referred to the 'cat and mouse' argument as well as the
Zhongguo tese theme. No-one seemed to know where China was
really heading.

In terms of their own social and economic conditions, there
remained much for the young intellectuals to complain about and
there were reasons to protest should the opportunity arise. In
some senses, the decline in the intellectuals' position looked set to
continue with more educational reforms proposed by the government which emphasised even more economic self-sufficiency for
education. The plans to sever the link between the possession of

a university or college diploma and secure state jobs was seen as a further threat. Graduates were not sure they would be adequately rewarded for their higher education, and financial anxieties were deepening.

Problems with the reform programme were perceived as more severe in 1989 than previously with rising inflation and other economic problems, and there was a growing lack of confidence in the leadership's ability to control the forces they had released upon Chinese society. Economic reforms had done little to alter unsatisfactory basic arrangements, according to the poster writers of June 1988, except to encourage corruption. This concern with corruption distinguished the 1989 campaign from previous ones and it was a key issue of the period. Officials could be influenced by 'gifts', a euphemism for bribes and this occurred at all levels.

Another factor added to the feeling that activism may have been more acceptable was the fact that thousands of students had 'got away' with protests late in December 1988 after some disturbances in Nanjing. The protests were ostensibly about the behaviour of African students living in Nanjing, criticised by their Chinese counterparts after a fight at a Christmas party. There were several main protests over a few days but as with other demonstrations in the 1980s, there was more than one issue involved. The fight between some African and Chinese students was the trigger but demonstrators once again expressed their dissatisfaction with their own conditions and the problems facing China at that time. Although officially criticised, there appeared to be no serious attempt to punish those involved and this may have led to some feeling of immunity from a backlash if the activism was viewed as patriotically inspired.

The death of Hu Yaobang on 13 April was the significant event which triggered the initial protests of the Beijing Spring. Considered as a fallen hero, his death warranted public mourning according to many young intellectuals. This traditional act conformed to their perceived historical role. It did seem, in the early stages, that the protests were to be tolerated, once more signalling to the participants that there may have been a faction in the leadership supporting their actions. After the first round of protests in mid-April, more would be likely to participate, with the 'safety in numbers' idea relevant and peer pressure encouraging classmates to join in or follow the 'tide'.

The presence of the foreign media was viewed as a form of protection with the reasoning being that if the world was watching, that is the international audiences of the news broadcasts, then the government would be deterred from taking action against demonstrators. Several told me of this belief in the safety brought by western media as they camped on Tiananmen Square and it was a key factor throughout the movement. Ultimately it was a serious miscalculation because the regime still chose to openly and violently crush them. On the other hand, media presence could act as a deterrent to political activism. The Chinese authorities increasingly used photographs and video clips to identify demonstrators[3] and the foreign media became the unwitting helpers in the subsequent punishment of participants, another unexpected result. The regime as well as the students used the technology to their own advantage.

These factors go some way in explaining why student protests in 1988 were localised and short-lived whereas in 1989 they spilled onto the streets of Beijing and elsewhere. There existed a predisposition for such action to be taken by this specific social group, as shown throughout this work, but the activists were not following social rules which dictated how they should behave. There was an element of manoeuvring, risk taking and negotiation, as previously stressed. Activism probably remained, however, a type of conformism with the repeated patriotic claims (*aiguozhuyi*) and denials of wanting to overthrow the government in contrast to the official description of the movement as a 'counter-revolutionary rebellion'. There appeared to be a prevailing belief that the corruption and inefficiency of the government and the CCP could be rooted out somehow and a better regime put in place. The adherence to such a view was another factor which probably encouraged young intellectuals to join the demonstrations. They were not viewing themselves as particularly radical or activist but expressing their views that changes were needed in order to save China from some disasters of reform and make their own position more tenable and acceptable.

With this shared belief in their own self-worth, Deng's generation took to the streets, not viewing themselves in the same way as their Red Guard or 'Democracy Wall' predecessors. They were patriotic and well educated and offered what they viewed as sensible suggestions to the government. It appeared that the time had come to show what they were worth and make their views felt. Some already had experience of protests and poster campaigns, either as bystanders or participants, and could become quickly involved. Their peer group networks were in place and they received tacit support from older intellectuals. As the events unfolded, however, it was shown that any activism outside the official discourse remained risky and even deadly.

They did not envisage, at least until near the end of the movement, that the CCP, with the old guard still in charge, could only judge them in the light of previous protestors and there would be an unavoidable and ultimately bloody generational clash. Finally, Deng's generation, for all their apparent calculations, political sophistication and economic pragmatism, became scarred just like previous generations of young intellectuals. The cycle of relaxation and repression was completed again and the legacy from the past placed firmly in the present.

Conclusion

It has been argued in this book that 'Deng's generation' existed as a social category recognisable by key trends in attitudes and behaviour. Several main spheres of interest have been examined, notably education, leisure and economics as well as politics. These were shaped by the early years of the reform decade with its associated shifts away from 'hard-line' Maoism towards market reforms and opening up to the outside world. Created and shaped by a new era and feelings of optimism after the previous decade of 'turmoil', those young people who became members of this generation were bound to have higher expectations in all areas of life, from jobs to personal freedoms with a greater likelihood of disappointment and frustration should these expectations remain unfulfilled. This has been a central point of this work and the hopes and disappointments have been discussed within the generational framework.

The potential value of the generation concept has been explored with reference to a small-scale case study conducted in China in the late 1980s. Viewing young intellectuals in this period as a distinctive part of the 1980s generation as well as a specific generation of intellectuals offers a way of understanding their key characteristics and leads to insights into the mass protest movement which swept the country in 1989. The difficulties associated with applying the generational concept in an empirical investigation, that is the identification of a generation and its own internal sub-divisions or units, can, it has been suggested here, be beneficial in understanding the social processes at work in the creation of generations. The social context and forces which shape generations and how they become distinctive from one another have also been illustrated by such a case study.

There remain some questionable points, however, such as who falls into this generation and who belongs to either the previous or the post-reform generation. My inclusion of older youth is accepted as contentious but has been argued in terms of whether or not they were more retrospective than prospective. Not all older educated youth would have belonged to Deng's generation in this framework and it has been seen that they were not as active as the younger members mostly because of their Cultural

Revolution experiences. They were caught in the middle of the changes, and thus could be allocated to Deng's generation, but only just. It was acknowledged that there were differences between the youngest and oldest sub-sections of the generation but nevertheless the context of reform, particularly the early educational reforms, brought them together.

The more obvious members of the generation were those still at school during the early 1970s who went straight to university. As the decade progressed, the younger members entering higher education can be seen as potential members of the post-reform generation. These youths have not been investigated here but it can be accepted that they were more likely to take the reform context for granted yet were probably deeply affected by the student movement and its tragic end in 1989. Tiananmen can be viewed as a generational watershed.

It may be a matter of opinion as to what historical or social forces and events create a distinctive generation and in the absence of clearly defined watershed events there may be a blurring of boundaries. Other forms of social classification, however, such as locating individuals within social classes, also have their problems. It can be seen that in the process of analysing concrete generations, the problems can actually assist in the understanding of inter- and intra-generational divides and units. In attempting to delineate generations, questions of social and historical movements have to be raised as well as their link to the predominant thoughts and actions of social groups.

Social class is regularly used in the study of different social groups because of its explanatory powers and its relative familiarity to sociologists. With more application to concrete examples, the concept of generation could illuminate various aspects of social behaviour and its possible value be explored more thoroughly. The example referred to here was shown to have both potential as well as limitations but given the special relevance of the generational perspective in the Chinese context, Deng's generation can be seen as a distinctive social group. Applying some of Mannheim's concepts certainly opened up an interesting line of enquiry which might otherwise have been closed. The concept of strategy was also utilised as a means of characterising the actions of Deng's generation along with their particular predispositions related to their own habitus.

The problems of reforms were shown to intensify the young intellectuals' sense of identity as a social group with a historical destiny and duty, as well as the status frustrations created by rapid economic and social changes. They supported reforms but wanted a bigger stake in them and the 1989 movement can be accepted as the ultimate outcome of their unmet aspirations which distinguished this generation from others. Having been groomed to be a 'vanguard' of social change, some of this generation sought to activate this role through protests, first of all small-scale localised ones then nationwide in 1989. The ideological clash between the generations became a physical and ultimately a deadly one.

The pro-democracy movement cannot be viewed entirely as the result of the generation gap but the generational characteristics of 1980s young intellectuals have been cited as important in explaining the events of this time. The movement also marked more clearly intra-generational units with the younger periphery often taking the leading role rather than their senior counterparts. Older people were involved either actively or passively since the issues were common to them as intellectuals.

One of the movements key players, Li Lu, when speaking about Tiananmen and its aftermath from exile in the USA, reaffirmed other commentators' opinions that there really was not much left of a dissident movement in China (BBC World Service, 4 June 1996). The immediate crackdown was severe and went on for many months, and every year after dissidents have been arrested, rearrested or harassed after being released from prison. One of the high profile leaders of the movement, Wang Juntao, for example, was released from prison in April 1994 and allowed to go to the USA suffering from ill health after his treatment. Liu Gang, another key person, served a six year prison sentence for his participation in the 1989 movement but even after being released his life was made difficult by the authorities and he felt compelled to leave China in 1996 (*Independent*, 4 May 1996:9). Wei Jingsheng, previously mentioned, is back in prison. He had only a brief spell of freedom in 1993 around the time when Beijing was bidding to host the Olympic Games in the year 2000 and was rearrested in the following April. Most of China's dissidents have been silenced.

Leaders of the protest movement and other participants who managed to escape found themselves as unexpected exiles. They had not anticipated that their activist strategy would lead to a life outside China. Some had expected instead to die as youthful martyrs in Tiananmen Square, like the prominent student leader Chai Ling. Death or imprisonment was the fate of unknown hundreds, perhaps thousands, but exile was an option for the fortunate ones. Many were active at first and spoke out against the Chinese regime, telling their own personal stories of the movement and their escape and trying to keep the interest alive (Li, 1990). Several overseas movements were established to campaign for democracy in China, such as the Federation of the Independent Chinese Student Unions in the USA, set up in the summer of 1989, and the Federation for a Democratic China, officially set up in Paris in September 1989 by notable exiles of the pro-democracy movement such as Wu'Er Kaixi, Yan Jiaqi and Chai Ling.

The initial enthusiasm was hard to sustain and a person cannot continue to relive terror and death. I looked closely at the face of one unexpected exile, Shen Tong, during a meeting in Los Angeles in August 1989, not long after his escape. He looked exhausted, forlorn and shocked, hardy able to speak clearly. He could speak little English at that time and needed an interpreter. Like many other such exiles, he had to make a new life for himself in the USA without forgetting the past. Writing about the events was one way of coming to terms with it and I can verify the therapeutic effect of putting pen to paper. New languages and skills had to be learned, jobs found and so on. Many had not sought or expected the status of political exiles but this is what they suddenly became upon escaping from China and they had to adapt. Being a student leader abroad is not the same as leading young people in China and it is not surprising that many abandoned their activism and turned to business or academic careers. Shen Tong attempted to return to China in 1992 but was turned away by the authorities.

The fourth of June also had a big impact on the lives of many overseas Chinese students. Many of the thousands studying abroad were probably hoping to be able to stay away for longer than their allocated time, as previously discussed, and 4 June gave them a good, if tragic, excuse to do so. They were assisted by host foreign governments of the UK, the USA, Canada and Australia, for example, who extended visas for half a year or more. The Canadian government in particular made it easier for Chinese students to become immigrants, another unanticipated outcome of the affair. Many may have harboured such desires and the Chinese government gave them more reasons for staying away by their continued repression of intellectuals in China.

The tide of going overseas continued after 1989. In the early 1990s it was estimated that there were around 50,000 overseas Chinese in the USA, nearly 20,000 in Japan and several thousand in Australia and Europe (CD, 7 Feb. 1991:3). Publicity concentrated on the problems for those left behind with this 'fad' among young Chinese people creating a 'new type of family life' (CD, *op. cit.*). Grandparents were often left with the children of sons and daughters who had gone abroad and the long-term repercussions of this still have to be fully investigated.

For those remaining in China, it seems that they are more interested now in making money than striving for democracy and that the government has been successful in diverting the attention of its citizens into this area, in line with its economic reforms. 'Youth dream of money not democracy' is a typical heading for articles about young intellectuals (*Independent*, 5 June 1996:11). The emphasis on money and materialism cannot be denied but when an interest in democracy is discouraged, it is not surprising that Chinese people, including young intellectuals, seek to further their personal and social interests in the permitted, legal ways rather than illegal ones that might entail the wrath of the authorities. There has simply been little choice about doing otherwise since 1989. Even to talk about democracy may be a 'waste of time' according to some but this does not mean the desire for political change has dissipated. There is also the view that economic change will lead to political change although this has not necessarily been the case as with other authoritarian states (Cherrington, 1993).

People have to live within the regime as it is and make what space they can for themselves and attempting to earn some money can further this aim. Also, as discussed in this book and pointed out by Li Lu, (BBC World Service, *op. cit.*) it is a strategy that began in the 1980s and was associated with young intellectuals even then. They were encouraged to be economically active and pragmatic and this was used to some extent during the pro-democracy movement when activists had to raise funds for their cause. At the present time in China it is difficult to raise money for political causes or an alternative political party, but the skills and activities now observable could possibly in the future be diverted as they were in 1989. For a while, the economic craze was overwhelmed by the democracy craze. A concern with money is not in itself a denial of the desire for democracy. As Li Lu states, it is one way of eking out some personal freedom in a society still tightly controlled by the state.

Every now and then there are some signs of this desire for political change and people do speak out. In late May 1996, a number of dissidents signed a petition calling upon the government to instigate political changes and allow more human rights including the release of political prisoners. This act was still quite 'brave' and 'risky' to use the adjectives of many of my own respondents from the 1980s.

But we must ask questions about the present generation of young intellectuals, such as whether they would be as impressed by such a petition drawn up by leading intellectuals, as their predecessors were in early 1989. There is a need to study them more closely and thoroughly as we have with Deng's generation It was initially difficult for foreigners to obtain first-hand information about them after the post-Tiananmen clampdown but results of surveys conducted by official bodies into young people's attitudes have been obtained. Rosen found that they had not suddenly become 'born-again' socialists because of intensified ideological work and reeducation campaigns. He writes that '. . . while the regime has been able to win outward compliance from students and youth in a number of areas, the authorities have made little headway in penetrating the belief systems of young people' (1993:310). In this sense, the ambivalent conformity of Deng's generation lives on in the 1990s generation with compliance based upon pragmatism rather than real conviction.

Another official decision which was intended to alter the attitudes of young intellectuals was to impose mandatory military training for students at the elite universities where much of the unrest was centred. Beijing University was made the 'test case' (Rosen, *op. cit*:317) with the entire first year group of over 700 young people sent to a military academy 160 miles from Beijing. They were not permitted to read anything to do with their chosen subjects but were subject to reeducation and propaganda intended to deter them from considering demonstrations like those of 1989. It was hoped that a dose of army life would make them different from their predecessors. The programme brought complaints from parents and university authorities and problems for the students singled out for what others saw as 'brainwashing'. This group may have been made more obedient but they do not comprise the whole of the next generation, and the authorities could not extend the programme to all universities. Cost and the subsequent lengthening of university education to five years have ruled this out. As one reaction of the government to make a mark on the next generation, it was bound to be short lived and small scale.

Other tried and tested means have been used to mould this generation into compliance such as the use of role models, an old tactic of the socialist regime. Some slightly updated model heroes have been offered, Xiu Honggang, for example, a soldier who attempted to apprehend a criminal on a bus and got stabbed for his troubles. His heroic deed was considered worthy of emulation by the government. Lei Feng, however, who had never been completely abandoned, was revamped and in the early 1990s had something of a comeback with attempts to publicise his good deeds and his red, socialist heart. There was even a cassette made of socialist songs to accompany the 'Learn from Lei Feng' movement, along with a karaoke version. The authorities were clearly trying to use the new technology to meet their own ends but the messages were basically the same and it is doubtful whether anyone was really listening amongst the new generation.

It was shown earlier in this book that few members of Deng's generation looked up to Lei Feng or saw much point in emulating his deeds. He was outdated even in the 1980s and by the 1990s had definitely become a 'hard sell' (Rosen, *op. cit*:320). The attempts to instil some sort of interest in this model hero and change young people's attitudes largely failed. The reform context, the emphasis on making money and the development of individual interests, were in conflict with the aim of promoting this selfless person.

It is clear that this is a materialistic generation with their interests in leisure activities probably stronger than political ones. Like their predecessors, they enjoy the *'gangtai'* culture of films, videos and pop songs. Their interest in foreign things is also similar to Deng's generation with them favouring these over domestic cultural products. This is seen as a cause of 'ideological confusion' and contributes to what is called 'national nihilism' (*op. cit*:329). Again, this can be seen as a continuation of the trends within Deng's generation.

Undoubtedly there are other continuities and it is suggested here that the post-reform generation of young intellectuals retain a deep sense of their historical destiny and special role which was so strong amongst Deng's generation, even though they like to watch foreign films and read detective books. There are bound to be links with the past although the 1990s generation will be aware of the problems of speaking out too loudly. Although they have been subjected to heavy doses of ideological work, commentators have pointed out its uselessness, with cynicism rife as it was even before 1989. Lip service is paid to the Marxist credentials of the regime whilst the realities of modern China as an economic power in the world are more valued.

It is probably true to say that the post-reform generation is even more open to the world than their immediate predecessors. They have been brought up in a time of varied contacts with foreigners and many aspects of foreign cultures in their midst. There has been a burgeoning of the economy, along with further widening of the gaps between rich and poor. China is increasingly a major player in the international economy. Hong Kong's return to the 'motherland' and the changing relationship with Taiwan are also important factors which will affect the nature of this generation. The '*gangtai*' culture looks set to expand and be more of a generational feature for the 1990s. This generation may develop a wider view of their Chinese identity to include their neighbours rather than restricting themselves to the mainland, but this needs to be investigated further. The effect of the inclusion of Hong Kong's young intellectuals into the post-reform generation is an interesting point of speculation. They were fairly outspoken against the regime and took a 'last stand over martyrs' on 4 June 1996 (*Independent*, 5 June 1996:11).

The present generation have had to be even more self-reliant economically with fewer prospects of state scholarships for higher education and no assurity of finding jobs upon graduation. It was announced at the end of April 1994 that free education at university level was to be abolished with everyone having to pay fees. The state assignment system was also finally being wound down with young people having to seek their own jobs and the *guanxi wang* phenomenon remains important.

The future is still uncertain with problems of law and order, overcrowded cities and increasing corruption as the socialist morality and controls break down. An ideological vacuum has been left unfilled, as in other societies which have recently experienced rapid economic and social, as well as political change. Russian youth, for example, strive to find ways to live in the changed reality of the post-*glasnost* period and Chinese youth do likewise although they are still constrained in many ways. They do not have the experience of political liberalisation. It may be the case that higher education is losing its appeal and certainly in the immediate post-Tiananmen period university enrolments were down on previous figures (Hayhoe, 1993:295).

The post-reform generation have a variety of influences working on them which may affect the trajectory of their actions but after considering their predecessors in some detail, it is probably true to say that they also wish to make their mark, to make their contribution to the 'motherland' and fulfil their historical role. This remains part of the habitus for intellectual youth in China. We have to wait to see what strategies they develop, whether they choose the business tide and attempt to increase China's economic power and influence in the world or instigate the political changes which so many of their predecessors have desired and even died for.

Appendix

METHODOLOGY: CONDUCTING RESEARCH IN THE PRC

From the outset, this research faced many of the well-documented problems common to other ethnographic studies in the PRC (Bernstein, 1977; Shirk, 1982; Chan, 1985; Croll, 1987; Pieke, 1987; 1992). These can be as basic as gaining entry to the country in the first instance because visas can be denied in the country of origin. This was difficult during periods when China was virtually closed, such as during the Cultural Revolution. When entry is possible, then access into suitable fieldwork situations for the purpose of data collection has to be sought. Official permission may be required and given the high degree of control over people's lives in China, only recently relaxed to some extent, plus the extensive bureaucracy, this can be difficult to obtain.

The opening up of China to foreign scholars after 1978 was negatively affected by the so-called 'Mosher affair' (Pieke, 1992:Appendix-1). Even though there was renewed cooperation between the Chinese side and foreign researchers, it is arguable that things 'never returned to the way they were', with fieldwork remaining 'the object of intense suspicion' (Pieke:2). Pieke has outlined useful approaches of avoiding the full of extent of official involvement in order to secure permission to undertake fieldwork.

If qualitative data is sought through interviews and participant observation, there are further problems in terms of contacting suitable interviewees and key informants. If the project is conducted in cooperation with Chinese authoritative bodies, then interviewees may be provided for the researcher. Such official intereviews raise questions about the formality and official interference. An alternative method frequently resorted to in the past has been to contact Chinese people who had emigrated, legally or illegally, from the mainland to places such as Hong Kong. Although there are a number of problems associated with such sources, the information has been valuable and indicative of what happened in the PRC during the closed years (Raddock, 1977; Shirk, 1982; Chan, 1985; Unger, 1982). Bernstein suggested that: 'As long as proper field research is not possible, interviews with former residents of the PRC remain a major source of information' (1977:15). Since many such youths fled to Hong Kong, particularly from nearby Canton, a ready supply of informants was available. Bernstein preferred the use of émigrés because they were acting freely and away from the CCP authorities.

In the 1980s, foreign researchers were more likely to be given the official go-ahead although still with a tight degree of control. It became easier for foreigners to work and travel throughout China and make contact with a variety of people. It was decided that this research would take advantage of the changed circumstances and it was possible to work as a teacher simultaneously to collecting first-hand data rather than using émigrés. Assuming the role of lecturer had several advantages. This approach was taken in order to minimise contact with official bodies such as those from the SEC and Chinese Academy of Social Sciences. Official permission was not sought to undertake the fieldwork, thus reducing the risk of initially being refused entry into China or the excessive involvement of Chinese authorities.

It was felt that official permission was unlikely given the sensitive nature of the project. Young intellectuals had been subjected to ideological work in the wake of the 1986–7 demonstrations and this research was undertaken only one year afterwards and was to involve views about reforms and politics in China. These were still controversial topics and not likely to be considered by the authorities as suitable for open discussion. Another reason for avoiding official bodies was my status as an independent researcher without institutional ties, apart from being an external Ph.D. candidate at a British university. I felt that this relative freelance status would not jeopardize other researchers or institutions if I was accused of conducting illicit fieldwork. I certainly did not wish to cause any problems for subsequent researchers and I was prepared to accept the responsibility for my own actions. I intended to leave the field as relatively untouched as possible.

Whilst not completely satisfied with this covert status, I felt it more or less unavoidable. I did not hide my intentions from any would-be key informants and interviewees, or from my colleagues at the college in Beijing where I was employed. This raises another factor in the decision to avoid official bodies: funding. This was to be a totally self-financing project, with no institutional backing from either Britain or China.

As with many other fieldwork projects, a series of compromises was necessary. I felt I had compromised some values about the need for openness when doing research because of the nature of Chinese society and politics. My ultimate decision was similar to that of Franz who also chose the 'inconspicuous' option. 'Anyone wishing to do research in China has to choose between two extremes. Either he seeks the green light from the very, very top, in which case archives and mouths open as though by magic, or he pursues history from below, as inconspicuously as possible. I chose the latter path. I descended to the "grass roots" as they say in China, and interviewed contemporaries in Peking and Shanghai' (Franz, 1982:xi).

All the above factors affected the nature of the research project, the methods of data collection and the actual data itself, as will be discussed. Like Franz's research, however, it 'came together' during the time I spent teaching and conducting fieldwork in China. There was no fixed research plan imposed at the outset. It was unclear, for example, exactly how much time would be available each week for research because of teaching commitments. The willingness of young intellectuals to be respondents was also an unknown variable in the first instance so it was not advisable to begin with a fixed target in terms of number of interviews to be conducted. The developmental nature of the research process meant that it was necessary to have a mix of research methods: observation, both participant and non-participant, and interviews, including one-to-one and group interviews. Informal discussion was also deemed a valid technique.

The collection of secondary data was an ongoing process with continual observation and monitoring of the context. Reactions of young intellectuals to contemporary events and opinions about them were solicited and recorded. Frequent class parties and informal discussions provided opportunities to gain further insights about the group under investigation through participant observation.

The interviews had to be arranged as soon as possible after arriving in the field, bearing in mind the difficulties of finding respondents and the identification of key issues which would form the focus of the interview. These potential issues had come to light in the work carried out prior to entering the field and they were confirmed as significant during the first few months. Living and teaching in a university facilitated the elucidation of these issues. The lack of official interference and constraints was also beneficial. It was felt that the expression of attitudes and opinions was more spontaneous as a result of being beyond authoritative bodies.

Some of the major drawbacks of my freelance status should be pointed out. Without official assistance or backing, everything had to be self-initiated 'from scratch', from finding suitable contacts in the field and respondents, to arranging interviews and finding a neutral place for interviewing, and so on. The covert nature of the research also presented difficulties, although as pointed out, those who agreed to participate in any way were informed of its objectives. Given the political situation, even in the relatively open year of 1988, there were still anxieties about participants being seen as in collusion with foreigners. The fact that I may have put some young Chinese people at risk, even though they had freely agreed to cooperate with me, was a cause of concern. Several young people came forward and acted as key informants and although aware that in assisting me they could have endangered their futures, they continued with this course of action.

This anxiety was heightened during the two poster campaigns when I was warned by informants to stop my investigation. I never lost sight of the knowledge that I could always leave the country whereas they could not. Several interviewees expressed their concern in a number of ways. One person looked around my apartment for 'bugging' devices before proceeding with the interview as he was convinced the authorities would be listening. I assured him that this was not the case but pointed out his option of leaving without saying anything. He chose to stay.

The nature of the research also gave rise to feelings of doubt and guilt which are not uncommon when undertaking in-depth social research of this kind where close contact and cooperation, even friendship, with the subjects is involved. I spent a good deal of leisure time with students and discussions we had on these social occasions were noted down in a field diary just as were many of the classroom ones. The problem then arose of including information which for the respondents may have been 'off the record'. It was very difficult to stop being the researcher because many interesting views and information arose in a variety of situations, such as during class parties which were really for leisure rather than work.

Common concerns of the group emerged even during these events which were recorded. This heightened the feeling of ambiguity because I was making notes daily about their behaviour and opinions. I accepted that this was unavoidable and frustrating but there was some consolation in the knowledge that the students were gaining some benefits by spending time with me such as improving their English and gaining information about going abroad.

After several months of getting to know people through informal discussions and teaching, an interview schedule was drawn up and potential interviewees approached. Finding a suitable, neutral place to conduct the interviews was a problem. It was felt that potential respondents would be deterred by coming to my apartment but it was difficult to find a suitable office for conducting interviews. Another possibility was visiting students and others on their own ground, that is, in the dormitories.

In the event, all of these were tried. An office was found by a key informant for interviews but this seemed rather official and the few interviews conducted there were not very relaxed. There was also some construction work going on nearby and the noise interfered with the tape recording. Several attempts were made at interviewing in student dormitories but there was very little privacy and again a good deal of background noise. The most successful place seemed to be in my apartment. It was not part of a foreign expert residence with no signing-in required and students could visit with anonymity. There were still fears that they were being watched and some interviewees did feel anxious but mostly these concerns were overcome.

The interviews were mainly conducted in English, some entirely so and others partially. The older respondents were mostly more proficient than their younger counterparts and could talk quite freely in English. Some interviewees were not able to express themselves in English and Chinese was then the medium. The questions were presented in Chinese where necessary and all except one was recorded. Some respondents began in English, wishing to gain some extra practice with their oral skills but subsequently switched to Chinese when they felt they could not explain themselves adequately. Whilst recognising that there were difficulties caused by my lack of fluency in Chinese and the respondents' varying levels of ability in English, the information gathered contained enough similarities to indicate trends in patterns of thoughts and prevailing views amongst young intellectuals.

Notes to Chapters

Introduction

1. The word '*re*' is variably translated as 'craze' or 'fever' and '*chao*' usually as tide.
2. The extended period of the Cultural Revolution will be used in this study, that is from May 1966 to Mao's death in September 1976. Although the major events in terms of factional fighting and disruption to education were over by mid-1968, the educational careers of young people remained affected by 'leftist' policies.

Chapter 1

1. The reform decade can be viewed as lasting from the Third Plenum of the Eleventh Central Party Committee in November 1978 to the end of 1988. Although *gaige kaifang* policies continued after this date, there were some periodic shifts. Attempts to slow down economic growth, for example, were becoming evident in the summer of 1988. The 1989 student movement also marks a turning point. The government maintained the reform programme but it could be argued that the second decade was in some ways qualitatively different from the first.
2. 'May Fourth' as a literary, political and social movement instigated by young intellectuals can be witnessed in the early years of the twentieth century, before the demonstrations of 1919 from which it gained its name.
3. For another interesting discussion of generational identities and differences from the point of view of young Chinese themselves in the 1990s, see Rice (1992) Chapter 7
4. The College or University Entrance Examinations are held annually over several days usually in July to decide who can enter higher education establishments.
5. English Corners sprang up throughout the 1980s as physical and linguistic spaces for learners of English to practise their vocabulary and skills. They also became meeting places and native English speakers were enthusiastically welcomed and questioned. The relative freedom of speech was, however, a cause for official concern and it was not surprising that some high profile English Corners, such as the one in Purple Bamboo Park near the university district in Beijing, was closed down in the aftermath of 4 June 1989 (Cherrington, R. 'State Silences "Speakers Corner"', *TES* 22.12 1989).
6. 'Roots, Consequence and Countermeasures: Analysis on the Students' Movement.' (Xuechao Fenxi: Yuanyin, Houguo ji Duice), *Zhongguo Fazhan yu Gaige*, (1988) 10, 35–40.
7. Personal or social networks (*guanxi wang*) were an integral part of many leisure, educational, economic and political activities. Such contacts could further a number of endeavours and social connections were often essential to get anything done. It can be viewed as a necessary part of various

strategies aimed at attaining a variety of goals such as entry into higher education and going abroad. Such practices have a long history in China and could be said to be a cultural trait (Kwong, 1994). It is not unique to the country and can be seen elsewhere as a route to scarce goods and resources. It does seem to be, however, particularly well developed by the Chinese. Inspite of 'vigorous campaigns . . . to uproot "feudal" elements of the Chinese culture' (Y. King, 1994:109) concepts such as *guanxi* remain strong. The communists were unsuccessful in their attempts to eradicate such practices and social networks operated in various ways both before and during the reform decade.

8. The names given here are all pseudonymns to protect the identities of the respondents.

Chapter 2

1. Previous 'down to the countryside movements' can include those during the 1930s (Bernstein, 1977).
2. Those working within the growing private business sector were termed '*getihu*' short for '*geti gong shanghu*' individual industrial and commercial households (Chan, 1992:64). 'The Chinese term *getihu* refers both to privately owned small businesses and to the business persons who run them. *Getihu* is sometimes rendered in English as "individual business" (person) or "self-employed business (person)" ' (Shi, 1993:153).

Chapter 3

1. Four modernisations: science and technology, defence, agriculture and industry.
2. Professor Fang Lizhi became something of a cause célèbre in the late 1980s. A famous astrophysicist, he was also a leading critic of the authoritarianism practised by the CCP and became associated with pro-democracy movements. He travelled outside China and had a relative degree of autonomy until the student movement of 1986–7 after which he was expelled from the Party. He was referred to as 'China's Sakharov' (Nathan, 1990:111). He fled China after the 1989 movement.
3. A series in GMRB (22 February to 10 April) for example, explained the trend in terms of the widening disparities between expectations and social realities and feelings of relative deprivation. This reportage discussed the origins of the phenomenon, relating it to social and economic problems facing young Chinese intellectuals. The series also appeared in other newspapers, notably *Zhongguo Qingnian Bao* and was later published as a booklet '*Shijie da Chuanlian*' (1988).
4. TOEFL: Test of English as a Foreign Language.

Chapter 4

1. There were the mahjong players (*mapai*) and the TOEFL candidates (*tuopai*) as well as 'dancers' (*wupai*) and 'drinkers' (*jiupai*) (Barme G. in Hicks, G. (ed.) 1990).

2. 'If it is a question of the economy, business or earning money, then the leitmotif is, "No matter whether it's black or white, so long as the cat catches mice" ' (Franz, 1982:2). This phrase of Deng Xiaoping was often used to imply that it was irrelevant whether China used capitalist or socialist economic devices as long as the country developed economically.

3. *'Gangtai'* – Xianggang (Hong Kong) and Taiwan.

4. Hou Dejian, a Taiwanese pop star who went over to the mainland in 1983, preferring it seemed the 'socialist motherland' to capitalist Taiwan. He was very popular throughout the 1980s and on the penultimate night of the 1989 pro-democracy campaign he joined three other prominent personalities on a symbolic hunger strike at the centre of Tiananmen, just before the troops moved in to crush the movement.

5. It is worth mentioning a similarity here between this and British classics serialised successfully by the BBC in the 1990s such as George Eliot's *Middlemarch* and Jane Austen's *Pride and Prejudice*.

6. 'What's the 90s gonna bring?' *Jiushi Niandai zenmeyang* by Xie Chengqiang in Jones, 1992:9.

7. Title of Song: *'Xin zhong de Taiyang'*.

Chapter 5

1. *Qing Ming* on 5 April is the time when the traditional Chinese ritual of honouring the dead takes place.

2. It is arguable that an in-depth official definition was not available until after this case study was completed. In the RMRB of 29 January 1991, there were references to 'Chinese characteristics socialism' in relationship to the state's Eighth Five Year Plan discussed at the 13th plenum of the CCP Central Committee, and reported on at length in this edition.

3. Other governments do this, for example in Britain after the 'Poll Tax riot' in London in April 1990.

Bibliography

Barmé, G. (1990) 'Confession, Redemption and Death: Liu Xiaobo and the Protest Movement of 1989' in Hicks, G. (ed.), 52–99

Bengtson, V., Furlong, M., and Laufer, R. (1974) 'Time, Aging, and Continuity of Social Structure: Themes and Issues in Generational Analysis', *Journal of Social Issues*, 30(2), 1–30

Bernstein, T. (1975) 'Introduction' in Seybolt, P. (ed.) *The Rustication of Urban Youth in China*. New York: M.E Sharpe

Bernstein, T. (1977) *Up to the Mountains and Down to the Villages: the Transfer of Youth from Urban to Rural China*. New Haven CT: Yale University

Berreman, G. (ed.) (1981) *Social Inequality: Comparative and Developmental Approaches*. Berkeley CA: University of California

Bourdieu, P. (1976) 'Marriage Strategies as Strategies of Social Reproduction' in Forster, E. and Ranum, P. (eds) *Family and Society*. Baltimore MD: Johns Hopkins University Press

Bourdieu, P. (1992).*Distinction: A Social Critique of the Judgement of Taste*. London: Routledge (translation by R. Nice)

Brake, M. (1985) *Comparative Youth Culture*. London: Routledge

Braungart, R. (1974) 'The Sociology of Generations and Student Politics', *Journal of Social Issues*, 30(2), 31–54

Brodsgaard, K. (1981) 'The Democracy Movement in China', *Asian Survey*, 21(7), 747–73

Brugger, B. and Reglar, S. (1994) *Politics, Economy and Society in Contemporary China*. Basingstoke: Macmillan

Chan, A. (1985) *Children of Mao: Personality Development and Political Activism in the Red Guard Generation*. London: Macmillan

Chan, S. (1992) 'Intellectuals and Reform' in Watson, A. (ed.), 88–116

Cherrington, R. (1988) 'Home-grown Cash Crop Flourishes', *TES* 15 July, 15

Cherrington, R. (1991) *China's Students: the Struggle for Democracy*. London: Routledge

Cherrington, R. (1993) 'And This Little Despot Went to Market', *New Internationalist*, November, 22–3

Cherrington, R. (1995) *Why Bother to Study? The Reform Generation of Educated Youth in 1980s China*. London: University of London, unpublished Ph.D. thesis

Cherrington, R. (forthcoming 1997) 'Generational Issues in China: a Case Study of the 1980s Generation of Young Intellectuals', *British Journal of Sociology*

Chow, T. (1967) *The May Fourth Movement: Intellectual Revolution in Modern China*. Cambridge MA: Harvard University Press

Clarke, J., *et al.* (1976) 'Subcultures, Cultures and Class: A Theoretical Overview' in Hall, S. and Jefferson, T. (eds) *Resistance Through Rituals: Youth Subcultures in Post-War Britain*. London: HarperCollins

Cleverley, J. (1985) *The Schooling of China*. Sydney: Allen & Unwin

Crawshaw, S. (1996) 'Students lose fear of Big Brother', *Independent*, 5 June, 11

Crow, G. (1989) 'The Use of the Concept of "Strategy" in Recent Sociological Literature', *Sociology* 23, 1–24

Dirlik, A. *et al.* (1989) *Marxism and the Chinese Experience.* New York: M.E. Sharpe

Dittmer, L. (1987) *China's Continuous Revolution:The Post-Liberation Period 1949–1981.* Berkeley CA: University of California Press

Djilas, M. (1957) *The New Class; an Analysis of the Communist System.* London: Thames & Hudson

Dore, R. (1976) *The Diploma Disease: Education, Qualifications and Development.* London: Allen & Unwin

Du, R. (1992) *Chinese Higher Education: A Decade of Reform and Development.* Basingstoke: Macmillan

Eisenstadt, S. (1956) *From Generation to Generation.* New York: Free Press

Feuchtwang, S. and Hussain, A. (eds) (1983) *The Chinese Economic Reform.* London: Croom Helm

Franz, U. (1982) *Deng Xiaoping.* Boston MA: Harcourt Brace Jovanovich

Frith, S. (1984) *The Sociology of Youth.* London: Causeway

Gardner, J. (1989) 'Development and Socialism in post-Mao China' in Scase, R. (ed.) 215–33

Garnham, N. and Williams, R. (1986) 'Pierre Bourdieu and the Sociology of Culture: an Introduction' in Collins, R. *et al.* (eds) *Media, Culture and Society: a Critical Reader.* London: Sage

Gasper, B. (1989) 'Keypoint Secondary Schools in China: the Persistance of Tradition?' *Compare*, 19(1), 5–20

Gittings, J. (1989) *China Changes Face.* Oxford: Oxford University Press

Gold, T. (1980) 'Back to the City: the Return of Shanghai's Educated Youth', *China Quarterly*

Gold, T. (1991) 'Youth and the State', *China Quarterly* 127, 594–612

Gold, T. (1993) 'Go with Your Feelings: Hong Kong and Taiwan Popular Culture in Greater China', *China Quarterly*, 136, 907–25

Goldman, M. (1992) 'The Intellectuals in the Deng Xiaoping Era' in Rosenbaum, A. (ed.), 193–218

Goldman, M. (1996) 'Politically-Engaged Intellectuals in the Deng-Jiang Era: A Changing Relationship with the Party-State', *China Quarterly*, 145, 35–52

Goldman, M., Cheek, T. and Hamrin, C. (eds) (1987) *China's Intellectuals and the State: in Search of a New Relationship.* Cambridge MA: Harvard University Press

Griffin, K. (ed.) (1984) *Institutional Reform and Economic Development in the Chinese Countryside.* London: Macmillan

Hall, S. and Jefferson, T. (eds) (1976) *Resistance Through Rituals: Youth Subcultures in Post-War Britain.* London: HarperCollins

Hamrin, C. and Cheek, T. (eds) (1986) China's Establishment Intellectuals. New York: M.E. Sharpe

Hayhoe, R. (ed.) (1984) *Contemporary Chinese Education.* London: Croom Helm

Hayhoe, R. (1989) *China's Universities and the Open Door Policy.* New York: M.E. Sharpe

Hayhoe, R. (ed.) (1992) *Education and Modernization: the Chinese Experience.* Oxford: Pergamon

Hayhoe, R. (1993) 'China's Universities Since Tiananmen: a Critical Assessment', *China Quarterly* 134, 291–309

Hebdige, D. (1979) *Subculture: the Meaning of Style.* London: Methuen

Hickrod, L. and Hickrod, G. (1965) 'Communist Chinese and the American Adolescent Subcultures', *China Quarterly*, 22, 171–80

Hicks, G. (ed.) (1990) *The Broken Mirror: China after Tiananmen*. Harlow: Longman

Hooper, B. (1985a) *Youth in China*. Harmondsworth: Penguin

Hooper, B. (1985b) 'The Youth Problem: Deviations from the Socialist Road', in Young, G. (ed.) *China: Dilemmas of Modernisation*. London: Croom Helm, 199–219

Hooper, B. (1991) 'Chinese Youth: The Nineties Generation', *Current History, (China)* 264–9

Israel, J. (1966) *Student Nationalism in China 1927–37*. Palo Alto CA: Stanford University Press

Jaschok, M. (1986) ' "Ripe Youths" or "Old Maids": Being a Single Woman is a Problem', *China Now*, (118), 34–41

Jenkins, R. (1992) *Pierre Bourdieu*. London: Routledge

Jenner, W. (1992) *The Tyranny of History: The Roots of China's Crisis*. London: Penguin

Jones, A. (1992) *Like a Knife: Ideology and Genre in Contemporary Chinese Popular Music*. Ithaca NY: Cornell

Jones, G. (1988) 'Integrating Process and Structure in the Concept of Youth: a Case for Secondary Analysis', *Sociological Review*, 36(4), 706–31

Kasschau, P. *et al.* (1974) 'Generational Consciousness and Youth Movement Participation: Contrasts in Blue Collar and White Collar Youth', *Journal of Social Issues*, 30(3), 69–94

Kelly, D. (1987) 'The Chinese Student Movement of December 1986 and its Intellectual Antecedents', *Australian Journal of Chinese Affairs*, no. 17, 127–42

Kelly, D. (1990) 'Chinese Intellectuals in the 1989 Democracy Movement' in Hicks, G. (ed.), 24–51

Kirby, S. (ed.) (1965) *Youth in China*. Hong Kong: Dragonfly

Kwong, J. (1994) 'Ideological Crisis Among China's Youths: Values and Official Ideology', *British Journal of Sociology*, 45(2), 247–64

Laufer, R. and Bengtson, V. (1974) 'Generations, Aging and Social Stratification: on the Development of Generational Units', *Journal of Social Issues*, 30(3), 181–206

Lee, G. (1993) 'Deathsong of the River: a Reader's Guide to the Chinese TV Series *'He Shang'*, *China Quarterly*, 135, 586

Lethbridge, H. (1965) 'Youth, Society and the Family in China' in Kirby, S. (ed.) 31–66

Levy, M. (1968) *The Family Revolution in Modern China*. New York: Athenaeum

Li, L. (1990) *Moving the Mountain: My Life in China from the Cultural Revolution to Tiananmen Square*. London: Macmillan

Liang, H. and Shapiro, J. (1983) *Son of the Revolution*. London: Chatto & Windus

Liu, A. (1976) *Political Culture and Group Conflict in Communist China*. Santa Barbara CA: Clio Books

Liu, W. (1991) 'Field Days', *China Now*, 138, 28–9

Luo, X. (1995) 'The "Shekou Storm": Changes in the Mentality of Chinese Youth Prior to Tiananmen', *China Quarterly*, 142, 541–72

Macartney, J. (1990) 'The Students: Heroes, Pawns, or Power-Brokers?' in Hicks, G. (ed.), 3–23

MacRobbie, A. (1991) *Feminism and Youth Culture*. Basingstoke: Macmillan

Mann, M. (1983) *Student Encyclopedia of Sociology*. London: Macmillan

Mannheim, K. (1952) *Essays on the Sociology of Knowledge*. London: RKP

Montaperto, R. (1972) 'From Revolutionary Successors to Revolutionaries: Chinese Students in the Early Stages of the Cultural Revolution' in Scalapino, R. (ed.) 575–605

Morgan, D. (1989) 'Strategies and Sociologists: a Comment on Crow', *Sociology* 23(1), 25–30

Murdock, G. and McCron, R. (1976) 'Consciousness of Class and Consciousness of Generation' in Clarke, J. *et al.* (eds) 192–208

Musgrove, F. (1968) *Youth and the Social Order*. London. Routledge Kegan Paul

Nathan, A. (1985) *Chinese Democracy: the Individual and the State in Twentieth Century China*. London: Tauris

Nathan, A. (1990) *China's Crisis: Dilemmas of Reform and Prospects for Democracy*. Columbia OH: Columbia University Press

O'Boyle, L. (1970) 'The Problem of an Excess of Educated Men in Western Europe 1800–50', *Journal of Modern History*, 42, 471–95.

O'Donnell, M. (1985) *Age and Generation*. London: Tavistock

Ownby, D. (1985) 'Changing Attitudes among Chinese Youths: Letters to *Zhongguo Qingnian*', *Chinese Sociology and Anthropology*, XVII, No. 4 1–113

Ownby, D. (1986) 'The Audience: Growing Alienation among Chinese Youths' in Goldman, M., Hamrin, C. and Cheek, T. (eds) 212–46

Parkin, F. (1979) *Marxism and Class Theory: a Bourgeois Critique*. Cambridge: Tavistock

Parsons, T. (1973) 'Youth in the Context of American Society' in Silverstein, H. (ed.) *The Sociology of Youth: Evolution and Revolution* New York: Macmillan

Pepper, S. (1990) *China's Education Reform in the 1980s: Policies, Issues and Historical Perspectives*. Berkeley CA: University of California Institute of East Asian Studies

Pepper, S. (1984) *China's Universities: Post-Mao Enrollment Policies and their Impact on the Structure of Secondary Education*. Ann Arbor MI: Michigan Center for Chinese Studies

Pepper, S. (1980) 'Chinese Education after Mao: Three Steps forward, Two Steps Back and Begin Again?', *China Quarterly*, 81, 1–65.

Pickvance, C. and Pickvance, K. (1994) 'Towards a Strategic Approach to Housing Behaviour: a Study of Young People's Housing Strategies in S.E. England', *Sociology* 28, 657–77

Pieke, F. (1987) 'Social Science Fieldwork in the PRC: Implications of the Mosher Affair', *China Information* 1(3) 32–7.

Pilcher, J. (1994) 'Mannheim's Sociology of Generations: an Undervalued Legacy', *British Journal of Sociology*, 45(3) 481–95

Pilkington, H. (1994) *Russia's Youth and its Culture*. London: Routledge

Postiglione, G. (1992) 'The Implications of Modernization for the Education of China's National Minorities' in Hayhoe, R. (ed.) 307–36

Raddock, D. (1992) *Political Behavior of Adolescents in China – The Cultural Revolution in Kwangchow*. Tucson AZ: University of Arizona Press

Rai, S. (1991) *Resistance and Reaction: University Politics in Post-Mao China*. Hemel Hempstead: Harvester Wheatsheaf

Rayns, T. (1992) 'Censor Sensibility', *Time Out*, 22 January 20–1

Remmling, G. (1975) *The Sociology of Karl Mannheim*. London: Routledge Kegan Paul

Rice, D. (1992) *The Dragon's Brood: Conversations with Young Chinese*. London: HarperCollins

Rose, G. (1982) *Deciphering Sociological Research*. London: Macmillan

Rosen, S. (1984) 'New Directions in Secondary Education' in Hayhoe, R. (ed.) 65–92

Rosen, S. (1985) 'Society and Reform in China', *Current History* 264–78

Rosen, S. (1992) 'Students and the State in China: The Crisis in Ideology and Organization' in Rosenbaum, A. (ed.) 167–92

Rosen, S. (1993) 'The Effect of Post 4 June Re-Education Campaigns on Chinese Students', *China Quarterly* 134, 310–34

Rosen, S. and Zou, G. (eds) (1990–1) 'The Chinese Debate on the New Authoritarianism', *Chinese Sociology and Anthropology*, Winter (23). no. 2. (1)

Rosenbaum, A. (ed.) (1992) *State and Society in China: the Consequences of Reform*. Boulder CO: Westview

Rozman, G (ed.) (1981) *The Modernization of China*. New York: Free Press

Scalapino, R. (ed.) (1972) *Elites in the People's Republic of China*. Seattle WA: University of Washington Press

Scase, R. (ed.) (1989) *Industrial Societies: Crisis and Division in Western Capitalism and State Socialism*. London: Unwin Hyman

Shambaugh, D. (1993) 'Introduction to Special Edition on "Greater China" ', *China Quarterly*, 136, 653–59

Sheridan, M. (1968) 'The Emulation of Heroes', *China Quarterly*, 33, 47–72

Shirk, S. (1982) *Competitive Comrades: Career Incentives and Student Strategies in China*. Berkeley CA: University of California Press

Singer, M. (1971) *Educated Youth and the Cultural Revolution in China*. Michigan: University of Michigan Press

Siu, H. and Stern, Z. (eds) (1983) *Mao's Harvest*. New York: Oxford University Press

Starr, J. (1974) 'The Peace and Love Generation', *Journal of Social Issues*, 30(2), 73–106

Taylor, R. (1981) *China's Intellectual Dilemma: Politics and University Enrolment 1949–78*. British Columbia: University of British Columbia

Thogersen, S. (1990) *Secondary Education in China after Mao: Reform and Social Conflict*. Aarhus: Aarhus University Press

Tournebise, J. and Macdonald, L. (1987) *Le Dragon et la Souris*, Paris: Christian Bourgois Editeur

Townsend, J. (1967) *The Revolutionization of Chinese Youth: a Study of Chung-Kuo Ch'ing-nien*. Berkeley CA: University of California

Tu, W. (ed.) (1993) *China in Transformation*. Cambridge MA: Harvard University Press

Tu, W. (ed.) (1994) *The Living Tree: the Changing Meaning of Being Chinese Today*. Stanford CA: Stanford University Press

Unger, J. (1982) *Education under Mao: Class and Competition in Canton Schools 1960–1980*. New York: Columbia University Press

Wang, J. (1989) *Contemporary Chinese Politics*. Englewood Cliffs NJ: Prentice Hall

Wang, L. (1994) 'Roots and the Changing Identity of the Chinese in the United States' in Tu, W. (ed.) 185–212

Watson, J. (ed.) (1992) *Economic Reform and Social Change in China*. London: Routledge

Wells, J. (1988) *Accents of English* (Part 1). Cambridge: Cambridge University Press

White, G. (1981) *The Political Role of Teachers in Contemporary China.* New York: M.E. Sharpe

White, G. (1983) 'Urban Employment and Labour Allocation Policies' in Feuchtwang, S. and Hussain, A. (eds)

White, G. (1993) *Riding the Tiger: the Politics of Economic Reform in Post-Mao China.* Basingstoke: Macmillan

Whyte, M. (1981) 'Destratification and Restratification in China' in Berreman, G. (ed.) 309–34

Willis, P. (1977) *Learning to Labour.* London: Saxon House

Wilson, R. and Wilson, A. (1970) 'The Red Guards and the World Student Movement', *China Quarterly* 42, 88–104

Wu N. (1993) *A Single Tear.* London: Hodder & Stoughton

Yahuda, M. (1979) 'Political Generations in China', *China Quarterly*, 80, 793–805

Yeh, W. (1990) '*The Alienated Academy: Culture and Politics in Republican China 1919–1937.* Cambridge MA: Harvard University Press

Ying, M. & Marsh, S. (1993) *China in the Era of Deng Xiaoping: a Decade of Reform.* Armonk: M.E. Sharpe

Zhu, Q. (1993) 'A Brief Analysis of the System of Indicators of Well-Off Society and Objectives for the Year 2000', *Social Sciences in China*, 2, 42–54

Chinese Language Sources

Hao B. (1988) 'Daxue Sheng de Yingan yi Jianchu Lu', *Gaojiao yu Rencai* 3, 13–16

Su, X. *et al.* (1988) *He Shang.* Beijing: Xiandai Chubanshe

Wang Z. (1988) 'Bian "Baoban Jiehun" ban "Ziyou Lianai"' , *Zhongguo Qingnian* May, 26–7

Zhang, W. (1988) 'Dandai Zhongguo Qingnian Jiazhi Guannian de Bianhua', *Wei Ding Gao* 14, 24–7

Zhang, Y. & Cheng, Y. (1988) *Di Si Dai Ren.* Beijing: Dongfang Chubanshe

Zhao, Y. (1988) 'Jiazhi de Chongtu' (pt.1), *Wei Ding Gao*, 8, 26–33

Zhao, Y. (1988) 'Jiazhi de Chongtu' (pt.2), *Wei Ding Gao*, 9, 19–21

Zhongguo Funu Tongji Ziliao 1949–1989 (1991) Beijing: Zhongguo Tongji Chubanshe

Zhuang, Q. (1988) *Shijie, Zhongguo, Daxue Sheng.* Beijing: Zhongguo Qingnian Chubanshe

Chinese Newspapers and Periodicals

Beiing Ribao
Beijing Wanbao
Gaojiao yu Rencai
Guangming Ribao (GMRB)
Hongqi
Qingnian Wenzhai

228 *Bibliography*

Qingnian Yanjiu
Renmin Ribao (RMRB)
Shehui Yanjiu (Beijing Daxue Shehui Xuexi)
Tuohong
Weiding Gao (Zhongguo Shehui Kexue Yuan)
Zhongguo Fazahn Yu Gaige
Zhongguo Funu
Zhongguo Qingnian Bao
Zhongguo Qingnian Zazhi

Audio Cassette

Hong Lou Meng (Dream of the Red Mansion) (1987) Beijing: Zhongguo Dianying
Chunbanshe

Index